Praise for *Leslie Beck's Longevity Diet*

"This book masterfully explores the relationship between the food we eat and its profound effect on the quality of our lives. It is an indispensable resource for all who understand that you are what you eat."

—Chef Michael Smith

"This is one of the most comprehensive and easy-to-read books on health and nutrition that I've read."

—Rick Gallop, bestselling author of *The G.I. Diet*

"Complete with excellent user-friendly recipes and all the information you will ever need. A must buy for those of us who believe in diet and health."

—Lucy Waverman, food columnist, *The Globe and Mail*

"Leslie Beck has transformed the lives of many active people by enabling them to acquire new levels of fitness as they develop lifelong physical and nutritional habits. This book will serve to inspire you to value health, nutrition and exercise, life long."

—John Stanton, founder of the Running Room

"This is a practical and sensible approach to health focusing on what we can control every day."

—Hayley Wickenheiser, three-time
women's hockey Olympic gold medallist

PENGUIN CANADA

LESLIE BECK'S LONGEVITY DIET

LESLIE BECK, a registered dietitian, is a leading Canadian nutritionist and the bestselling author of ten nutrition books. Leslie writes a weekly nutrition column in *The Globe and Mail*, is a regular contributor to CTV's *Canada AM*, and can be heard one morning a week on CJAD Radio's *The Andrew Carter Show* (Montreal).

Leslie has worked with many of Canada's leading businesses and international food companies and runs a thriving private practice at the Medcan Clinic in Toronto. She also regularly delivers nutrition workshops to corporate groups across North America.

Visit Leslie Beck's website at www.lesliebeck.com.

MICHELLE GELOK is a Canadian registered dietitian currently based in Abu Dhabi, United Arab Emirates. Michelle writes health and nutrition articles for a variety of publications in Canada and the UAE. Her work has appeared in *Chatelaine*, CBC Online, *Aquarius* magazine and *The National* newspaper, where she was a weekly columnist. Michelle has worked extensively with Leslie Beck since 2004, developing over three hundred recipes for her last four books, *The No-Fail Diet, Foods That Fight Disease, Heart Healthy Foods for Life* and *Leslie Beck's Longevity Diet*. Visit Michelle's website at www.michellegelok.com.

Also by Leslie Beck

The Complete Nutrition Guide for Women

The Complete A–Z Nutrition Encyclopedia

Heart Healthy Foods for Life

Foods That Fight Disease

The No-Fail Diet

The Complete Nutrition Guide to Menopause

Healthy Eating for Preteens and Teens

Leslie Beck's Nutrition Guide to a Healthy Pregnancy

10 Steps to Healthy Eating

Leslie Beck's Nutrition Guide for Women

Leslie Beck's Nutrition Encyclopedia

Leslie Beck's Nutrition Guide to Menopause

LESLIE BECK'S LONGEVITY DIET

The Power of Food to Slow Aging and
Maintain Optimal Health and Energy

LESLIE BECK RD

Michelle Gelok RD
Recipe development and nutritional analysis

PENGUIN
CANADA

PENGUIN CANADA

Published by the Penguin Group

Penguin Group (Canada), 90 Eglinton Avenue East, Suite 700, Toronto, Ontario, Canada M4P 2Y3
(a division of Pearson Canada Inc.)

Penguin Group (USA) Inc., 375 Hudson Street, New York, New York 10014, U.S.A.
Penguin Books Ltd, 80 Strand, London WC2R 0RL, England
Penguin Ireland, 25 St Stephen's Green, Dublin 2, Ireland (a division of Penguin Books Ltd)
Penguin Group (Australia), 250 Camberwell Road, Camberwell, Victoria 3124, Australia
(a division of Pearson Australia Group Pty Ltd)
Penguin Books India Pvt Ltd, 11 Community Centre, Panchsheel Park, New Delhi – 110 017, India
Penguin Group (NZ), 67 Apollo Drive, Rosedale, North Shore 0745, Auckland, New Zealand
(a division of Pearson New Zealand Ltd)
Penguin Books (South Africa) (Pty) Ltd, 24 Sturdee Avenue, Rosebank, Johannesburg 2196, South Africa

Penguin Books Ltd, Registered Offices: 80 Strand, London WC2R 0RL, England

First published 2011

1 2 3 4 5 6 7 8 9 10 (WEB)

Copyright © Leslie Beck, 2011

This publication contains the opinions and ideas of its author and is designed to provide useful information
in regard to the subject matter covered. The author and publisher are not engaged in health or other
professional services in this publication. This publication is not intended to provide a basis for action in
particular circumstances without consideration by a competent professional. The author and publisher
expressly disclaim any responsibility for any liability, loss, or risk, personal or otherwise, which is incurred
as a consequence, directly or indirectly, of the use and application of any of the contents of this book.

Manufactured in Canada.

LIBRARY AND ARCHIVES CANADA CATALOGUING IN PUBLICATION

Beck, Leslie (Leslie C.)
Leslie Beck's longevity diet : the power of food to slow aging and maintain optimal health and energy /
Leslie Beck.

Includes index.
ISBN 978-0-14-317187-4

1. Longevity—Nutritional aspects. 2. Aging—Nutritional aspects.
3. Health. 4. Nutrition. I. Title.

RA776.75.B435 2011   613.2   C2010-905824-0

Visit the Penguin Group (Canada) website at **www.penguin.ca**

Special and corporate bulk purchase rates available; please see
www.penguin.ca/corporatesales or call 1-800-810-3104, ext. 2477 or 2474

*This book is dedicated
to the memory of my grandparents,
Alfred and Dorothy Coulter,
who both enjoyed long and healthy lives.*

"You can never live to be 100 if you stop living at 65."

—GEORGE BURNS, WHO LIVED TO ENJOY HIS 100TH BIRTHDAY

Contents

PART 2 EAT RIGHT TO LIVE LONGER   49

Acknowledgments

If it were not for the commitment of my dedicated team, my clients, my husband, my family and friends, this book could not have been completed. The following people deserve a very special thank you for their invaluable contributions that made this book a reality.

Michelle Gelok, a registered dietitian whose creative culinary skills brought to *Leslie Beck's Longevity Diet* a mouth-watering menu of delicious, nutritious and lower-calorie meals. Michelle developed, tested and analyzed each recipe in this book. Her passion for food and healthy cooking is evident in every recipe you'll taste.

Michelle Onlock and Laura Hanson, my incredibly efficient, professional and enthusiastic assistants who, through their dedicated teamwork, made it possible for me to run my busy private practice as I wrote this book. Thank you for your steadfast support.

Andrea Magyar, and the entire team at Penguin Group (Canada), who saw the value in this book and made it come to life.

Lynn Schellenberg, whose editorial skills helped make a scientific topic interesting, fun and easy to understand. I appreciated your encouraging comments, suggestions and dedication to this project.

My private practice clients, who never fail to motivate me to continue my learning and professional growth.

Darrell, my husband and my closest friend, whose never-ending optimism, love and patience brought balance to my life as I researched and wrote this book.

Introduction

If asked, most of us would probably agree that we wish to live a long and healthy life. We want to see our children become happy and successful adults. We hope to play an active role in our grandchildren's lives and proudly watch them grow up. And we look forward to crossing off as many items on our bucket lists as possible. Adding healthy years to our lives can help ensure that we reach these milestones and fulfill these desires.

We don't dream of living longer just to feel old and fragile when we get there. Instead, we want to spend those extra years feeling *young*. We hope that when we reach our eighties, nineties, and even beyond we'll be mentally agile, physically active and free of nagging aches and pains. We want to live as many years of a long life as we can in good health and with plenty of energy. And science tells us that's something largely under our control.

In fact, contrary to what many might believe, genetics don't dictate our life expectancy. Only 20 to 30 percent of the aging process is determined by the genes you're born with. That's good news because it means as much as 80 percent of how well you age is up to you. In other words, your lifestyle choices are, for the most part, in command of the pace of aging. Overwhelming evidence supports the notion that you can extend your "healthspan"—the number of years you will live healthfully and free of disease. By improving your diet and other lifestyle habits, it's entirely possible to compress the biological decline of aging that makes us feel "old" into the last few years of a very long life.

It's well established that eating the right foods and avoiding the wrong ones, along with maintaining a healthy weight, can lower your risk for many illnesses associated with aging, including high blood pressure, heart disease, stroke, type 2 diabetes, osteoporosis, cataracts, arthritis and a number of cancers. Our lifestyle habits have a profound effect on our health. It's estimated that if every one of us ate healthfully, stayed lean and exercised regularly, 80 percent of heart disease cases and 60 percent of diet-related cancers could be prevented. And think about type 2 diabetes: almost all cases—90 percent—could be prevented by lifestyle changes, yet, sadly, we're witnessing an epidemic of the disease in this country.

Yes, eating right can help ward off chronic, disabling diseases as we get older. That's certainly one important way proper nutrition can *increase* your life expectancy. But the right diet can also *delay* the aging process—by fighting triggers of aging inside your cells, such as inflammation and oxidative stress. Cutting-edge research shows that the foods you eat also have important effects at the genetic level to slow aging. Certain foods and food components have the ability to keep your genes fit and youthful. And, in every species studied so far, the right diet can activate longevity genes and extend lifespan! In other words, your diet has the potential to allow you to be biologically *younger* than your chronological age.

Eating for longevity means more than just including the healthiest foods possible in your diet. It also means excluding—or at least limiting—foods that can accelerate the aging process. And, very importantly, if you want to live longer, and healthier, you'll need to keep your calorie intake in check. *Leslie Beck's Longevity Diet* is a comprehensive nutrition and diet guide to help you greatly improve your chances of living healthier and longer. But it's more than a nutrition plan designed to slow aging. You'll also learn about other lifestyle habits and personality characteristics you can cultivate that are associated with successful aging.

How to use *Leslie Beck's Longevity Diet*

The information and practical advice in this book will help increase the likelihood of living longer, healthier and younger. In Part 1, "The Secrets to Successful Aging," you'll learn about the contribution that genetics and lifestyle factors make towards living a long and healthy life. And you'll discover the lifestyle secrets of people who live in the world's five longevity hot spots, called *Blue Zones*. You'll learn their habits—from diet to exercise to mental outlook—so that you can model your lifestyle after these exceptionally healthy and long-lived people. You'll also find out the top six habits or "longevity factors" that contribute to a healthy "ripe old age," determined through years of scientific study.

Part 2, "Eat Right to Live Longer," offers everything you need to know in order to plan the healthiest diet possible to slow aging. I discuss the science—how certain foods, vitamins, minerals and antioxidants work in your body to actually counteract aging. I tell you about the top 25 foods that promote longevity and then suggest quick, practical and tasty ways to add them to your diet. You'll also hear about the foods to dodge or eat with caution, because they can speed up the aging process. As well, this part of the book contains information about certain nutrition supplements that can keep your cells and your genes healthier as you age.

You'll find very specific diet advice in Part 3, "Leslie Beck's Longevity Diet." This section explores the fascinating link between calorie intake and lifespan. You'll read how decades of research findings have linked restricting calories to *extending lifespan* in every single species tested—from yeast cells to mice to rhesus monkeys. You'll learn that this dietary regimen—one that reduces calories while providing optimum nutrition—turns on longevity genes that halt aging and increase resistance to disease. You'll also find out that calorie restriction is currently being studied in humans, and with very promising results!

In Part 3 I also outline a specific diet plan you can use to promote your own longevity—a plan that's based on the principles of calorie restriction and that uses meals and dishes featuring the delicious, power-packed longevity foods of Part 2. With this plan you'll learn how to determine the calorie level that's right for you and how to choose foods that are brimming with nutrients and antioxidants. My Longevity Diet is designed to deliver optimal nutrition and the best food combinations in meals and snacks to increase energy and prevent feeling hungry. Before you begin following my Longevity Diet, I encourage you to run through five easy steps as a means of getting started, and then I provide eight "strategies for success" to help you keep on track. And if incorporating a few of these simple steps is as far as you want to go, that's just fine, too. Incorporating these diet tips into your lifestyle—along with the other healthy habits outlined in earlier chapters—will go a long way towards adding healthy years to your life.

Over 60 recipes that promote longevity

Part 4, "The Longevity Diet Recipes," offers an array of delicious, easy-to-prepare, taste-tested recipes to help you turn longevity foods into delicious meals and snacks. Each recipe was created, tested and analyzed by Michelle Gelok, a registered dietitian who has worked with me for the past six years. And each recipe is accompanied by an analysis that provides a breakdown of the calorie, fat, protein, carbohydrate, fibre and sodium content per serving, along with information on which vitamins and minerals it serves up. I hope you'll enjoy adding these lower-calorie, nutrient-rich and mouth-watering dishes to your diet. You can use these recipes as a foundation for your new Longevity Diet lifestyle. I also encourage you to revisit my tips in Part 2 on how to add each longevity food to your meals and snacks to come up with even more ways to keep these super foods at the centre of your diet.

In 400 B.C. Hippocrates said, "Let food be thy medicine and medicine be thy food." Flash-forward to 2011. We've come a long, long way from using foods to treat diseases caused by vitamin or mineral deficiencies. Today, poor health is caused, in large part, by over-eating unhealthy foods and by under-eating nutritious foods. And we're learning that the foods you eat—and how many calories you consume each day—are strongly tied to your life expectancy. While we have a lot more to learn about diet and longevity, I hope you'll use the information in this book to help you live a healthier and, very likely, a longer life.

Leslie Beck, RD
Toronto, 2010

PART 1

THE SECRETS
TO SUCCESSFUL
AGING

1

Aging is within your control

As a dietitian in private practice, I'm asked by clients on a daily basis to help them adopt the healthiest diet possible. And for many of them, it's not just about losing weight, lowering cholesterol or managing blood sugar. Although these are very important goals that motivate people to eat better, there's another underlying motivation that propels people to make permanent lifestyle changes: the desire to live a healthier, longer life.

Many of my clients are baby boomers, members of the generation born between 1946 and 1964. Today they're between 46 and 64 years old and looking for ways to enjoy their upcoming retirement years actively and in good health. In fact, the number of Canadians who are aged 55 to 64 and approaching their retirement has never been as high as it is today. And their awareness that they're getting older, that their bodies are not invincible and that they are not immortal prompts many of them to take stock of their lifestyle habits so that they may live better, longer.

Today people are seeking ways to evade the health problems that strike so many men and women in their older years, such as diabetes, high blood pressure, heart attack, stroke and certain cancers. My clients in this age range tell me that they want to be able to continue playing a round of golf or running in a 5-kilometre race for years to come. They want to be active with their grandchildren and to be able to travel to dreamed-about destinations. The bottom line: They want to do whatever they can to retain, or improve, their energy level, physical fitness and health—not only for today but also for their later years.

Don't get me wrong—people don't think they can prevent grey hair or wrinkles by changing their diet or taking up exercise. After all, aging is a natural process. But what we do know is that a whole host of healthy habits—in particular, eating well—can forestall some of the consequences of aging that subtract healthy years from our lives.

Aging is universal

Aging is a process that all living organisms experience and it runs a fairly predictable course.

The deterioration of bodily functions with age is an outcome of the changes to molecules, cells and organs in the body over a lifetime. Not one bodily system is left unscathed by the aging process.

The amount of collagen and elastin in our skin decreases, so that it becomes thinner and wrinkled. The lenses in our eyes become more rigid, impairing our ability to focus on near objects and inevitably leading to a prescription for reading glasses. The loss of muscle fibres and other micro-scopic changes in muscle cells result in a gradual decline in physical strength and mobility. Our bones thin, making us more vulnerable to fractures if we fall. Our blood vessels accumulate fat deposits and become less flexible, resulting in hardening of the arteries, or atherosclerosis. Lung tissue loses elasticity and the muscles of the rib cage shrink, reducing our capacity to breathe in oxygen-rich air. The intestinal tract becomes less efficient at producing enzymes that break down and digest foods. Even our senses of taste and smell wane with age.

We're living longer but we're not breaking records

This gradual decline of bodily functions over time, known as *senescence*, affects every organ in the body. While aging is an inevitable process, can we slow down the process so our bodies remain biologically younger longer? After all, our *life expectancy*—the average age we can expect to live to—has increased dramatically over the past century. In 1900, when tuberculosis and pneumonia were the top killers, the average life expectancy was 48. Today, thanks to improvements in sanitation and food and water, as well as the advent of vaccines and antibiotics, Canadians are living to an average age of 80.7 years.

Even recently we've witnessed an increase in life expectancy. The average 65-year-old male can expect to live another 18 years, two years more than what a man of this age could have looked forward to a decade ago. The average 65-year-old woman can expect 21 more years of life, a year longer than she might have expected in 1997. Factors such as greater access to health care, advances in medicine and better diets are likely responsible for our increased longevity.[1]

The one thing that has not changed, however, is our *maximum lifespan,* which is simply the maximum number of years an individual from a given species can live. It's defined by the age of the oldest living member of the species. For humans, the accepted maximum lifespan is 122 years, achieved by Jeanne Clement of Arles, France, who died on August 4, 1997. She outlived her husband, her daughter and her only grandson. Whether Madame Clement had remarkable genes or was lucky enough to elude the numerous illnesses that claimed so many others during her lifespan is unknown. Whatever the reason for her long life, she set a benchmark for maximum human lifespan, one that has yet to be surpassed.

HEALTHY HABITS OR GENETICS?

Eventually, we all come face to face with aging. After all, no one lives forever, and relatively few live well past 100. It seems there are fixed limits on our biological clocks such that no medical or pharmaceutical advance will help us live past our maximum lifespan. But that doesn't mean we're destined to live our older years in poor health. Most of us are well aware that smart lifestyle choices can dramatically reduce the odds of succumbing to health conditions such as high blood pressure, heart disease, stroke, type 2 diabetes, obesity and certain cancers. Hundreds of studies have linked a nutritious diet, a healthy weight, regular exercise and not smoking with a lower risk for many chronic diseases associated with aging. What's more, it's well accepted that making healthy lifestyle changes can even *reverse* some health conditions including high blood pressure, high cholesterol and pre-diabetes.

Okay, so it's no surprise that healthy habits can ward off disease as we age. But here's the big question: Is it possible to *delay* biological aging? Can we live longer and experience the vast majority of those years in good health? Can we extend our healthy and vigorous years well into our nineties? Is it feasible to compress the functional decline of aging that makes us feel "old" into the last few years of a very long life?

It's undeniable that clean living can add healthy years to your life. The California Seventh-day Adventists, for example, not only have a lower risk of heart disease and certain cancers than other Americans, they also live 10 years longer than expected, due in large part to their vegetarian diet and exercise habits.[2] And that's only one example. Scientists from the United Kingdom reported that among 20,000 men and women studied, those who exercised regularly, abstained from smoking, limited their daily alcohol intake to two drinks and ate at least five servings of fruits and vegetables a day lived, on average, 14 years longer than people who didn't.[3] In Chapter 2, "Live Healthy to 100: Lessons from the World's Longevity Hot Spots," you'll learn how the elite of the aged—those who live a century or more free of disease—manage to enjoy a longer and healthier life.

One has to wonder why some people age faster or more slowly than others. Why is it that some of us celebrate our hundredth birthday in good health while others succumb to aging much earlier in life? Does it have to do with our genetic makeup, our diet and exercise habits, our mental outlook on life—or a combination of these factors? The answer to this question is what gerontologists (the scientists who study aging) are trying to uncover. Over the last fifty years, gerontologists have proposed several theories of aging, many of them interconnected. Some of these theories focus on the genes we're born with and others focus on the environment we live in and expose our bodies to. What seems very clear is that no single theory explains the aging process. Rather, multiple factors are involved that play out in different ways and at several levels in the body.

Does biology control your lifespan?

To understand how the foods you eat—and don't eat—might speed or delay the aging process, it's first important to become familiar with the theories of aging, which fall into two groups. *Programmed theories* contend that aging follows a predetermined biological timetable. *Damage or error theories* assert that environmental damage to our body accumulates over time and causes aging. What follows is a brief and simplified rundown of the major theories— keep in mind that many of them are interlinked.

PROGRAMMED THEORIES
Programmed theories hold that our bodies are hard-wired to age and die: Once we achieve maturity, "aging genes" kick in that begin our path to the grave. These theories view aging and death as a necessary part of evolution. If a species did not have the capacity to age and die, then it would not be forced

to reproduce to survive. In other words, if we were to live forever there would be no evolution. Aging, therefore, must be inherent in us and not simply the result of wear and tear over time.

THE PROGRAMMED LONGEVITY THEORY asserts that the sequential switching on and off of certain genes controls the changes of aging.

THE HORMONE THEORY OF AGING holds that the changes caused by our hormonal system as we get older are the most important factors in aging. As we age, our hormonal systems become less efficient, leading to changes such as female menopause and male andropause. With the loss of estrogen during menopause, women's bones become weaker and their blood-cholesterol level rises, increasing the risk of osteoporosis and heart disease. A decline of testosterone can lead to fatigue, loss of energy and physical agility, as well as a higher risk of heart disease. Growth hormone, which plays a role in muscle strength and bone health, also declines with age. Although hormonal changes do occur with aging, it's not known if they control the pace of aging or are a consequence of other changes in the body.

THE IMMUNE SYSTEM THEORY OF AGING proposes that the rate of aging is under the control of our immune system. Our immune system is our body's primary defence against bacteria, viruses, toxins and cancer cells. The theory holds that with age our immune cells decline in number and in their ability to function properly. A vulnerable immune system increases the potential for foreign invaders to harm our body and to cause aging and even death.

DAMAGE OR ERROR THEORIES

The second group of major theories on aging is made up of the damage or error theories. Most scientists have discredited the idea that the aging process cannot be altered. Conventional wisdom now holds that aging is simply a wearing out of the body over time as its normal maintenance and repair systems gradually give out. Damage or error theories propose to link the effects of accumulated assaults on our bodily systems to the aging process. As you read on, you'll see there are similarities among the several different damage or error theories.

THE WEAR AND TEAR THEORY holds that the effects of aging are caused by damage to the body over time. Eventually, cells and body systems wear out from continued use. Once they wear out, they can no longer function properly. A good example of wear and tear is osteoarthritis, a progressive disease of aging that targets weight-bearing joints, especially the knees and hips. It's caused by the breakdown of cartilage, a tough but flexible connective tissue that covers the surface of joints, allowing bones to slide over one another, reducing friction and preventing damage. Over time, repeated use and stress can cause the cartilage to crack and wear away, leading to painful and stiff joints.

THE RATE OF LIVING THEORY contends that a species' lifespan is related to an organism's metabolic rate, or the speed at which it processes oxygen. According to this theory, every organism is endowed with the ability to expend a fixed amount of energy in its lifetime. After this energy is used up, organisms will suffer from accumulated wear and tear more rapidly and eventually die. Species that use oxygen faster because they have higher metabolic rates age and die sooner than species with slower metabolisms. To date, there is no evidence that a species' metabolic rate dictates its life expectancy.

THE CROSS-LINKING THEORY attributes aging to the gradual accumulation of cross-linkages between proteins in cells. The first step in cross-linking is the attachment of a glucose (sugar) molecule to a protein. This event sets in motion a chain of reactions that result in proteins binding together, or becoming cross-linked, which impairs their structures and changes the way they work. Over time, cross-linked proteins, called *advanced glycation products* or AGEs, accumulate in the cell and eventually disrupt its function. AGEs also stiffen body tissues, which makes them function less efficiently. For example, AGEs in blood vessel walls cause them to stiffen.

AGEs can also bind to receptors, another kind of protein molecule, on cell walls and trigger inflammation and the formation of free radicals inside cells. Scientists have linked AGEs to some of the deterioration associated with aging, including cataracts, Alzheimer's disease, heart disease and impaired kidney function. Although we can't stop cross-linking, we can slow it down. Researchers believe that when blood sugar is elevated, more cross-linking occurs. This means that taking steps to prevent diabetes—or to manage it, if it's an existing condition—can help slow the formation of AGEs and aging.

THE FREE RADICAL THEORY asserts that aging can be attributed to random accumulated damage done to cells by free radicals, which are highly reactive oxygen compounds. High levels of free radicals in the body bring about what's called *oxidative stress* (more on this in a minute). Free radicals are routinely produced within our cells as a by-product of oxygen metabolism. But they can also be created in our bodies by exposure to cigarette smoke, sun and air pollution.

Normally, cells utilize antioxidants such as certain enzymes and vitamins C and E to combat harmful free radicals. But some free radicals manage to escape these built-in defence systems and damage DNA, lipids (fat) and proteins. As our body ages, it produces more and more free radicals and its own antioxidants are unable to fight this process, which results in cellular damage. A good metaphor for the damage oxidative stress causes to the body is a cut apple when it's exposed to air. Over time, the apple will turn brown and deteriorate because oxygen in the air triggers chemical reactions in the flesh of the apple.

The lipid (fat)-rich cell membrane, which protects a cell's vital machinery from the outside environment, is especially vulnerable to the attack of free radicals. If levels of vitamin C and E are depleted, repeated free radical damage to a cell's membrane can cause cross-linking of lipids to proteins and the formation of *lipfuscin*, known as "age pigment." Grains of this yellowish-brown pigment can be found in all aged cells, and its predictable accumulation is thought to be the most reliable marker of chronological age. Research is ongoing to determine if antioxidant-rich foods or supplements can slow down aging in humans.

THE SOMATIC MUTATION THEORY of aging states that what matters most in the aging process is what happens to our genes after we inherit them. From infancy to old age, our cells are continually dividing. Each time a cell divides there's a chance that some of its genetic material, the DNA, will be copied incorrectly. Such alterations in DNA are called *mutations*, and they can have damaging effects on protein function and, ultimately, on how our body functions. As the theory goes, aging is the result of the gradual accumulation of random mutations that can occur from radiation and other environmental toxins. It's possible that longevity is influenced by the proficiency of our DNA to repair itself, a process that relies on proper nutrition.

Do your genes control your lifespan?

Aging isn't determined by biology alone. There's little doubt of a genetic connection to longevity. Yet, your genes don't control life expectancy as much as you might think. Based on research conducted among Danish twins, Scandinavian researchers calculated that the contribution of genetics to aging is only 20 percent to 30 percent.[4] (In other words, as much as 80 percent of how well you age is up to you and will depend on your environment, lifestyle and health-related behaviours.) While your DNA alone does not determine your lifespan, it does play an important role, as gerontologists are discovering.

Genetics may play more of a leading role in the longevity of healthy centenarians, people who live a full century or more. Research from Beth Israel Deaconess Hospital and Harvard Medical School revealed that siblings of New England centenarians have death rates about one-half of the national average. What's more, centenarians also have a striking family history that supports a genetic component to longevity. Compared to other Americans, male siblings of centenarians are at least 17 times as likely to reach 100 themselves, and female siblings are at least eight times as likely.[5]

Most people who reach their 100th birthday or beyond enjoy relatively good health, not getting sick until right before the end of their lives. Yet not all escape the chronic diseases that normally hit most people after mid-life. Data from the New England Centenarian Study found that about 40 percent of centenarians experienced one illness in their lifetime, but they overcame them with fewer complications. Centenarians are also less likely to spend time in the intensive care unit and to require less expensive care when they do get sick. What seems to set these resilient individuals apart are great genes combined with healthy living and, no doubt, a little luck.

GENETICS 101

To understand how your genes help control the pace of aging, let's first review what exactly it is that genes do inside each and every cell of your body. Within the nucleus, or centre, of your cells are roughly 30,000 genes arranged along strands of DNA. (DNA is organized as twenty-three pairs of chromosomes.) Each gene is simply a specific sequence of DNA that holds the code to make a protein that has a very specific regulatory function in the cell, such as a hormone, a cell receptor or an enzyme. The progression from a gene code to an actual protein involves two steps: *transcription* and *translation*.

During transcription, DNA unwinds in the area that encodes the gene of interest once it has received a signal from the cell that the particular protein is needed. The code is then transcribed, or recorded, into a molecule called *messenger RNA*. The messenger RNA then exports this genetic information from the nucleus to another area within the cell, where it's translated into a specific protein. Together, transcription and translation make up the process called *gene expression*. Simply put, gene expression is the action of a specific gene in producing messenger RNA and, ultimately, a very specific protein. It's what these proteins do—or don't do—that intrigues gerontologists.

The proteins made by genes carry out many functions in the body, many of which are related to the aging process. Some proteins fight free radicals and repair damage to DNA, while others help regulate blood sugar or mitigate stress in cells. If you think heredity dictates your genes and that the genes you're born with don't change, think again. It's true that you're born with 30,000 genes, but these genes can be more active or less active in cells, producing more or less of a specific protein. What's fascinating is the fact that certain dietary factors can activate or deactivate certain genes, including genes associated with longevity. In other words, components of your diet can affect when a gene is turned on, how powerfully it's activated and how it interacts with its neighbouring genes. Researchers are learning that certain lifestyle factors can help keep our genes fit, increasing the odds we'll live a longer, healthier life.

THE DISCOVERY OF LONGEVITY GENES

By studying the cells of various organisms—yeast, roundworms, fruit flies and mice—researchers have isolated a number of genes linked to a longer lifespan. These simple, short-lived organisms are easy to study and can provide helpful clues to human aging. Genes known by names such as daf-2, amp-1, clk-1 and pit-1 have been shown to affect the lifespan of laboratory organisms and their ability to withstand stress. Studying the genetic makeup of these life forms led scientists to discover one of the first longevity genes, called SIR2, in baker's yeast cells. (SIR stands for Silencing Information Regulator. It's a gene that regulates the deactivation or "silencing" of certain chemical signals sent by cells.)

Aging in yeast is determined by how many times the mother cell divides to produce daughter cells, which typically occurs twenty times. Some yeast cells can live longer, prompting scientists to wonder if a certain gene was responsible for these cells growing older (dividing more than twenty times). When they studied unusually long-lived yeast cells, they found that a mutation in one gene caused it to code for proteins containing an enzyme called SIR2. When a copy of the SIR2 gene was added to the yeast cell, specific activities that typically lead to cell death were subdued (that is, the chemical signals that would have triggered these activities were "silenced") and the yeast cell's lifespan was extended by 30 percent. Researchers have learned that restricting a yeast cell's food availability is one way to increase the activity of SIR2 genes. As you'll read in Chapter 8, "The Calorie-Longevity Connection," curbing calorie intake may also extend human lifespan.

LONGEVITY GENES IN HUMANS These experiments in yeast cells eventually led to the discovery of a family of longevity genes, called sirtuins, in species ranging from bacteria to mice to humans. The first human version of the yeast SIR2 gene identified by scientists was a gene called SIRT1. It encodes a protein called SIRT1 that has the same activity as SIR2 but also seems to silence a wider range of proteins in the cell that bring about aging. So far, seven longevity genes, named SIRT1 through SIRT7, have been discovered. (The "T" in SIRT1, SIRT2, SIRT3 and so on is short for the two—2—of SIR2.) When confronted with calorie restriction, these genes become activated to keep cells alive and healthy by coordinating a variety of hormonal networks, regulatory genes and other genes.

SIRT1, the most studied sirtuin in mammals, turns off a number of age-promoting activities in human cells when calories are limited. Sister genes SIRT3 and SIRT5 reside in the mitochondria, the power plant in every cell that processes oxygen and converts substances from the foods we eat into energy for essential cell functions. Here, these genes enable cells, when the cells are subject to a lack of food, to make use of other energy sources effectively. In a nutshell, when food is limited, the sirtuin genes coordinate multiple actions in our cells to shut down the aging process.

THE TELOMERE—LONGEVITY CONNECTION

Individual lifespans also appear to be tied to strands of DNA called *telomeres*, genes that preserve the tips of the chromosomes. These short sequences of DNA "bookend" chromosomes and protect their ends from damage, much as the plastic tips on the ends of your shoelaces prevent them from fraying. Telomeres function by preventing chromosomes from losing little bits of DNA at their ends; they allow cells to divide while holding the important genetic material intact.

But each time a cell divides its telomeres erode slightly and become shorter. Eventually, telomeres become so short that their host cell stops dividing and lapses into what's called cell senescence. (As you might recall from earlier in this chapter, *senescence* refers to the loss of biological processes that occurs with aging.) As a result, vital tissues and organs begin to fail and the classic signs of aging ensue. Shorter telomeres have been linked not only to the aging process but also to cancer and earlier death. The erosion of telomeres, however, is counteracted by an enzyme appropriately named *telomerase*. This enzyme adds small sequences of DNA to telomeres, preserving chromosome length and cell function.

Research suggests that telomeres are one piece of the puzzle that accounts for why some people can live to a ripe old age in good health. Studies in animals have determined that longer telomeres are associated with a longer and healthier life, and the same appears to be true for humans. The New England Centenarian Study revealed that "healthy" centenarians had significantly longer telomeres than their peers in poor health. Centenarians who functioned independently and did not suffer from high blood pressure, congestive heart failure, heart attack, stroke, dementia, cancer, lung disease or diabetes were considered healthy. Those deemed to be less healthy had physical function limitations and at least two of the health problems listed above.[6]

Another study published in 2010 from the Albert Einstein College of Medicine of Yeshiva University determined a clear link between telomere length and living to 100. The researchers studied telomere length in Ashkenazi Jewish centenarians and their children, and in a control group of children of parents with average life expectancies. (Ashkenazi Jewish people are from central and Eastern Europe; the majority of the study participants were born in the United States or moved there before World War II.) The researchers found that compared to the control group, the centenarians and their children had significantly longer telomeres and were better able to maintain telomere length as they grew older. What's more, longer telomeres were associated with better cognitive function, healthier blood-cholesterol levels and protection from age-related diseases. The study revealed that participants who lived an exceptionally long life had inherited mutated genes that made the enzyme telomerase extra active and able to maintain telomere length more effectively.[7]

DIET AND TELOMERE LENGTH Heredity isn't the only factor that influences telomere length. Environmental and lifestyle factors can speed up telomere shortening. Oxidative stress—the damage to DNA, proteins and lipids caused by free radicals—shortens telomeres and, as we've already seen, contributes to aging. In fact, telomeres are particularly vulnerable to free radical attack, which produces damage that often cannot be properly repaired. Things that cause inflammation in the body, such as obesity, an unhealthy diet, physical inactivity and cigarette smoking, are also believed to accelerate telomere shortening and biological aging. That's because inflammatory reactions in the body generate oxidative stress and significantly hamper the ability of telomerase to maintain telomere length.

It's not surprising, then, that a growing number of studies have shown that certain foods and nutrients preserve the length of our telomeres as we age. Studies have found that multivitamins, foods rich in vitamins C and E, omega-3 fats in fish oil, whole grains and dietary fibre are associated with longer telomeres. On the flip side, a high intake of linoleic acid—a fatty acid plentiful in soy, corn and sunflower oils—has been linked with shorter telomeres in women. A large waistline, too, has been associated with shortened telomeres. In a study of 2284 healthy women, those in the top category of waist circumference—32 inches or greater—had shorter telomeres than the women whose waists measured 28 inches or less.[8] The findings from this ongoing research hint strongly that tweaking your diet is an important strategy to thwart telomere shortening, allowing you to live longer—and in better health. You'll learn more about foods and supplements that promote longevity in Chapter 5, "Top 25 Foods for Longevity."

Let's now return to the question I posed earlier in this chapter: Is it possible to slow, or delay, the aging process? The answer is a resounding yes. In the following chapters I will outline diet, nutrition and other lifestyle approaches that can help you prolong your healthy years by turning on longevity genes and fighting triggers of cellular aging. While it's unlikely you'll beat Jeanne Clement's record of 122 years, these strategies can help you live healthfully and with more vigour right into your nineties. How well you will age, it seems, is truly up to you.

2

Live healthy to 100: Lessons from the world's longevity hot spots

By now it's clear that a long, healthy life depends largely on good habits. Sure, the genes your parents passed down to you play a part in how well your body reacts to the passage of time. But scientists have learned that living life well is even more important. They've studied regions where people live significantly longer than anyone else on earth. These longevity hot spots are called *Blue Zones*, and their inhabitants live not only exceptionally long but remarkably active and healthy lives, well into their nineties and beyond.

People in Blue Zones are ten times more likely to reach the age of 100 than folks living in North America. And they suffer substantially less heart disease and cancer than we do. Why do the inhabitants of these regions stand a better chance of living healthfully to 100? Are the clues to their longevity hidden among their genes? Are medicine and modern technology responsible? Do lifestyle factors such as diet, exercise and mental outlook play a role? Or is a combination of these factors at work?

Scientists, demographers and journalists have sought answers to these questions by studying and interviewing the citizens of Blue Zones. Insights gleaned from Blue Zone residents provide powerful lessons in living longer. Turns out, these people don't take particular medications, vitamin pills or special elixirs to extend their lifespan. Learning how Blue Zone centenarians eat, move, think, connect with others and, in general, take care of themselves can help us add vital years to our lives.

Five Blue Zones have been identified and thoroughly researched by Dan Buettner, an explorer and journalist working in partnership with the National Geographic Society. These regions are:

✓ Sardinia, Italy
✓ Okinawa, Japan
✓ Loma Linda, California
  Icaria, Greece
  Nicoya Peninsula, Costa Rica

With funding from the U.S. National Institutes of Health, Buettner and a team of scientists spent more than five years of onsite investigation gathering information on lifestyle characteristics that might explain the extraordinary Blue Zone longevity. The most heavily studied Blue Zones are Sardinia, Okinawa and Loma Linda and though they are cultures and continents away from each other, it turns out their inhabitants share a number of characteristics.

Sardinia, Italy

This large island located in the Mediterranean Sea lies 120 kilometres off the coast of Italy. Here, in the island's mountainous villages, men reach the age of 100 at an astounding rate: double what's seen in the rest of Italy. The AKEA Study, short for *A Kent'Annos,* an old Sardinian greeting meaning "May you live to be 100," confirmed that the island has the highest percentage of people within Italy who have passed the 100-year mark.[1] The fact that Sardinians keep pretty much to themselves, have a low immigration rate and have stable daily routines and practices made them an ideal population to study for the genetic and lifestyle traits linked to extreme longevity and successful aging. And it seems there's a lot to learn about the centenarian way of life in this mountainous Blue Zone.

DIET The study found that the traditional Sardinian diet was simple, conservative and healthy, consisting of food produced from the land. Homegrown fruits and vegetables such as tomatoes, eggplant, zucchini, potatoes and protein-rich fava beans were a constant in Sardinian meals. Bread, goat's milk and cheese made from sheep's milk were also dietary staples. (Interestingly, research suggests that goat's milk might help promote longevity. Its unique fatty acids have the ability to limit cholesterol deposits in body tissues. What's more, goat's milk may do a better job than cow's milk at keeping bones strong as we age.[2]) The Sardinians ate meat at most once a week and only if the family could afford it. They drank one or two glasses of red wine with the evening meal, a time when the family was reunited. The grapes they used for wine making were grown on the island and contained a high concentration of flavonoids, antioxidants thought to offer protection from heart disease.

EXERCISE The researchers learned that in Sardinia, physical activity wasn't something people had to schedule, it was simply a way of life. Before economic affluence arrived in the 1950s, farming and breeding sheep represented the only sources of income for a Sardinian family. Men would spend full days doing hard physical work, tilling fields or walking for miles to herd sheep to pasture. During the winter months, shepherds would set out on long treks, herding their sheep from mountainous land to lowland pastures. While men worked outdoors from early morning to night, women raised the children, maintained the house and took care of the finances. (Some experts speculate that Sardinian men might experience less heart disease and greater longevity partly because they weren't weighed down with the stresses of running a household.) A trip to the market or visiting a relative usually involved a long walk.

CULTURAL ATTITUDES It's thought that another factor contributing to so many Sardinians' centenarian status is a disposition that helps ease stress. Researchers have noted the Sardinians' sense of purpose in life and their positive outlook and sense of humour. They also have a strong commitment to their families. Elders are respected for their experiences, their knowledge and their contribution to raising their families. And unlike so many elderly North Americans, they're looked after by younger family members rather than by retirement and long-term care facilities.

GENETICS While lifestyle and cultural factors undoubtedly contribute to the extreme longevity experienced by Sardinians, especially Sardinian men, genetic destiny also plays a role. The Sardinian Blue Zone is in a remote, mountainous region that was quite difficult to access until a few decades ago. Its geography discouraged immigration and encouraged marrying into each other's families. If you look in a Sardinian phone book, you'll find relatively few last names. The vast majority of today's Sardinians are, in fact, related to the island's original settlers. Such isolation from the rest of the world means there's been little, if any, variation to the gene pool. Instead, genes that favour longevity have been strengthened over generations.

The fact that Sardinians didn't intermarry much with other Mediterranean people also served to suppress genetic traits that could weaken the body's resilience to illness. The limited gene pool of Sardinians gives researchers a unique opportunity to discover specific genes associated with long life. Italian scientists are in the process of determining on which chromosomes such longevity genes may reside. Some are examining genes located on the Y chromosome—a sex chromosome passed from father to son—after observing that the number of Sardinian males and females who live to 100 is virtually equal. (In North America, female centenarians outnumber their male counterparts four to one.)

Best practices: Sardinian longevity factors
✓ Daily fruits and vegetables
Goat's milk
Little red meat—no more than once per week
Red wine with evening meal—one or two glasses
✓ Daily walking
Commitment to family
✓ Positive mental outlook
Strong sense of purpose

Okinawa, Japan

This lush, subtropical archipelago of 161 islands, stretching 1300 kilometres between the Japanese mainland and Taiwan, is home to the longest-lived people in the world. The unusually high number of lean, youthful-looking and mentally alert centenarians living in the Japanese state of Okinawa has intrigued researchers for decades. The Okinawa Centenarian Study, which began in 1975 and continues today, has documented extraordinary life expectancies and remarkably low rates of heart disease and cancers among its participants.

Compared to mainland Japanese, elderly Okinawans have much lower blood-cholesterol levels and younger blood vessels. Compared to North Americans, they have 90 percent less chance of breast cancer, 80 percent less chance of prostate cancer and half the risk of ovarian and colon cancers.

Okinawans have a lifelong lean body mass index (BMI) and gain very little weight as they age. They also have stronger bone densities and experience 20 percent fewer hip fractures than their mainland peers. What's more, Okinawan elders have higher levels of sex hormones, including DHEA (dehydroepiandrosterone—a hormone secreted by the adrenal gland), estrogen and testosterone, than do similarly aged Americans, indicating Okinawans are actually biologically younger.[3,4] (Sex hormones naturally decline as we grow older; the waning of sex hormones has been associated with a number of age-related changes.)

Today there are 740 centenarians living in Okinawa—50 per 100,000 residents—and 90 percent are women. Most of them are active, in good health and living independently.[5] That's quite impressive when you consider that Canada is home to roughly 14 centenarians per 100,000 citizens and most are in poorer health.[6] The Okinawans beat world records in longevity for decades until 2000, when life expectancy statistics started to decline. Since World War II, younger Okinawans have been living more like North Americans, exercising less and abandoning their traditional diet for processed foods and higher-fat fare. Concern that the island's younger generations will not live nearly as long as their grandparents has led to a massive government-funded health education campaign, urging Okinawans to return to their traditional lifestyle. Indeed, thirty years of research has clearly shown that the way Okinawa's elders have lived for most or all of their lives stacked the odds in their favour of living very long and healthy lives.

FOOD AS MEDICINE The traditional Okinawan diet has received much scientific scrutiny for its longevity-promoting potential. The long-lived people of Okinawa, strongly influenced by China, believe that the food they eat is the "medicine for life." Notions of healing power through food are embodied in three characteristics of their diet. The first is called *shingi gusui*, meaning "infused medicine." Okinawan infusions are essentially broths, made of many different ingredients infused together to be used as a herbal medicine. The Okinawans pay great attention not only to the sequence in which the ingredients are added to the broth but also to the combinations of foods used.

Indeed, the combination of foods is the second characteristic of Okinawan healing foods. One broth still widely used today combines pig's liver and vegetables and is given to people when they are sick. Another popular combination is freshwater fish and a bitter vegetable called *nigana,* which are infused together to promote recovery from fatigue. There may be wisdom in the Okinawan system of infusing multiple foods together for the purpose of healing—a mountain of scientific evidence suggests nutrients and other food components work in tandem to reduce the risk of many age-related diseases. In other words, the whole—or combined—effect is greater than the sum of its separate effects.

Finally, the Okinawans put their belief in the medicinal power of food into practice every day. By incorporating many foods thought to restore health into their everyday diet, Okinawans endeavour to build stamina, maintain vitality and lead a healthy lifestyle.[7]

DIET Explanations for the Okinawans' exceptional longevity may very well be found at the dinner table. Daily traditional foods are simple and obtained from the land, and many are exceptional sources of disease-fighting vitamins, minerals and *phytochemicals*—chemical compounds in plants that offer resistance to disease and other health benefits. Unlike North American meals, which are based on meat and potatoes, the majority of Okinawan meals centre on plant foods, mostly vegetables and soy. You might be surprised to learn that rice isn't a staple starchy food for Okinawans. Instead, a type of sweet potato, satsuma-omi, makes up 93 percent of the everyday diet in Okinawa. Traditional meals include sweet potato and miso soup and a snack might be a steamed sweet potato. Compared to white rice, satsuma-omi contains more fibre, B vitamins, vitamin C, calcium and potassium. It's estimated that the farmers in Okinawa consumed about 700 milligrams of vitamin C per day from this staple food alone—almost eight times the recommended daily intake for men! These purple-coloured sweet potatoes are also rich in natural compounds called *anthocyanins*, antioxidants linked to disease prevention.

Okinawan elders don't eat much meat, no more than one ounce (30 grams) per day. Less than 10 percent of their diet consists of meat, mainly pork and poultry. Pork, served at religious occasions and holidays, has long been considered a longevity food. Okinawans use all parts of the pig, including its feet, which are boiled into soups and stews. Pigs' feet offer not only protein but collagen, which animal research suggests provides health benefits in the form of lowering blood-triglyceride (fat) levels. Besides pork and poultry, the Okinawans eat almost no other meat, and virtually no eggs or dairy products either. Fish, plentiful in heart-healthy omega-3 fatty acids, is eaten several times a week.

The everyday Okinawan diet is also plentiful in various types of seaweed, which are rich in minerals such as calcium, as well as in fibre and essential fatty acids. Vegetables such as spinach, cabbage, green peppers, carrots, sweet bell peppers and onions, all abundant in vitamins A and C and fibre, are eaten daily too. In fact, Okinawans eat at least seven servings of vegetables each day, and two to four fruit servings. Soy, in the form of tofu and miso (a fermented soybean paste used in cooking), is eaten in large amounts—two servings daily—delivering vegetarian protein and natural chemicals called *isoflavones*, estrogen-like compounds believed to help shield older Okinawan women from hot flashes, osteoporosis and heart disease. Tea, an exceptional source of antioxidants called *catechins*, is consumed daily. When it comes to alcohol, however, Okinawans are not big drinkers. On average women drink no more than one ounce of hard liquor per day, and men consume two drinks daily.

While Okinawans eat a variety of nutrient-rich foods, they don't eat a lot. They have a tradition called *hara hachi bu*, which literally translates to "eight parts out of a full ten." In other words, Okinawan elders don't overeat. Instead, they eat until they're 80 percent full. It's estimated that Okinawans eat roughly 10 percent to 20 percent fewer calories each day than mainland Japanese, who in turn consume roughly 20 percent fewer calories each day than North Americans.[8,9] Their low calorie intake may have a lot to do with their longevity. As you'll read in Chapter 8, for all species tested—including rhesus monkeys, who share 95 per cent of our genes—cutting back on calories is one of the few ways found to dramatically extend lifespan.

EXERCISE Just as it was for the Sardinians, exercise is rooted in the everyday lives of Okinawans and incorporates activities that target aerobic, strength and flexibility fitness. Martial arts, such as karate and tai chi, traditional dance, walking and gardening keep Okinawans both physically and mentally fit and connected to their spiritual beliefs. Gardening reinforces their belief in the healing energy of plants. Okinawans use traditional dance, which they learn from a very young age, to tell stories celebrating ancient times. Tai chi and karate demand a combination of mental energy and physical skill, strength and endurance. Daily exercise, a natural part of Okinawan life, has helped keep these elders lean and fit throughout their long lives.

CULTURAL ATTITUDES When it comes to personality, Okinawan elders have a lot in common with their peers living in Sardinia. They lead a low-stress lifestyle and maintain a positive outlook on life. They possess strong coping skills and a deep sense of spirituality, meaning and purpose to life. Women are highly valued in Okinawan society for their key role in keeping alive the cultural tradition of basho-fu weaving—which produces very light, breathable fabric from banana fibre. In exchange for their participation in this cottage industry, middle-aged and older women are respected and honoured and paid wages for their labour. It's thought that Okinawan women's lifelong productivity and active engagement in society are among the reasons why they age so successfully.[10] And other research supports the notion that social status plays a role in longevity. In the village of Ohgimi, where basho-fu weaving has long been linked with its cultural identity, researchers found that older women who reported having a lower social role had a significantly higher risk of dying within the study period than did their peers who had a higher social role.[11]

GENETICS DNA may be one factor contributing to the good health Okinawan elders and centenarians enjoy. Certainly, the brothers and sisters of long-lived Okinawans also tend to live long, healthy lives. The Okinawan Centenarian Study revealed that siblings of Okinawan centenarians, when compared to members of the general population at the same age, have a "mortality advantage"—that is, they are half as likely as their peers to die at that age. This "advantage" continued until they were 90 years old, translating into nearly twelve additional years of life! The research group also found that Okinawan centenarians have a gene called HLA (human leukocyte antigen) that helps guard them from inflammatory and autoimmune diseases.[12,13] But genetics isn't the whole story. When Okinawans grow up in other countries and change their lifestyle habits, they lose their longevity and take on the same risk for heart disease as those in their new home. Researchers believe that Okinawans have the best combination for longevity—both genetic and lifestyle advantages.

Best practices: Okinawan longevity factors

✓ Plant-based diet
✓ 7+ vegetable servings per day
Seaweed daily
Soy (tofu, miso) daily
Little meat—no more than one ounce per day
Tea daily
Alcohol in moderation
Daily exercise
Positive mental outlook
Strong sense of purpose
✓ Deep sense of spirituality

Loma Linda, California

Spanish for "beautiful hill," Loma Linda is located in the San Fernando Valley of southern California, halfway between Los Angeles and Palm Springs. Since 1976, this community of 21,000 has garnered international fame for its exceptionally healthy residents who manage to outlive all other Americans. And in this case, longevity may have nothing at all to do with genes. The majority of people living in Loma Linda are Seventh-day Adventists, a faith that encourages its members to live a healthy lifestyle. The Adventist church, of which there are 24 million adherents worldwide, expects its followers to be non-smokers, to abstain from alcohol and to eat a vegetarian diet. Many Adventists also avoid beverages containing caffeine.

While individual Adventists' compliance to this health philosophy varies, Loma Linda Adventists are almost entirely a non-smoking population. Most are non-drinkers too, and those who do imbibe do so infrequently. But they diverge in how strictly they follow a vegetarian diet. Only a small percentage are total vegetarians, or vegans, who avoid all animal foods including meat, poultry, fish, eggs and dairy. Most California Adventists are lacto-ovo vegetarians, who eat dairy and eggs, but avoid meat, poultry and fish, or they are semi-vegetarians, who eat meat less than once per week.

Over the past forty years, research conducted among California Seventh-day Adventists has revealed that this population is far healthier and lives longer than anyone else in California and in the United States. They have a significantly lower risk of heart disease, diabetes and most cancers. Adventist men live 7.3 years longer on average than other Californian men, and Adventist women outlive their state peers by 4.4 years. What's more, compared to non-Adventist Californians, Adventists who have the healthiest lifestyle habits—those who exercise the most, follow a vegetarian diet and have a healthy weight—gain an extra ten years of life expectancy.[14–16]

At the time of writing this book, the Adventist Health Study-2 is underway among 97,000 Seventh-day Adventists living in the United States and Canada. This ten-year project, which began in 2002, is examining the link between lifestyle and a number of chronic diseases. The study is expected to uncover what foods help prevent cancer, heart disease, diabetes, Alzheimer's disease and arthritis. The research team is also investigating the roles that genetics and religious faith play in physical health and longevity.

DIET As described above, most Seventh-day Adventists living in Loma Linda follow a lacto-ovo vegetarian diet. That means they shun meat, poultry and fish but include eggs and dairy products such as milk, yogurt and cheese in their diet. About 20 percent are semi-vegetarians, eating meat infrequently— less than once per week. And the vast majority avoids alcoholic beverages.

The Adventist Health Study, which ran from 1974 to 1988, revealed that vegetarian Adventists experienced much better health and had a longer life expectancy than their meat-eating Seventh-day Adventist peers.[17] Two other large-scale studies from the United Kingdom and Germany have turned up similar results: The vegetarians' risk of dying during the study period was up to 50 percent lower than the non-vegetarians'.[18,19] It seems that a vegetarian diet, in particular the California Seventh-day Adventists' diet, protects from disease and increases life expectancy. But are these benefits due to the avoidance of certain foods that may harm health? Or do Adventist vegetarians live longer because they eat a variety of healthy foods and food components?

The answer to both of these questions is yes. According to research for the Adventist Health Study led by Dr. Gary Fraser from the Loma Linda School of Public Health, diet can take much of the credit for the exceptional health of Seventh-day Adventists. By studying the varied eating styles of 34,192 California Seventh-day Adventists, he set out to determine which foods helped lower the risk of obesity, diabetes, arthritis, high blood pressure, heart disease, stroke and a number of cancers.[20,21]

Overall, vegetarian Adventists fared better than meat-eating Adventists. In this mostly non-smoking population, eating meat—mainly beef— increased the risk of obesity, hypertension, rheumatoid arthritis, fatal heart attack, colon cancer and bladder cancer. Risks for fatal heart attack, colon cancer and bladder cancer were significantly higher when beef was eaten at least three times per week. What's more, compared to Loma Linda Adventists who eat meat at least once every week, non–meat eaters lived longer. On average, Seventh-day Adventist women lived 2.5 years longer than their non-vegetarian counterparts, while men gained an extra 3.2 years of life.

There were other factors, besides lack of meat, that explained the better health and longevity experienced by vegetarian Adventists. These folks ate more whole-grain bread, tomatoes, legumes (dried beans, peas and lentils), nuts, dried fruit and fresh fruit than did non-vegetarian Adventists. Meat-eating Adventists preferred white bread and consumed alcohol more often than their vegetarian peers. Specifically, the following foods were found to help guard against disease among Seventh-day Adventists. (You'll learn

Health benefits of the Seventh-day Adventists' diet

Food	Health Benefit
Nuts	Eating nuts four to five times per week—versus once or less—reduced the risk of heart disease by 50 percent. (Nuts' protective effect on the heart was also observed among the non-vegetarians.)
Whole-grain bread	People who preferred whole-grain bread were 44 percent less likely to develop heart disease and 12 percent less likely to die of a heart attack than were white-bread eaters.
Dried fruit	Dried fruit contributed to the lower risk of prostate cancer observed among vegetarian Adventist men. Dried-fruit eaters also appeared to have a lower risk of pancreatic cancer.
Fruit	Total fruit intake offered strong protection from lung cancer.
Tomatoes	Tomatoes helped guard against prostate cancer among vegetarians.
Legumes	These foods guarded against colon cancer but only among Adventists who ate meat. Eating legumes at least three times per week compared with less than once lowered the risk of colon cancer by 67 percent in meat-eating Seventh-day Adventists. Legumes were also linked to a lower risk of pancreatic cancer.
Soy milk	Drinking soy milk more than once a day was found to reduce the risk of prostate cancer by 70 percent among Adventist men.

plenty more about these and other longevity foods in Chapter 5, "Top 25 Foods for Longevity.")

Following a vegetarian or mostly vegetarian diet, low in fat and plentiful in fruits and vegetables, has unquestionably helped many Californian Seventh-day Adventists maintain a lean body weight, which, in and of itself, may help explain their longevity. We certainly know that carrying excess body fat around the abdomen ups the risk of heart disease, diabetes and certain cancers. The size of your waistline is a good measure of visceral fat, the type of deep fat that packs itself around your organs and secretes chemicals that increase the body's resistance to the blood-sugar-clearing hormone insulin and cause inflammation throughout the body. Indeed, research from the Adventist Mortality Study has revealed that middle-aged (25 to 54 years) and older (55 to 84 years) California Adventists who were overweight or obese had a higher risk of dying from any cause than their leaner peers—even after physical activity was accounted for.[22]

EXERCISE Unlike in Sardinia and Okinawa, physical activity is not an intrinsic part of daily life in urban Loma Linda. But that doesn't mean these Seventh-day Adventists are all couch potatoes. In fact, among 27,530 Californian Seventh-day Adventists only 22 percent said they were inactive, while 61 percent (almost two-thirds) were moderately active. People who reported moderate and intense levels of regular activities such as walking, hiking and swimming had lower risk of dying during the study than their sedentary counterparts. What's more, the protective effect for moderate activity persisted beyond age 80.[23,24] Walking 3 to 4 1/2 miles (5 to 7 km) per hour, five or more days of the week, is considered "moderate" physical activity. So, while daily exercise isn't built in to the Adventist lifestyle, regular physical activity is part of the Loma Linda longevity phenomenon.

RELIGION The reason why California Seventh-day Adventists live longer than their fellow Americans may be explained by factors other than their vegetarian diet and non-smoking status. Living in a tight-knit religious community may also have something to do with it. Studies have found that, even after the researchers account for a number of healthy lifestyle habits, church attendance—regardless of one's faith—still predicts greater longevity. It seems there is something about religion or spirituality that positively affects health. ✓ Regular church goers have lower levels of stress hormones and may be better equipped to face life's challenges. Research has found too that people who are guided by spiritual values and feel their life is part of a greater plan have stronger immune systems, lower blood pressure and less risk of heart attack and cancer. They also recover faster from illness and live longer.

Feeling a deep sense of purpose and connection in one's life also appears to be a longevity factor. The Adventist religion encourages its members to give back to the community by engaging in volunteer activities. Participating in charitable acts serves to give Adventists a sense of purpose and meaning in life. And living in a community with others who share their religious beliefs helps keep them connected to something higher than themselves. Interacting and spending time with like-minded people serves to reinforce the philosophy they've chosen to live by.

Best practices: Seventh-day Adventist longevity factors

Vegetarian diet or little meat (less than once per week)
✓ Nuts
✓ Legumes
✓ Whole grains
✓ Fruit and dried fruit
✓ Tomatoes
Avoidance of alcohol (or very little)
Non-smoking
✓ Moderate physical activity
✓ Strong sense of religion
Deep sense of purpose and connection

Icaria, Greece

The tiny Greek island of Icaria in the Eastern Aegean Sea is one of the more recent locations to be considered a Blue Zone. Dan Buettner and his team of researchers learned that Icaria has one of the highest percentages of 90-year-olds anywhere in the world. In fact, nearly one in three of the island's residents live into their nineties. What's more, these long-lived people have dramatically lower rates of heart disease and cancer, and they experience very little dementia.

Turns out the Icarians share many of the habits of other Blue Zone residents. They live a low-stress lifestyle that embraces the Greek Orthodox religion. Living in small communities helps them to create and support strong social connections. And the Icarian lifestyle necessitates daily exercise, be it gardening or walking to church or the market or to visit family and friends. Their Mediterranean-style diet is rich in heart-healthy olive oil and antioxidant-rich green vegetables. They drink goat's milk, plentiful in health-promoting compounds. They also drink herbal teas every day, many of which contain compounds that help keep blood pressure low. Thirty-minute naps are part of their daily routine. (You'll learn more about sleep and longevity in the next chapter.)

Best practices: Icarian longevity factors
✓ Mediterranean diet rich in olive oil
✓ Dark green vegetables
  Goat's milk
  Herbal teas
  Daily exercise
✓ Low-stress lifestyle
✓ Connection to community members
  Strong sense of religion

Nicoya Peninsula, Costa Rica

The northwest coast of Costa Rica is home to a high number of people that live into their nineties and hundreds. In fact, this region boasts more healthy elders than anywhere else in Costa Rica. What's more, the Nicoya Peninsula has the lowest death rate among middle-aged people than any other Blue Zone studied to date.

Scientists studying the oldest residents of the Nicoya Peninsula have identified a high-fibre diet rich in beans and corn as one of the reasons for their unusually long lives. And, unlike North Americans, they eat lightly, enjoying their smallest meal at the end of their day. Physical work is a part of daily life. The Nicoya centenarians also have a strong sense of family. As couples, they tend to live with other family members from whom they get support. Researchers have also noted that the elders of Nicoya have strong social networks and feel a sense of purpose to their lives—they feel needed and enjoy contributing to help other people in the community.

Best practices: Nicoyan longevity factors
✓ High-fibre diet
✓ Legumes and corn
✓ Small meals
  Physical work as part of daily life
  Commitment to family
  Tight social networks
  Strong sense of purpose

While the long-lived people inhabiting these five different Blue Zones are separated by thousands of kilometres and vastly differently cultures, in many ways they are closely connected. They share a number of lifestyle practices that certainly seem to help them live longer than most people. Members of each community eat a plant-based diet and very infrequently—or never—eat red meat. Alcohol intake is moderate in Sardinia, Okinawa, Icaria and the Nicoya Peninsula, and most Loma Linda Adventists don't drink at all. And in contrast to the North American lifestyle, overeating is uncommon in these longevity hot spots. Blue Zone residents appear to eat only enough calories to stay lean.

Finally, in each community a sense of purpose, faith and spirituality pervades its members and bonds them together. In the following chapters, you will learn how to bring these—and many more—powerful longevity factors into your life.

3

Six habits for successful longevity

It's the underlying message of this book: Maintaining health and vitality into your nineties and beyond is, for the most part, up to you. You might not realize it, but the seemingly benign choices you make every day can influence your life expectancy and, more importantly, the number of *healthy* years you will live. Those minor daily decisions—to order a cheeseburger or grilled chicken salad, to drive or walk to the store, to ignore or discuss a family dispute, to schedule your annual medical exam or put it off until work calms down—can have a bearing on your lifespan.

The long-lived Blue Zone residents discussed in Chapter 2 have given us many clues to the factors related to longevity. And numerous scientific studies have established the link between lifestyle habits—as well as personality traits—and life expectancy. You'll read below how your sleep habits, exercise level, stress management practices, social connections, leisure activities, outlook on life and, of course, your eating habits can shorten—or extend—your lifespan.

Through years of research, scientists have learned that six important factors are powerfully connected to living a long and healthy life. In the sections that follow, you'll discover what these longevity factors are and how they can alter the pace of aging. You'll learn what you need to do differently, if anything, to delay the aging process. Essentially, you'll find out how to *live* to live longer.

Longevity factor #1: Eat a plant-based diet

What you eat—and how much you eat—are undeniably linked to longevity. This link makes sense since a typical diet supplies your body with more than

25,000 bioactive compounds such as amino acids (the building blocks of protein), fatty acids, fibre, vitamins, minerals and thousands of natural plant chemicals called phytochemicals, which work in many different ways to fight off damage caused by aging and help prevent diseases. Phytochemicals are naturally occurring compounds found in plant foods—"phyto" comes from the Greek word for plant. Vegetables, fruit, whole grains, legumes and nuts produce phytochemicals to protect themselves from bacteria, fungi, viruses and cellular damage. When we consume these plant foods their phytochemicals defend our bodies from disease too. Scientists have identified thousands of phytochemicals in the foods we eat. In fact, there may be more than one hundred different phytochemicals in just one serving of vegetables. Some of the main subgroups of phytochemicals include carotenoids (present in carrots and spinach), flavonoids (in apples and green tea), indoles (in broccoli and cabbage) and sulphides (in onions and garlic).

Remember that while some foods have preventative, age-defying properties, others can actually lessen your chances of living a long and healthy life by harming cells and upsetting your body's metabolic and chemical balance. There's no question, knowing which foods to eat and which ones to avoid can help add years to your life.

Research around the globe has discovered that certain ways of eating—or dietary patterns—are strongly linked with longevity. The low-fat and nutrient-rich diet of the residents of Okinawa, Japan, has contributed to their very long average life expectancy. A vegetarian diet has also been associated with successful aging. And the typical diet followed by people living in Mediterranean countries—plentiful in fruits, vegetables and olive oil—is thought to have helped them age better and live longer. As well, findings from many studies have made it clear that compared to our Western diet pattern emphasizing meat, refined carbohydrates and sweets, a so-called "prudent" way of eating is related to a higher life expectancy.

There's an underlying theme connecting all of these dietary patterns—they are all plant-based. Each one accentuates fruits, vegetables, whole grains, nuts and legumes while taking the focus off animal foods such as meat and poultry. Compared to a meat-centred diet, one that's plant-based provides more fibre, antioxidants and phytochemicals, as well as numerous vitamins and minerals. A plant-based diet is also considerably lower in saturated fat and cholesterol, two factors that raise levels of low-density lipoprotein (LDL) blood cholesterol—the "bad" kind of cholesterol. The bottom line: There's ample evidence to support the health benefits of a plant-based diet.

WHAT DOES A PLANT-BASED DIET LOOK LIKE?

A plant-based diet isn't necessarily vegetarian, although it can be. The extent to which you minimize your intake of animal foods is up to you. If you don't want to give up animal foods entirely or all at once, you can gradually add more vegetarian meals to your diet on a regular basis. For some people, making the transition to a plant-based diet means eating a 4 ounce (120 g) steak rather than their usual 10 ounce (300 g) cut. For others, it means adding cooked lentils to pasta sauce instead of ground meat. And for some, it might mean pouring soy beverage over their breakfast cereal instead of cow's milk. The main point is this: Make vegetables, legumes and whole grains the main attraction of your meals. And if you're already following a plant-based diet, that's great! The following chapters will highlight which particular foods you need to eat more of—and less of—for successful aging.

THE CALORIE–LONGEVITY CONNECTION

When it comes to longevity, there's more to diet than the foods you include and the ones you limit. That's very important, but there is also the question of how much food you eat. In other words, the number of calories you consume each day can have a direct impact on your life expectancy. It's a concept called "calorie restriction" and it's been around since the 1930s. So far, animal studies have shown that maintaining a low-calorie diet over the long term can dramatically lengthen lifespan—in all species tested, including yeast, worms, flies, mice, dogs and primates. On a reduced-calorie diet, animals live longer than it had been thought possible—up to 30 percent longer—and remain more youthful, energetic and remarkably healthy.

The underlying premise of calorie restriction is to eat fewer calories while consuming all the necessary protein, vitamins and other nutrients. It's believed to extend lifespan in two ways. First, cutting calories reduces the production of free radicals, highly damaging forms of oxygen linked to aging. It also seems to increases the resistance of cells to stress, helping them live longer.

Whether calorie restriction can help humans live 30 percent longer remains to be seen. But studies conducted so far have found that limiting calories certainly blunts aging. Researchers found that people who practised calorie restriction on their own for six years scored vastly better than did control subjects on all major risk factors for heart disease, including blood cholesterol, triglycerides, blood pressure and inflammation. In Chapter 8, "The Calorie-Longevity Connection," you'll learn the promising results from a large, ongoing U.S. study investigating the effects of a calorie-restricted diet in healthy humans. And I'll show you how to apply calorie restriction to your diet, safely and healthfully, to help you slow down the signs of aging.

Longevity factor #2: Stay physically active

It's hardly news that regular physical activity keeps you healthier and fit. Countless studies have demonstrated that being active reduces the risk of developing a number of diseases including diabetes, cancer, heart attack and stroke. As a matter of fact, leading a sedentary lifestyle is considered an independent risk factor for heart attack. That means that being a couch potato—aside from other risk factors like smoking, high blood pressure and high cholesterol—increases your odds of suffering a heart attack.

But can exercise actually slow the aging process? It's a good question, and until recently we thought that regular exercise fought aging only by reducing the risk of age-related illness and controlling weight. Well, it turns out there's added incentive to add physical activity to your daily routine: Exercise can help you stay younger for longer. Imagine at 80 having the muscle mass, strength and bone density you did when you were in your fifties? Or playing tennis and hiking without any joint pain? Believe me, it is possible to live an active, healthy life longer than you ever expected. But there's a catch: You need to get your body moving. There's no doubt that regular exercise is a secret weapon against the normal course of aging.

Aging does cruel things to the body. Our muscles slowly atrophy, a process called *sarcopenia* that begins in middle age, making us weaker. Our bone mass dwindles, causing our skeleton to lose height. With thinner bones, you're more likely to fall and fracture a wrist, an arm or, worse, a hip. Your joints take a hit too. Cartilage, the rubbery tissue that connects bone to tendon, becomes brittle and weak. Aging joints mean sore, stiff joints. Not a pretty picture. But here's the good news: Exercise can combat many of these not-so-nice but natural changes that occur as we grow older.

EXERCISE AND LONGEVITY

You've already learned that exercise, as a natural part of daily life, is central to the lives of elders and centenarians living in Blue Zone communities. But you don't have to be born in Sardinia or Okinawa to reap the life-promoting benefits of exercise. Studies closer to home suggest that being fit can add years to your life, whereas being inactive can lead to premature death. In one study of 4634 people living in Massachusetts, U.S., participating in a high level of physical activity from age 50 onwards not only boosted life expectancy but increased the number of years lived free of heart disease. Compared to less active people, men and women who reported the highest level of daily exercise gained an extra 3.5 years of life.[1] The Harvard Alumni Health Study of 13,485 men found that those who burned 2000 to 3000 calories per week through exercise lived almost two years longer than sedentary individuals.[2]

There's additional evidence that becoming active in middle life increases longevity. Researchers at the Harvard Public School of Health looked at the health of 13,535 American women who had reached the age of 70 or older without any health ailments. Those who had higher levels of physical activity beginning at midlife were substantially less likely to suffer an illness or any physical or cognitive impairment as they aged. It was regular, moderate-intensity midlife exercise that made all the difference to successful aging. Those who regularly walked at a moderate pace, starting from midlife, had a better chance of exceptional health than those who walked at an easy, slow pace. What's more, moderate walking improved later-life health in both lean and overweight women. (However, those who kept their weight down and exercised more vigorously than moderate walking experienced the best health.) The bottom line: Fitter people live longer, even if they have a few extra pounds around the middle.[3]

GIVE YOUR DNA A WORKOUT One way exercise might increase your lifespan is by keeping your DNA healthy. In Chapter 1, I discussed telomeres, those short sequences of DNA that cap the ends of your chromosomes, protecting them from becoming damaged so that cells remain vital. If you'll recall, every time a cell divides, its telomeres become shorter and shorter, until eventually the cell dies. Longer telomeres have, in fact, been linked to a longer life in animals and humans. It turns out that exercise can counteract telomere shortening. In a study of twins living in the United Kingdom, women and men who were sedentary had shorter telomeres than their active peers, regardless of their age. Compared to people who were inactive, those who exercised three hours per week had telomeres the same length as sedentary people ten years younger.[4] In other words, if you lead a sedentary life you may be biologically ten years older than your active cohorts!

STRENGTHEN YOUR BICEPS Adding weights to your workout routine can also reverse muscle aging. As we age, genes that control the health of our muscle cells change. Those involved in muscle cell repair, DNA repair and cell death become *up-regulated,* or more active, as we get older. Genes that help the mitochondria, the engine inside each cell, convert nutrients into muscle fuel become less active with age. To determine if exercise could reverse muscle decline all the way down to the genetic level, scientists studied the genes of healthy young adults and healthy older adults. After six months of strength training twice weekly, the genetic profile of the older folks' muscles closely resembled that of the younger individuals. A total of 179 genes were affected by exercise and returned to impressive, younger levels. What's more, the leg muscles of the older group became 50 percent stronger than before training.[5]

Regular exercise isn't meant just for the young. Getting active at any age can promote longevity and improve your health in later years. Nobody wants to spend their last five or more years weak and frail in a nursing home—and the latest research on aging has shown us there is no need for it to be that way. But preventing that dismal nursing-home scenario demands action now. If exercise isn't part of your life, you can change that right away. Let the facts about how exercise can keep you biologically younger and healthier inspire you to start moving now, so that you can enjoy an energetic old age.

WHAT KIND OF EXERCISE—AND HOW OFTEN, HOW HARD?

By now you're probably wondering what type of exercise you need to do to extend your life. There's no question that strength training, also called resistance training, can help you hold on to your muscle mass as you age by offsetting sarcopenia, that gradual process of muscle decline. Resistance training can even help you regain lost muscle mass. And as you learned earlier, this type of exercise can keep your muscle cells youthful by influencing the activity of genes. But you need to do more than lift weights a few times each week to live longer.

Aerobic, or cardiovascular exercise, is also important. It helps keep your blood vessels younger by slowing the rate at which they become stiff. As your arteries stiffen with age, your blood pressure gradually climbs. Regular cardio workouts also help your body use glucose (sugar) efficiently, keeping diabetes at bay. Working out on a regular basis—both cardio and resistance training—is also good for your brain. Study participants who engage in a regular exercise program are sharper—they have enhanced mental focus and a slower decline in cognitive function—and they cope better with conflict.

Finally, you need to include exercise that helps keep your joints flexible and your muscles relaxed. Flexibility exercises such as gently bending, reaching and stretching your muscles may not add years to your life but they will most definitely add life to your years. Being flexible helps reduce muscle soreness after exercise, improves your posture, reduces back pain and helps circulate nutrients and oxygen to your muscles. And the more flexible you are, the less likely you'll get injured during exercise, allowing you to be active day after day.

It's beyond the scope of this book to lay out a detailed exercise program that promotes longevity. I strongly recommend you consult a certified personal trainer to help you develop a plan based on your fitness level and ability. A personal trainer will help you set achievable goals, ensure you are exercising correctly and motivate you along the way. In the meantime, the guide below will give you an idea of what to work towards.

STRENGTH TRAINING, 2 TO 4 TIMES PER WEEK Research suggests that virtually all of the health benefits of resistance training can be obtained in two 15- to 20-minute sessions per week. If your goal is to build muscle strength, you'll need to work out longer and more often. There are many different ways to add resistance training to your fitness program.

Activities and exercises for building strength

At home	At home or the gym	At the gym/ community centre
• Heavy yard work • Raking and carrying leaves • Climbing stairs	• Push-ups • Chin-ups • Abdominal crunches • Squats • Lunges	• Free weights (dumbbells, barbells) • Nautilus machines • Cybex machines • Spinning • Pilates

As you get stronger, it will become easier and easier to lift the same amount of weight or to perform the same number of push-ups. Throughout your program, you must periodically (and gradually) increase the amount of work your muscles perform so that further improvements can be made. That means you need to increase the amount of weight you lift or the number of push-ups and sit-ups you do.

GUIDELINES FOR SAFE STRENGTH TRAINING

- Warm up with five minutes of light aerobic activity and stretching to get your circulation going and your joints moving.
- Ask a personal trainer to show you proper technique to protect your back and joints.
- Breathe regularly when doing an exercise.
- Rest for at least one day between strength training sessions.

CARDIOVASCULAR EXERCISE, 4 TO 7 DAYS PER WEEK There are plenty of different aerobic activities that get your lungs, heart and blood vessels in shape, such as brisk walking, hiking, jogging, cycling, swimming, dancing and cross-country skiing. If you prefer the gym, you'll have a number of different machines and a variety of aerobic classes to choose from. The key is finding things you like to do and mixing it up so you don't get bored.

While it's clear that cardiovascular exercise helps you live longer, it's less clear whether exercise intensity plays a role. In other words, how hard do you need to work out to live longer? There's some evidence that higher-intensity cardio exercise is better than low-intensity activity. The Harvard Alumni Health Study mentioned earlier revealed that greater calorie expenditure from moderate and vigorous exercise increased longevity. Participation in light activities, such as slow walking, regardless of the number of calories burned, wasn't related to life expectancy. However, men who participated in moderate physical activity—like brisk walking—lived longer than their peers who engaged in light activities. But men who lived the longest in the study were those who worked out the hardest—they burned more calories through regular vigorous exercise such as running and cycling.

EXERCISE INTENSITY You can use your heart rate to track exercise intensity. First you'll need to determine your maximal heart rate, the maximum number of times your heart beats in one minute. There's a simple formula you can use to estimate your maximal heart rate (MHR): 220 minus your age in years. Low-intensity exercise is performed at 50 percent to 60 percent of your maximal heart rate, moderate intensity at 60 percent to 70 percent, and high-intensity at 75 percent to 85 percent.

By multiplying these numbers by your maximal heart rate, you can determine your heart rate zone for each exercise intensity. For example, if your maximal heart rate is 170 and you want to work out at a moderate intensity, you'll need to keep your heart rate between 102 and 119 beats per minute (the math: 170 x 0.6 = 102; 170 x 0.7 = 119). I recommend investing in a heart rate monitor to wear during exercise. It will tell you whether you're going too easy, too hard or just right. While a higher intensity may increase lifespan, not all your workouts need to be vigorous. You should include a variety of intensity levels in your weekly routine since each exercise intensity level draws on different energy systems and as such can offer different health benefits. Low-intensity light aerobic exercise burns mainly fat while high-intensity hard aerobic exercise burns glucose (sugar). While it's true that working out at a lower intensity burns fat as fuel, this isn't the best intensity to work at if you're trying to lose weight. Exercising at higher intensities will help you shed pounds faster because you burn more calories. You'd have to exercise longer to get the same calorie burn from a low intensity workout. In fact, some research suggests that exercising harder burns more calories both during and *after* your workout.

Ultimately, how hard you should work depends on your current fitness level. If you're a beginner, work at a lower range to burn more overall calories. If you're an exercise veteran, you can exercise more vigorously. If you have an exercise restriction due to an injury, a health condition or medications, be sure to check with your doctor before starting an exercise program.

FLEXIBILITY, 4 TO 7 DAYS PER WEEK Stretching is often the most overlooked part of a fitness program. But the beauty of flexibility exercises is that they can be performed relatively quickly at any time of the day. It's easy to take a five-minute stretch break in the middle of your day. And many of the activities you perform each day—vacuuming, yard work, gardening—help to maintain your flexibility. Sports like golf, bowling and curling also include a flexibility component. Classes such as tai chi, yoga and pilates are also fantastic ways to increase your flexibility.

It's best to do some light activity for five minutes before you stretch. This increases your body temperature and your range of motion. Or do your stretching after a cardio workout, when your muscles are warmed up. Stretching cold muscles may cause injury. Think of your muscles like plastic: Plastic is hard to stretch when it's cold, but add a little heat and the plastic becomes softer and more pliable. Your muscles behave the same way. During exercise, your muscles generate heat and they become more pliable.

Stretch slowly and smoothly without bouncing or jerking. Use gentle continuous movement or stretch-and-hold for 10 to 30 seconds, whichever is right for the exercise. Stretch to the limit of the movement but not to the point of pain. You should aim for a stretched, relaxed feeling. And don't hold your breath. Keep breathing slowly and rhythmically while holding the stretch. If you're not sure what to do, get help from a fitness expert at your gym. Or pick up a book on stretching at your local bookstore.

Longevity factor #3: Exercise your brain

After extensive interviewing and cognitive testing of New England centenarians, researchers learned something surprising. Many of these men and women still had remarkable thinking ability. In fact, one-quarter of these century-old people were completely free of any mental disorders such as dementia. While many factors are thought to be responsible for their preserved brain power—a healthy diet, regular physical exercise, genetics—staying mentally active plays a key role.

Just like your muscles, your brain needs regular exercise to stay healthy as you age. As we get older the brain can atrophy in the same way muscles can. With the passing of years, the brain becomes less able to withstand damage caused by aging and other factors (e.g., smoking), causing signs of memory loss. The brain's resilience to endure neurological damage with age is called *cognitive reserve*. You can think of cognitive reserve as your brain's ability to create new neural pathways and to make connections that can be used as a "backup savings account" to allow you to draw on at a later date. And the bigger your brain's saving account, the better you'll protect your memory and perhaps even fend off damage caused by Alzheimer's disease.

Just because your cognitive reserve diminishes with age doesn't mean you're destined to live your elder years scatterbrained and forgetful. Hardly; in fact, researchers believe it's entirely possible to maintain—and increase— your cognitive reserve. Your brain has what's called plasticity, meaning it has a lifelong ability to create new neuronal pathways based on new experiences. To build your cognitive reserve, researchers agree, you need to lead a mentally stimulating life. In other words, keep your mind active throughout your life. Just like your muscles, if you don't exercise it your brainpower will atrophy.

BUILD YOUR COGNITIVE RESERVE

The earlier you begin building your cognitive reserve the better. But it's never too late to start. Exercises to strengthen brainpower should offer challenge and novelty. If an activity bores you, it's doing nothing to stretch your mind. Teaching your brain new things as simple as driving a new route to work or trying a new recipe can help boost cognitive reserve. If you're more adventurous you might even consider learning to play an instrument or a new language. The more activities you do, the better—the effect is cumulative. Use the ideas below to stimulate your intellect on a daily basis.

- *Play word games.* Do the crossword or Sudoku puzzle in your daily newspaper. Or browse the shelves of your local bookstore for books on brain teasers, puzzles and word games. Board games count too. Rather than watching television after dinner, challenge a family member to a game of Scrabble. Or play a strategy board game such as Monopoly, Risk or Ticket to Ride to exercise your grey matter.
- *Test your memory.* Write down a list of things—names of Canadian prime ministers, U.S. state capitals, vitamin C rich foods, and so on—and then memorize it. An hour later, see how many you recall. Don't make this exercise too easy. For greater brain stimulation, try to learn something new.
- *Solve math problems in your head.* Try to do simple arithmetic in your head without the help of pen and paper or a calculator.
- *Pick up a new hobby.* Learn a new skill that involves hand-eye coordination such as knitting, needlework, sewing, painting or building a puzzle. Consider taking on a new sport that combines mental and physical prowess such as golf or martial arts.

Longevity factor #4: Get proper sleep

A good night's rest: It's something everybody needs and many people yearn for. Think about how you feel after a solid eight hours of uninterrupted sleep: more alert, more energetic, happier and better able to cope with life's daily stresses. Now think about how you feel when you lack sleep—tired, lethargic, irritable, unmotivated and less productive. Sleep deprivation can make your whole body feel worn out—your muscles feel weary, your eyes throb, your appetite fades, even your digestive system becomes sluggish. The fact that proper rest makes us feel better certainly suggests there's a strong link between sleep and health.

There are reasons why our bodies aren't programmed to be awake 24/7. During sleep our body restores, repairs and rejuvenates itself. Many of our body's major restorative functions—muscle growth, tissue repair, protein synthesis and growth hormone release—occur during our sleep. Scientists also believe that sleep plays an important role in brain function. It is critical for brain development in infants and children. In adults, sleep is related to changes in brain structure and organization that affect our memory, ability to learn and capacity to perform a variety of mental tasks.

SLEEP AND LIFE EXPECTANCY

The health cost of poor sleep might be greater than you think. Study after study has found that decreased sleep increases the risk for dozens of illnesses and health problems including obesity, high blood pressure, heart disease, stroke, diabetes, breast and colon cancers and depression. It's not surprising, then, that researchers have determined that regularly failing to get enough sleep can shorten your life expectancy. A recent review of 23 studies concluded that short sleepers (getting less than seven hours' sleep per night) had a greater risk of dying from any cause compared to those who slept seven to eight hours per night.[6]

Missing sleep has a number of harmful effects on your body. Studies have determined that too little sleep raises blood pressure, impairs blood-sugar control, generates inflammatory compounds and increases levels of a stress hormone called cortisol. Sleep deprivation can also wreak havoc on weight control. Sleep deprivation increases the body's production of ghrelin, the hormone that tells us we're hungry, and decreases production of leptin, the hormone that tells us we're full.

It's not only short sleepers who may have a shorter lifespan. People who sleep more than nine hours each night have also been shown to have a higher risk of dying from any cause. Compared to people who get seven to eight hours per night, long sleepers are 38 percent more likely to die from cardiovascular disease and 21 percent more likely to have a cancer-related death.[7] The link between long sleep and mortality is not well understood. It's believed that long sleepers experience more fragmented sleep, which, in turn, can increase inflammation in the body.

HOW MUCH SLEEP?

If sleep is one key to a longer life, how much do you need each day? The amount of necessary sleep varies from person to person but most adults need between seven and nine hours of sleep since studies indicate that increased disease risk kicks in with less than seven hours. Children and teenagers should strive for nine to ten hours of sleep each night. The trouble, of course, is getting that sleep, with the Internet, e-mail, television and household chores competing for our time. And with age, our sleep becomes shallower, causing us to wake up more often.

Since the detrimental health effects of too little sleep develop over time, it's important to make proper sleep a priority now. If you don't get seven to nine hours of shut-eye each night, the following tips can help improve your sleep.

- *Establish a pre-sleep routine.* Reading a book, drinking a cup of chamomile tea or taking a warm bath can all help to slow the mind and the body, preparing them for sleep. Stop watching television or doing office work at least one hour before bedtime. Instead, do something that helps you turn your mind off and relax.
- *Control your sleep environment.* Keep your bedroom dark and quiet and make sure it is not too warm or too cool. If you need to lower the volume on outside noise, consider using earplugs or a white-noise appliance— even a small fan can do the trick. Use heavy curtains or shades to block outside light.

  Turn your bedside clock away from you so you can't see the time if you wake up in the middle of the night. Knowing that you have only a few hours until morning can cause stress and make it harder to fall back asleep.

  Finally, use your bedroom as a place to sleep—don't use it for watching television, eating, exercising, working or other activities associated with wakefulness.
- *Stick to a consistent sleep schedule.* As much as possible, go to bed and wake up at the same times each day to help set your body's internal clock. Try to stick to this schedule on weekends, too, to avoid feeling sleepy on Monday.
- *Avoid naps.* Late-afternoon naps can make it difficult to fall asleep at night. If you need to nap, limit your snooze to 30 minutes and make sure it's over before 4 P.M.

- *Avoid late-night meals.* Avoid eating a heavy meal during the two hours before bedtime. If you eat close to bedtime, your sleep will be more fragmented because your body is busy digesting. And the more fat you eat at your evening meal, the more likely you will experience sleep disruptions. If you are prone to heartburn, avoid spicy meals that can trigger symptoms and prevent you getting a good night's sleep.
- *Limit caffeine.* Caffeine blocks the action of adenosine, a brain chemical that induces sleep. If you're having trouble sleeping, aim for no more than 200 milligrams a day, and preferably less. (One 8-ounce cup of coffee has 80 to 175 milligrams of caffeine; the same serving size of tea has 45 milligrams.) Avoid caffeine in the afternoon and evening.
- *Avoid alcohol.* Although drinking alcoholic beverages can make you feel drowsy, a few hours later alcohol acts as a stimulant that will awaken you during the night. Alcohol can also impair REM (rapid eye movement) sleep, the portion of sleep thought to be important for memory. Limit alcohol to one to two drinks per day and avoid drinking three hours before bedtime.
- *Manage stress.* If stress is keeping you awake at night, practise relaxation techniques. Learn to breathe deeply, meditate or practise yoga. If these techniques don't work for you, consider speaking with a stress management counsellor.
- *Exercise early.* Regular exercise helps you fall asleep faster and relieves stress. Exercise should be done at least three hours before bedtime. A workout right before bed can make falling asleep more difficult.

Longevity factor #5:
Maintain a positive attitude

There's no doubt that your outlook on life can have an impact on longevity. That's certainly what researchers have learned by interviewing centenarians. People who manage to live to a ripe old age tend to be an optimistic bunch. As a matter of fact, there's a growing body of scientific evidence to back up the notion that having a positive attitude helps you live longer. Studies have shown that people who see the glass half full tend to have fewer heart attacks, be less vulnerable to cancer and have a lower risk of dying from any cause during the study periods, compared to people who view the glass half empty.

One of the first studies to document a strong connection between personality and longevity was conducted in 1000 Dutch men and women aged 65 to 85 years. Compared with their pessimistic peers, older adults who had the highest level of optimism had half the risk of dying. What's more, they were also 77 percent less likely to die from heart disease even after the researchers accounted for traditional cardiovascular risk factors such as body weight, high blood pressure and high cholesterol.[8] A more recent study published in 2010 found that, among 23,216 adults, those who were the least pessimistic about life had half the risk of suffering a stroke than their pessimistic counterparts.[9] And there's more. A review of 83 studies investigating optimism and health concluded that optimism is a significant predictor of living longer and many positive health outcomes.[10]

OPTIMISM: THE MIND—BODY CONNECTION

What's at work here? Why are people with sunny dispositions healthier and more likely to live longer? For starters, optimistic folks tend to be more physically active, sleep better, smoke less and drink less than pessimistic people. Optimists most likely cope with stress differently too. Their temperament prevents them from being too overwhelmed by things. And they tend to take advantage of new opportunities, a trait that helps keep their minds active and healthy.

But there's more to the story than how one deals with the stress life presents us. Having a positive attitude actually affects the body's chemistry. Compared to pessimists, optimistic people have lower levels of inflammatory compounds in their bloodstream, chemicals linked to a number of diseases.[11] And they have lower levels of cortisol, a stress hormone that when elevated for a prolonged period can impair blood-sugar control, weaken the immune system, decrease bone density and increase abdominal fat. It's also thought that having a positive outlook on life can down-regulate—quiet— your automatic nervous system, the network of nerves that control heart rate, blood flow and breathing. In this way, being optimistic may help keep blood pressure in check.

Not everyone is naturally optimistic. Some people are more inclined to worry over things they can't control and others may be more skeptical about life's opportunities. Optimists look for the light at the end of the tunnel. They see possibilities that allow them to take action to solve problems, experience success in their work and improve their relationships. They deal with the rough spots and move on. Optimists don't think that nothing bad will ever happen—rather, they hope life's good moments will outweigh the bad ones. Compared to people with a negative outlook, optimists are happier, more hopeful, have more energy and tend to be satisfied with life.

HOW TO BE MORE OPTIMISTIC

Being optimistic is a choice you make and it's a choice that can help you live a longer, healthier life. If negative thinking tends to pervade your outlook, there are ways to help you start seeing the glass half full. Even optimists need to make an effort every so often to reframe their outlook.

- *Use positive self-talk.* Frame the way you see the world in a positive manner. Make a list of positive affirmations and post it where you'll see it every day. Statements like "I always have a choice," "Anything is possible," "I look for the positive in every situation" and "I control my attitude" can shape a positive outlook on life.
- *Live for the day.* Remember that life is short. When you start to feel down or worried about the future, remind yourself that the only day you have for certain is today and every minute counts. If you live life day by day, it's much easier to let go of the past and stop fretting over the future.
- *Smile more often.* Believe it or not, studies have found that putting a happy look on your face, even if you don't want to, actually does make you feel more positive about the future. Similarly, as funny as it sounds, walk with a bounce in your step. Pessimists tend to take small steps slowly. By speeding your pace you'll feel more energetic and purposeful.
- *Surround yourself with positive people.* Don't let negative people drain your energy. Spend time with friends who view life positively, who have fun and make you feel happy. If you can't avoid a pessimist, learn how to not let that person bring you down.
- *Put yourself first.* It's important to pay attention to your personal needs even if you are busy taking care of kids, a spouse and parents. By allowing yourself to do things that make you feel good—going for a run, getting a massage or having dinner with an old friend—you'll have more energy and happiness to give to others.
- *Give back to others.* Volunteer your time and energy to others in need and causes you care about. Even small acts of thoughtfulness, like offering your seat on the bus to someone or letting somebody jump ahead of you in line, can make you feel positive about yourself and those around you.

Longevity factor #6:
Stay connected to others

You may not realize it but the social networks you develop in your life can play a role in how long you'll live. Think back to the Blue Zones discussed in the previous chapter. In each longevity hot spot, social contact plays a central role in daily life. Sardinians and Okinawans have strong ties to family and the community at large. Elders are cared for by younger family members and they are respected for their wisdom, experience and contributions to the family. In the Seventh-day Adventist community of Loma Linda, California, residents connect with one another through regular church attendance and volunteer work.

Research conducted in other parts of the world has also revealed that social contact with friends, relatives and the greater community predicts a longer active life. Studies have revealed that people with few social ties are more likely to die before those with extensive contacts. As well, men living alone appear more likely to die sooner than their married peers.[12]

Maintaining a vital role in one's extended family can also help you live longer. Elderly persons living in Spain who felt their role in their children's lives was important had a 30 percent lower risk of dying over the fifteen-year study compared to those who felt they played only a small role.[13] And research from Australia hints that having many friends is beneficial for a longer life. People with the widest network of good friends and confidants outlived those with the fewest friends by 22 percent. The protective effect of friends continued throughout the decade-long study, regardless of other profound life experiences such as the death of a loved one.[14]

How your social connections extend your lifespan isn't well understood. Friends and family members may encourage older people to take better care of themselves by eating healthfully, exercising more, cutting down on smoking or seeking medical treatment sooner for health problems. Maintaining close social contacts can also help people get through difficult times by offering coping mechanisms and having a positive effect on mood.

It's not always easy to keep up meaningful social ties as we age. Divorce, widowhood and the death of close friends is an unfortunate but real part of life. However, there are a number of ways to stay connected to others as we grow older. Many of the options below may also promote longevity by improving your physical and mental fitness level.[15]

- *Pursue social activities.* Wine tastings, lecture programs, even travelling with friends can help you expand your social network and stay connected to others.
- *Get involved.* Take on projects that require you to have regular contact with others, like planning a gathering for a club, organizing a card- or game-playing night with friends or helping out with a church supper.
- *Look for community programs.* Take advantage of programs and services offered at community and senior centres.
- *Volunteer.* Donate your time to a cause you believe in such as a charity, a local school, a library or a museum.
- *Consider group exercise.* Join a walking or biking club or a fitness or yoga class at a community fitness centre.
- *Enroll in a course.* Take an adult-education or college course in a topic that interests you. You'll meet new people and build your cognitive reserve at the same time!
- *Adopt a pet.* Animal companionship can bring happiness, love and meaning into our lives. Local animal shelters are full of potential furry friends looking for a home.

The power to live longer is, to a large degree, in your hands. According to the research findings that inspired this chapter, there are many ways you can alter your lifestyle to help increase your life expectancy: You can eat less meat and more plant foods, exercise your muscles and brain regularly and establish healthy sleep habits. Changing how you think about the world and connecting with those around you may also help add healthy years to your life. As you've just read, there's no single habit that's linked to successful longevity. All six lifestyle habits described in this chapter are thought to play an important role. When it comes to nutrition and longevity, the following chapters will help you transform your diet into one that will help you live better, longer.

PART 2

EAT RIGHT
TO LIVE LONGER

4

How foods help you live longer

The power of everyday foods is impressive. What you eat—and don't eat—on a regular basis can dramatically delay the onset of aging and age-related diseases such as heart disease, stroke, type 2 diabetes, certain cancers, cataracts, even Alzheimer's disease. Almost every day we hear how eating certain foods can help prevent one health problem or another. Foods such as fish and whole grains guard against heart disease, nuts and low-fat dairy products lower elevated blood pressure, leafy green vegetables shield your eyes from cataracts and berries slow down cognitive decline. And that's only a few examples of foods that help thwart aging.

The foods you eat contain hundreds of powerful substances capable of unlocking the key to longevity. Vitamins, minerals, antioxidants and phytochemicals all play an important role in keeping your body healthy—and younger—as you age. These microscopic protective compounds promote longevity by forestalling signs of aging at the cellular level. And they do so in a number of different ways.

For instance, your body needs small amounts of more than thirty different vitamins and minerals, on a daily basis, to facilitate thousands of metabolic reactions that keep your cells and tissues healthy. And since your body can't produce these vital compounds on its own, it relies on your diet to get them. In the appendix "A Guide to Vitamins and Minerals," you'll find the vitamins and minerals listed along with your daily requirements and best food sources.

Protein is also essential to healthy aging. Protein-rich foods such as poultry, fish, dairy products, legumes and soy supply amino acids that help conserve your muscle mass as you age. Protein, along with many vitamins, minerals and certain types of fat, is also needed to maintain a strong immune system as you grow older. If you recall from Chapter 1, many experts attribute the rate at which we age to a natural decline in the number and functioning of our body's immune cells. Safeguarding an aging immune system by eating a nutrient-packed diet can help prevent illness caused by viruses, bacteria and parasites. But that's not all. A resilient immune system is also better able to detect and kill off cancer cells.

There are other ways the copious protective compounds in foods can add years to your life. Your dietary choices can combat the very processes believed to contribute to the vast majority of age-related disease: oxidative stress, inflammation and insulin resistance.

A healthy diet can counteract oxidative stress

One of the main theories of aging revolves around the concept of oxidative stress, the body's imbalance between the production of highly reactive oxygen molecules called free radicals and its ability to detoxify these compounds or repair the harm they do. Your body constantly reacts with oxygen as you breathe and as your cells produce energy. In the process, harmful free radicals are formed that make contact with other molecules in cells. Free radicals can injure proteins, cell membranes and genes, which can lead to changes in the body associated with aging.

Oxidative damage has been implicated in many age-related diseases including atherosclerosis, heart attack, cancer, Alzheimer's disease, arthritis, cataracts and macular degeneration. (Macular degeneration is a disease that attacks the central part of the retina called the macula, which controls fine, detailed vision.) Free radicals also harm the mitochondria of cells, their energy-generating power plants, making cells less effective at producing the energy they need to keep functioning and alive.

FREE RADICAL DAMAGE ACCUMULATES WITH AGE As we get older we become more susceptible to the long-term effects of free radical damage. To counteract oxidative stress, our bodies produce enzymes—antioxidants—that mop up free radicals, neutralizing them before they can cause further damage. But your body's ability to produce antioxidants can become overwhelmed by other things that create free radicals, such as illness, an unhealthy diet and exposure to pollution and cigarette smoke.

That's where your diet comes in. Many foods, especially fruits and vegetables, are excellent sources of antioxidants and help your body ward off free radical damage and minimize the impact of aging. Vitamins C and E, beta carotene, selenium and thousands of phytochemicals in foods possess strong antioxidant action.

FOODS THAT FIGHT FREE RADICALS Which foods have the strongest antioxidant power? According to experts at the Jean Mayer USDA Human Nutrition Research Center on Aging at Tufts University in Massachusetts, they're foods that score high on an antioxidant test called ORAC (short for Oxygen Radical Absorbance Capacity). ORAC is a test-tube analysis that measures the ability of foods, your blood and just about anything else to fend off free radicals. As a matter of fact, eating high–ORAC foods has been shown to raise the antioxidant power of human blood by as much as 25 percent (fresh spinach produced the biggest rise, followed by vitamin C, strawberries and, lastly, red wine). Scientists have also demonstrated the ability of high–ORAC foods to prevent some long-term memory loss in middle-aged rats and to protect their tiny blood vessels from oxidative damage.[1]

Later, you'll learn more about how many of the foods that scored high on the ORAC test (listed in the table "Top-scoring ORAC Foods") can hold back the aging process.

Top-scoring ORAC Foods

Fruits	Vegetables
Prunes	Kale
Raisins	Spinach
Blueberries	Brussels sprouts
Blackberries	Alfalfa sprouts
Strawberries	Broccoli
Raspberries	Beets
Plums	Red peppers
Oranges	Onions
Red grapes	Corn
Cherries	Eggplant
Kiwifruit	
Pink grapefruit	

A healthy diet can prevent and reduce inflammation

Inflammation is a very hot topic in medical research. Study after study continues to uncover the many ways in which chronic, low-grade inflammation harms the body. In fact, inflammation is now recognized as a major determinant of numerous age-related diseases including heart attack, stroke, Alzheimer's, diabetes, metabolic syndrome and arthritis, to name only a few. But inflammation isn't always a bad thing. The truth is, we need a healthy balance of inflammation to stay well.

INFLAMMATION AND AGING *Acute inflammation* is the short-term response of your body's immune system that allows you to heal from wounds and infection. For example, if a cut on your finger becomes infected, your immune system releases cells to seek out foreign invaders and repair the resulting damage. The redness, swelling, heat and pain you feel are actually good things—they are signs that your body's immune system is hard at work. Once its work is done and healing takes place, your immune system turns off this inflammatory response. It's when this response isn't turned completely off that problems arise.

Chronic inflammation is characterized by the ongoing release of inflammatory immune compounds. Think of it as the body's healing process in overdrive. The important thing to know is that prolonged inflammation can damage healthy tissues, such as artery walls and joint cartilage. It can also induce gene mutations that promote cancer development. Let's use heart disease as an example of inflammation run amok. When artery walls absorb cholesterol from your bloodstream this causes a buildup of fatty plaque. In an attempt to heal this damage, your body sends inflammatory cells to blood vessel walls. But your blood vessel walls can also release other chemicals that cause further inflammation and damage. Inflammation can be made worse if you smoke or have high blood pressure. Eventually, this chronic, low-grade inflammation may trigger a blood clot, which, in turn, can cause a heart attack or stroke.

Chronic inflammation can be caused by many factors, including a bacterial or viral infection, cigarette smoking, lack of sleep, sun exposure, a diet high in saturated (animal) fat, high blood pressure, elevated blood sugar and carrying too much body fat around your middle (abdominal obesity). Each of these factors can trigger the release of chemicals and activate cells involved in inflammation.

MEASURING INFLAMMATION There is a blood test that measures inflammation in your body: it's called *CRP* (C-reactive protein). CRP is a protein that's made by the liver during the acute phase of inflammation. It's also produced by abdominal fat and blood vessels that feed the heart. The amount of CRP produced by the body varies from person to person and is affected by your genetic makeup and lifestyle. People who smoke, have high blood pressure, are overweight and don't exercise tend to have higher CRP levels, whereas lean individuals who exercise tend to have lower levels.

Another test, called *hs*-CRP (high-sensitivity C-reactive protein), is used to detect very low levels of CRP in the blood. Doctors use this test in seemingly healthy people—e.g., people who have normal blood-cholesterol levels—to determine their risk of cardiovascular disease. The CRP test, on the other hand, is ordered for people at risk for bacterial or viral infection, or for those with chronic inflammatory diseases, such as rheumatoid arthritis, to see if the disease is responding to treatment and if inflammation in the body is decreasing.

FOODS AND INFLAMMATION Foods fit into three categories: they're either pro-inflammatory (e.g. they promote inflammation), neutral or anti-inflammatory. There are many compounds in foods that fight inflammation: antioxidants, omega-3 fatty acids, monounsaturated fat and phytochemicals called flavonoids are just a few. Foods rich in these substances, such as berries, green tea, salmon and olive oil, subdue inflammation in the body by promoting the production of anti-inflammatory immune compounds. In doing so, these foods help protect cells from signs of aging.

Pro-inflammatory foods include those high in saturated and trans fats, as well as high-glycemic foods like refined (white) starches and sweets, which spike your blood glucose. A steady intake of fatty meats, deep-fried fast food, refined grains, sweets and sugary beverages will favour the release of inflammatory chemicals in your body. You'll learn more about which foods to limit and avoid in Chapter 5.

A healthy diet can keep insulin levels low

Scientists are learning that insulin, the hormone that clears sugar (glucose) from your bloodstream, is a direct player in the aging process. And they're learning that something called the *insulin signalling pathway* plays a pivotal role in longevity. In fact, this pathway has been shown to extend longevity in species ranging from fruit flies to humans. Think of a signalling pathway as like a theatrical play with a cast of actors, each playing a very specific role in the play's story. The actors in the insulin signalling pathway include insulin itself, insulin receptors, enzymes and transporter proteins inside cells. The plot, like any theatrical production, unfolds in stages.

THE INSULIN SIGNALLING PATHWAY In the first act you eat a meal that includes, let's say, pasta, which is rich in carbohydrates. Your body digests these carbohydrates and breaks them down into small sugar units called glucose, which are then absorbed across the wall of your small intestine into your bloodstream. This influx of glucose tells your pancreas to produce and secrete insulin into the blood in order to move the sugar into your cells where it's needed for energy. By doing this, your blood-glucose level returns to normal.

In act two, insulin in the blood binds to its receptor on the surface of a cell, which then transmits a flurry of signals that activate a number of enzymes inside the cell. These enzymes go to work, allowing glucose transporters to shuttle glucose from the blood to fat cells and muscle cells. In the final act, the glucose level in cells increase and glucose in the bloodstream decreases. That, very simplistically, is the insulin signalling pathway, which in reality is extremely complex and involves many chemical players.

As we age, our cells become less sensitive to the action of insulin, which can lead to a condition called *insulin resistance*. In insulin resistance, the body becomes insensitive to the effect of insulin and as a result is less able to remove glucose from the bloodstream. With more sugar remaining in the bloodstream than normal, the pancreas compensates by working harder and harder to produce more and more insulin in an attempt to keep blood sugar under control. Insulin resistance, which can be worsened by overweight and a sedentary lifestyle, is a potent risk factor for type 2 diabetes, a disease that can steal five to ten years from your life.

LESS INSULIN LEADS TO A LONGER LIFE Interestingly, healthy centenarians have been shown to have less insulin resistance—as well as lower levels of oxidative stress—than their peers under 90. Studies have found that centenarians living in southern Italy have greatly enhanced insulin sensitivity and have lower blood-insulin levels than other elderly citizens.[2,3] Also intriguing are findings from a study of 466 healthy adults, aged 28 to 110, which revealed that 90- to 100-year-olds were far less likely to have insulin resistance than younger study participants.[4] This strongly suggests that having an efficient insulin response helps you live longer.

Scientists believe that maintaining low levels of insulin in the blood, which reduces insulin signalling inside cells, can help clear the way to a long and healthy life. Boston researchers showed that mice genetically engineered to lack an enzyme called Irs-2 in brain cells—an enzyme that conveys the insulin signal inside the cell—lived almost half a year longer than normal mice despite being overweight. They were more active in their old age, they held on to their youthful metabolic rate and they retained higher levels of antioxidant enzymes. On the other hand, mice with normal levels of the Irs-2 enzyme aged less gracefully—they had more sluggish metabolisms, became more sedentary and had lower levels of blood antioxidants after eating meals. The researchers concluded that the engineered mice lived longer because the diseases that normally kill them—cancer, heart disease and diabetes—were postponed by reducing insulin signalling in the brain.[5]

FOODS AND INSULIN LEVELS The best way to keep insulin levels low in the brain—and in the rest of the body—is to eat a healthy diet, maintain a lean body weight and get regular exercise. When it comes to diet, what's most important is choosing low-glycemic carbohydrate foods—foods that release their glucose gradually, instead of quickly, into the bloodstream and, as a result, don't cause your insulin level to spike. (The faster your blood sugar rises after eating, the more insulin your pancreas pumps into your blood-stream to move glucose in your cells.)

Nutritionists use a scale called the glycemic index (GI) to rank carbohydrate-rich foods by how fast they raise blood sugar levels compared to pure glucose, which is ranked 100. As you just learned, foods with a high GI value are digested quickly and cause a rapid rise in blood sugar, and there-fore, an outpouring of insulin. A steady intake of high GI carbohydrates can lead to chronically elevated blood glucose and insulin levels and eventually insulin resistance, a precursor for type 2 diabetes.

Foods that are ranked high on the GI scale (70 or higher) include white bread, whole-wheat bread, baked potatoes, refined breakfast cereals, instant oatmeal, cereal bars, Pop Tarts, raisins, dates, ripe bananas, carrots, honey and sugar.

Foods with a low GI (less than 55) release sugar more slowly into the bloodstream and don't produce a rush of insulin. Examples include grainy breads with seeds, steel-cut oats, 100 percent bran cereals, brown rice, sweet potatoes, pasta, apples, citrus fruit, grapes, pears, legumes, nuts, milk, yogurt and soy milk.

The Glycemic Index Value of Selected Foods

Less than 55 – Low GI	55–70 – Medium GI	Greater than 70 – High GI

Bread and crackers

Pumpernickel bread, whole-grain	46
Sourdough rye bread	53
Cracked wheat	53
Linseed Rye, Rudolph's	55
Pita bread, white	57
Whole meal rye bread	58
Rye bread	65
Rye crispbreads	64
Stoned Wheat Thins	67
Breton Wheat Crackers	67
Light rye, Silverstein's Bakery	68
Whole-wheat bread	69
Melba toast	70
White bread	70
Water crackers	71
Bagel, white	72
Wonder, enriched white bread	73
Kaiser roll	73
Soda crackers	74
Rice cakes	82
Baguette, French	95

Breakfast cereals

All Bran Original, Kellogg's	42
All Bran Buds w/ Psyllium, Kellogg's	47
Red River	49
Oat Bran	50
Porridge made from steel-cut oats	52
Special K	54
Porridge made from rolled oats, large flake	62
Cream of Wheat	66
Oatmeal, instant	66
Grape Nuts	71
Raisin Bran	73
Bran Flakes	74
Cheerios	74
Cream of Wheat Instant	74
Corn Bran, Quaker	75

Shredded Wheat/Weetabix	75
Corn Flakes	81
Crispix, Kellogg's	87

Cookies, cakes and muffins

Sponge cake	46
Banana bread	47
Oatmeal cookies	55
Blueberry muffin	59
Digestive biscuits	59
Oat bran muffin	60
Angel food cake	67
Oatmeal muffins, made from mix	69
Arrowroot cookies	65
Graham crackers	74

Pasta, grains and potato

Barley	25
Fettuccine, egg	32
Spaghetti, whole-wheat	37
Spaghetti, white	41
Rice, white, converted, Uncle Ben's	45
Bulgur	46
Corn, sweet	53
Potato, sweet, mashed	54
Rice, brown	55
Rice, long-grain, white	56
Rice, basmati	58
Potato, new, unpeeled, boiled	62
Couscous	65
Millet	71
Rice, short-grain	72
Potato, french fries	75
Potato, white-skinned, baked	85
Potato, instant, mashed	86
Rice, instant	87
Potato, red-skinned, boiled	88
Potato, red-skinned, mashed	91

Legumes, nuts and seeds

Soy beans	18
Kidney beans	27
Lentils	30
Black beans	31

Lentil soup, canned	34
Chickpeas, canned	42
Baked beans	48
Black bean soup	64
Split pea soup	66
Almonds	15
Peanuts	14

Fruit and unsweetened juices

Cherries	22
Grapefruit	25
Peach	28
Apricot, dried	31
Apple	34
Pear	38
Tomato juice	38
Apple juice	40
Orange	42
Grapes	43
Orange juice	46
Mango	51
Banana	52
Kiwifruit	53
Pineapple	59
Raisins	64
Cantaloupe	65
Watermelon	72
Dates, dried	103

Milk products and milk alternatives

Yogurt, low-fat, aspartame	14
Milk, whole	27
Milk, skim	32
Yogurt, low-fat, sugar	33
Soy beverage, full-fat	33
Milk, chocolate	34
Ice cream, premium	39
Soy beverage, low-fat	44
Ice cream, regular	61
Tofu-based frozen dessert	115

Snack foods and sugary drinks

Potato chips	54
Popcorn	55
Cola	58
Corn chips	72
Sports Bar, PowerBar, chocolate	58
Gatorade	78
Pretzels	83

Sugars

Fructose (fruit sugar)	23
Lactose (milk sugar)	46
Honey	58
Sucrose (table sugar)	65
Glucose	100

Source: Foster-Powell K et al. International tables of glycemic index and glycemic load values: 2002. *Am J Clin Nutr* 2002; Vol. 76(1): 5–56.

Many of the anti-aging foods you'll read about in the next chapter—nuts, legumes, whole grains and fruit—have a low glycemic value.

But there's more to preventing high insulin levels than simply choosing healthy, low-glycemic carbohydrates. Portion size is important too. After all, if you eat a heaping plate of whole-wheat pasta, which is a low-glycemic food, you'll end up with a lot of glucose entering your bloodstream. This flood of glucose will then trigger the release of excessive insulin to deal with it. In other words, eating appropriate-sized portions and watching your calorie intake are major strategies to help maintain lower levels of blood insulin. In Chapter 8, I'll explain how your daily calorie intake can impact longevity. But now it's time to turn to Chapter 5 to learn about the "Top 25 Foods for Longevity."

5
Top 25 foods for longevity

There's no doubt that eating a nutrient-packed and antioxidant-rich diet is essential to helping you live a longer, healthier life. And there's no time to waste: the sooner you start, the greater the benefit. Taking steps right now to adopt the healthiest diet possible—along with the key longevity habits discussed in Chapter 3—will pay off much later in life. But you don't have to wait to reap the benefits. Adding these nutrition superstars to your diet will make you feel great right now. So let's get started.

On the pages that follow you'll learn about 25 incredibly healthy foods that have the potential to slow biological aging. (I've listed them in alphabetical order.) These foods are must-haves in a diet that's designed to slow the aging process because they act on multiple levels to slow aging. They provide unique antioxidants, vitamins and minerals that bolster our immune system, defend against free radicals, maintain a healthy blood-glucose and insulin level, and help keep chronic inflammation at bay.

I've given you plenty of quick and easy ways—no recipes required!—to add these nutritious foods to your diet. Making them a regular part of your meals will help you follow a plant-based diet—you'll notice that, with the exception of salmon, every single one is a plant food! They're the very foods you will be including in my Longevity Diet outlined in Chapter 9. You'll also find delicious recipes featuring these longevity foods in the last section of this book.

Almonds

Most of us have heard that almonds are good for us. Many studies have shown that eating a small handful of almonds each day lowers LDL (bad) cholesterol levels. And it's not just almonds that are good for your heart. A recent review of twenty-five studies concluded that all nuts help lower blood-cholesterol levels, even in people with normal cholesterol levels. And the more nuts you eat, the more benefit you get.[1] Almonds, however, deserve a special mention. Most of their fat is monounsaturated, the type that helps lower LDL cholesterol and raise good HDL cholesterol. (HDL stands for high density lipoprotein.) But that's not all—monounsaturated fat can reduce inflammation in the body and improve insulin sensitivity in people with diabetes.

Almonds are also rich in vitamin E, a potent antioxidant that protects cells from being oxidized by harmful free radicals. In fact, one serving of almonds (23 nuts) supplies nearly three-quarters of a day's worth of vitamin E. Vitamin E defends your brain cells and your LDL cholesterol from free radical damage. When your LDL cholesterol particles become oxidized, they're more dangerous because they can stick more readily to artery walls. Almonds are also an excellent source of magnesium and potassium, two minerals that help keep your blood pressure in the normal range. Finally, almonds are a low-glycemic food, which means that they help slow the rise in blood sugar after eating.

A word of caution: Almonds are easy to overeat. If you eat them by the handful you're likely to consume extra calories your waistline doesn't need. The best way to eat almonds—or any type of nut for that matter—is by controlled portions. Pre-portion one serving (1 ounce or 23 almonds) in a snack-sized Ziploc bag. To prevent weight gain, you will also need to subtract a similar number of calories from your diet. Substitute nuts for less healthy foods like cookies, ice cream, soft drinks, potato chips and refined starchy foods.

NOTABLE NUTRIENTS IN ALMONDS
(PER 1 OUNCE/30 G OR 23 ALMONDS)
163 calories, 14 grams (g) fat (9 g monounsaturated fat), 3.5 g fibre, 11 international units (IU) vitamin E, 75 milligrams (mg) calcium, 76 mg magnesium, 200 mg potassium

QUICK TIPS TO ADD ALMONDS TO YOUR DIET
- Add slivered almonds to a bowl of oatmeal, cold breakfast cereal or yogurt and berries.

- Start your day with a slice of whole-grain toast spread with almond butter and topped with sliced banana.
- Add ground almonds or almond butter to a breakfast smoothie.
- Sprinkle casseroles and steamed green beans with slivered or chopped almonds.
- Mix ground almonds into homemade turkey burgers.
- Toss slivered almonds into a green or spinach salad.
- Enjoy fresh apple slices spread with almond butter for a midday snack.
- Take a snack-size resealable bag of raw almonds, dried apricots and raisins to snack on at the office.

Recipes
Almond Orange Granola Parfait, page 225
Field Berry Almond Pancakes, page 228

Avocado

While technically a fruit, the avocado actually derives 84 percent of its calories from fat. But here's the good news: Avocados contain mainly monounsaturated fat. And just like almonds, avocados have been shown to lower LDL (bad) cholesterol in people with high cholesterol. What's more, avocados can also help raise your good, HDL cholesterol. Avocados are packed with potassium and they deliver lutein and zeaxanthin, two phytochemicals that guard against cataract and macular degeneration. Once consumed, lutein makes its way to the eye, where it protects both the retina and the lens from oxidative damage.

But there's more. Avocados are an excellent source of folate, a B vitamin that keeps the DNA of your cells in good repair. Half an avocado provides one-quarter of a day's worth of folate (the recommended daily intake of folate is 400 micrograms). Folate also helps rid the body of homocysteine, an amino acid that's produced during certain metabolic reactions. Normally homocysteine is transformed into harmless compounds with the help of folate and other B vitamins. But a lack of these vitamins can hamper the natural breakdown of homocysteine, causing it to accumulate in the bloodstream. Having too much homocysteine is linked with a higher risk of atherosclerosis, heart attack, stroke and possibly even Alzheimer's disease.

When adding avocado to your diet, think of it as an added fat: a little goes a long way when it comes to calories. Consider one-eighth of an avocado equivalent to 1 teaspoon (5 ml) of vegetable oil or 1 Fat Serving (as you'll learn in Chapter 9).

NOTABLE NUTRIENTS IN AVOCADO
(PER ONE-HALF)
161 calories, 14.7 g fat (9.8 g monounsaturated fat), 487 mg potassium, 81 micrograms (mcg) folate, 3 IU vitamin E

QUICK TIPS TO ADD AVOCADO TO YOUR DIET

- As a change from nut butter, spread a slice of whole-grain toast with ripe avocado. Add pepper to taste.
- Garnish black bean soup or turkey tacos with chopped avocado.
- Mix chopped avocados, red onion, tomatoes, cilantro and fresh lime juice to make a salsa to serve with grilled fish or chicken.
- Spread ripe avocados on whole-grain bread as a healthy replacement for butter or mayonnaise when making a sandwich.
- Instead of cheese, add slices of avocado to your next sandwich.
- Combine sliced avocado, sliced fennel, orange segments and fresh mint for a delicious salad. Top with fresh chopped parsley and drizzle with a teaspoon (5 ml) of extra-virgin olive oil.

Recipes
Black Bean and Avocado Salad with Toasted Cumin Dressing, page 247
Grilled Chicken with Tomato Cilantro Citrus Salsa, page 282
Shrimp, Mango and Avocado Salad, page 255

Beets

These colourful root vegetables owe their deep crimson hue to anthocyanins, powerful phytochemicals shown to have cancer-fighting properties. In animal studies, these phytochemicals activated the body's antioxidant enzymes to fight free radicals. It's true that beets have more natural sugar than any other vegetable, but they're still low in calories. And they're a great source of potassium and folate.

Beets are also a good source of betaine, a compound that's derived from a B vitamin–like compound called *choline*. Betaine protects cells from aging in a few ways. First, like folate in avocado, it helps remove homocysteine from the blood. Betaine also helps the liver process fats and protects liver cells from chemical damage. Finally, betaine in beets reduces inflammation in the body. In one study, researchers found that people who consumed the most betaine from their diet—versus the least—had 10 percent lower homocysteine levels, 19 percent lower C-reactive protein levels and 12 percent lower concentrations of another inflammatory chemical called tumour necrosis factor alpha.[2] (As you'll recall from Chapter 4, C-reactive protein, or CRP for short, is an inflammatory compound produced in the body.)

Some people shy away from beets because it takes time to prepare them. I suggest roasting or boiling whole beets in advance. That way, it takes only minutes to heat up them up for a side dish or to add them to a salad when it's meal time.

What's the best way to cook beets? Beets can be cooked in a variety of ways, but I prefer to roast my beets in the oven or on the barbecue. If using the oven, preheat to 400°F (200°C). Wash and scrub the whole beets to clean off any dirt. Leave the beets whole unless you have extra-large ones (if extra-large, cut in half). Trim off the stems and ends of the beets. (Save the nutrient-rich beet leaves to add to soup or to sauté as a side dish.) Wrap beets, in a single layer, in aluminum foil. Make sure the foil is tightly sealed.

Roast for approximately 1 to 1-1/2 hours or until tender and easily pierced with the tip of a paring knife. Remove beets from oven and allow to cool. When they are cool enough to handle, peel the skins off. They should peel easily by hand but you can use a paring knife if you prefer.

NOTABLE NUTRIENTS IN BEETS
(PER 1/2 CUP/125 ML COOKED)
37 calories, 0.1 g fat, 8.5 g carbohydrate, 1.7 g fibre, 259 mg potassium, 68 mcg folate

QUICK TIPS TO ADD BEETS TO YOUR DIET
- Add grated raw beets to a green salad or a healthy coleslaw made with shredded cabbage and carrots. Grated raw beets can also be added to a wrap sandwich.
- Beets can be added to a medley of oven-roasted winter vegetables. Because beets take longer to cook than other vegetables, pre-roast them, then add them to the other vegetables near the end of their cooking time.

- Sauté chopped roasted beets in olive oil, fresh orange juice and grated orange rind for a delicious side dish. Sprinkle with chopped chives. (This is one of my favourite ways to serve beets!)
- Create your own salad using chopped beets. Try endive topped with chopped beets, chopped apple and raisins. Or serve sliced beets over a bed of greens and top with roasted walnuts and a few crumbles of goat cheese.
- Scan your cookbooks for a healthy borscht recipe, a traditional Russian soup whose main ingredient is beets.

Recipes
Beet, Apple and Ginger Soup, page 256
Roasted Beets with Honey Balsamic Glaze, page 266

Berries: Blackberries, blueberries, cranberries, strawberries, raspberries

These bite-sized fruits top most "super food" lists and for good reason. For starters, they're low in calories, contain virtually no fat and provide important nutrients. Berries deliver vitamin C and folate, vitamins needed for immunity and healthy DNA. In fact, one serving of strawberries provides a full day's worth of vitamin C! Even better, berries taste delicious and require little prep work to add them to your diet.

Berries' real claim to fame is their outstanding antioxidant concentration. Blackberries, strawberries, raspberries, blueberries and cranberries ranked among the top fifty of a long list of one thousand foods measured for their total antioxidants per serving.[3] And the antioxidants in berries are pretty powerful. With the exception of prunes and raisins, blackberries, strawberries, raspberries and blueberries outscore all other fruits for their ability to neutralize harmful free radicals.

Berries contain a number of different phytochemicals linked with disease prevention. *Ellagic acid*, plentiful in strawberries and raspberries, acts as an antioxidant and also helps the body deactivate cancer-causing substances. This phytochemical has been shown, too, to slow the growth of cancer cells. In lab studies, ellagic acid prevents cancers of the skin, bladder, lung, esophagus and breast. Anthocyanins, abundant in blueberries, have been shown to inhibit the growth of lung, colon and leukemia cancer cells in the lab. Another powerful berry antioxidant is *pterostilbene*, of which blueberries are an outstanding source. Pterostilbene appears to influence metabolic processes that reduce the risk of both cancer and heart disease.

Eating berries on a regular basis can help keep your eyes young as you grow older. That's because they supply lutein, a phytochemical that reduces the risk of cataracts and age-related macular degeneration, the leading cause of blindness in older adults. The darker the berry (e.g., blueberries and black-berries), the more lutein you'll find.

Phytochemicals in berries can also keep your heart healthy as you age. As antioxidants, these compounds stall the oxidation of LDL cholesterol, improve the function of blood vessel walls and help prevent the formation of blood clots. What's more, berries have been shown to stave off inflammation by inhibiting the action of an enzyme called cyclo-oxygenase. And if that's not enough, preliminary animal studies hint that diets rich in blueberries and strawberries may also slow down aging in the brain.

NOTABLE NUTRIENTS IN BERRIES
(PER 1 CUP/250 ML SERVING, THE STRAWBERRIES SLICED)
Blueberries: 84 calories, 0.5 g fat, 21 g carbohydrate, 3.6 g fibre, 114 mg potassium, 14.5 mg vitamin C, 9 mcg folate
Blackberries: 62 calories, 0.7 g fat, 14 g carbohydrate, 7.6 g fibre, 42 mg calcium, 233 mg potassium, 30 mg vitamin C, 36 mcg folate
Cranberries: 46 calories, 0.2 g fat, 12 g carbohydrate, 4.6 g fibre, 13 mg vitamin C, 85 mg potassium
Raspberries: 64 calories, 0.8 g fat, 14.7 g carbohydrate, 8 g fibre, 31 mg calcium, 186 mg potassium, 32 mg vitamin C, 26 mcg folate
Strawberries: 53 calories, 0.5 g fat, 12.7 g carbohydrate, 3.3. g fibre, 254 mg potassium, 98 mg vitamin C, 40 mcg folate

QUICK TIPS TO ADD BERRIES TO YOUR DIET
- Toss a handful of fresh or dried berries over a bowl of breakfast cereal.
- Mix fresh berries into a bowl of hot whole-grain cereal such as oatmeal, brown rice or millet.
- Stir fresh berries into low-fat yogurt with 1/2 cup (125 ml) of 100 percent bran cereal for an antioxidant-rich, high-fibre breakfast.
- Add fresh or frozen berries to muffin, pancake and waffle batters.
- Mix sliced strawberries and blueberries with cinnamon, lemon juice and maple syrup, and serve over whole-grain pancakes or waffles.

- Enjoy a breakfast smoothie made with skim milk or unflavoured soy milk, fresh or frozen berries and a tablespoon of ground flaxseed.
- Make breakfast pizza by spreading plain non-fat Greek-style yogurt over a whole-wheat pita and topping it with fresh berries.
- Add sliced strawberries, rich in vitamin C, to a spinach salad; the vitamin C will help your body absorb more iron from the spinach.
- Add dried berries such as blueberries and raspberries to a leafy green salad.

Recipes
Blueberry Raspberry Smoothie, page 233
Field Berry Almond Pancakes, page 228
Pumpkin Spice Muffins with Carrots and Blueberries, page 309
Raspberry Ginger Muffins, page 311
Rye Breakfast Bars with Flaxseed and Cranberries, page 230
Sweet Potato Cranberry Drop Biscuits, page 239
Strawberry Kiwi Smoothie, page 236

Black beans and other dried beans

There's no question that all types of dried beans—black beans, kidney beans, garbanzo beans (chickpeas), navy beans and so on—are good for you. Studies have found that people who include beans in their diet on a regular basis have a lower risk of heart disease, high blood pressure and type 2 diabetes. Research has also revealed that eating beans regularly is linked with protection from prostate cancer.

Beans contain a package of healthy ingredients that work together to keep you healthy. They're rich in vegetarian protein, packed with fibre and contain low-glycemic carbohydrate. They're also one of the very best food sources of folate and magnesium you can find. What's more, beans have a number of disease-fighting phytochemicals, including saponins, protease inhibitors and phytic acid, which protect cells from genetic damage that can lead to cancer.

While all beans are good for you—and you should make an effort to add them to your diet—black beans stand out for a few reasons. Gram for gram, black beans have more antioxidant activity than any other bean, rivalling many antioxidant-rich fruits and vegetables. Black beans also supply nearly 40 percent of your daily requirement for manganese, a mineral that's needed to make superoxide dismutase, a key antioxidant enzyme in your liver. And compared to other beans, they rank high for their magnesium and fibre content.

But don't stop with black beans. Sure, they're higher in antioxidants, but chickpeas, kidney beans, navy beans, pinto beans and lentils are all rich in plant protein, low-glycemic carbohydrate and fibre. In fact, in this chapter I've featured lentils as a longevity food too, for reasons you'll soon learn. You'll also find two delicious chickpea recipes in this book.

NOTABLE NUTRIENTS IN BLACK BEANS
(PER 1/2 CUP/125 ML SERVING)
114 calories, 0.5 g fat, 20 g carbohydrate, 7.5 g fibre, 60 mg magnesium, 305 mg potassium, 128 mcg folate

Is there a way to shorten the cooking time of dried beans? All dried beans are prepared in the same way: First they're cleaned and soaked, and then they're cooked to make them ready for your favourite bean dish. To reduce the time it takes to cook dried beans, use the *quick-soak method*. Place cleaned black beans in a large pot with three times the volume of cool water. Bring beans and water to a boil for two minutes and then remove pot from the heat. Cover and let stand for one hour, then drain the beans and rinse in a colander. Now they're ready to cook.

To cook, add 3 cups (750 ml) of unsalted water for every 1 cup (250 ml) of soaked beans. The water should be 2 inches (10 mm) above the top of the beans. Bring the beans to a gentle boil and then reduce to a simmer, partially covering the pot. Gently stir beans occasionally during cooking. Skim off any foam that develops during cooking. Black beans will cook in 30 to 45 minutes; they then can be used in soups, salads, tacos and dips.

If you're crunched for time, buy canned black beans. All you have to do is open the can, drain the beans in a colander, and then rinse them under cool running water. Rinsing canned beans removes sodium as well as some of the gas-producing carbohydrates.

QUICK TIPS TO ADD BLACK BEANS TO YOUR DIET
• Toss cooked black beans into a pasta or brown rice salad.
• For a hearty lunch, serve homemade black bean soup instead of the usual chicken noodle, or add cooked black beans to other soups to boost their fibre and nutrient content.

- Make a three-bean salad by mixing black beans with red and white kidney beans. Add chopped parsley, diced red onion and black pepper. Toss with a balsamic vinaigrette.
- Use black beans in addition to red kidney beans when making your favourite chili recipe.
- Add black beans to tacos and burritos. Use half the amount of lean meat you normally would and make up the difference with beans.
- For a Southwestern dip, purée in the food processor 1 can (19 oz/540 ml) of rinsed black beans, half a small red onion, 1 tablespoon (15 ml) balsamic vinegar, 2 teaspoons (10 ml) lime juice, fresh cilantro, 1-1/2 teaspoons (7 ml) of olive oil and 1/2 teaspoon (2 ml) of cumin. Serve with raw vegetables or whole-wheat pita chips. For a crowd, double the ingredients.

Recipes
Black Bean and Avocado Salad with Toasted Cumin Dressing, page 247
Black Bean Hummus, page 237
Chana Masala, page 297
Lemon Chickpea Soup, page 259
White Bean, Garlic and Arugula Wrap, page 303

Broccoli

As a member of the cruciferous family of vegetables, broccoli is closely related to cauliflower, Brussels sprouts and turnip. These vegetables derive their name from their four-petalled flowers, which look like a crucifer or cross. (The word *cruciferous* comes from the Latin word for cross.) Like other cruciferous vegetables, broccoli contains potent anti-cancer phytochemicals called glucosinolates. Once consumed, glucosinolates are broken down by bacteria in your digestive tract and transformed into compounds called isothiocyanates. Some glucosinolates also transform into isothiocyanates when you chop or chew cruciferous vegetables.

The most famous isothiocyanate, called sulforaphane, is abundant in broccoli and broccoli sprouts. In fact, more than 125 papers have been published on the anti-cancer properties of sulforaphane. Scientists have learned that sulforaphane helps remove carcinogens from the body by turning on certain genes that speed up the production of detoxification enzymes in the liver. As a result, the liver is able to clear potentially carcinogenic substances more quickly. Another isothiocyanate derivative from broccoli, allyl isothio-cyanate, has been shown to halt tumour cell division and stimulate the death of cancer cells.

Broccoli delivers a hefty dose of yet another phytochemical called kaemp-ferol. In a study of 66,940 healthy women over 18 years, those who consumed the most kaempferol, versus the least, were 40 percent less likely to develop ovarian cancer.[4] But that's not all. Studies have revealed that people who eat the most cruciferous vegetables versus the least, including broccoli, have a much lower risk of breast, prostate, pancreatic, colon and lung cancer.

There's another reason to add broccoli to your diet: Compared to other cruciferous vegetables, it leads the pack when it comes to vitamin C and folate content.

NOTABLE NUTRIENTS IN BROCCOLI
(PER 1/2 CUP/125 ML COOKED)
15 calories, 0.1 g fat, 2.9 g carbohydrate, 1.1 g fibre, 21 mg calcium, 139 mg potassium, 39 mg vitamin C, 28 mcg folate

What's the healthiest way to cook broccoli? To consume the most phyto-chemicals from broccoli and other cruciferous veggies, eat them raw. Cooking these vegetables can inactivate the enzyme that transforms glucosinolates into active isothiocyanates. What's more, glucosinolates are water soluble, so if you boil your broccoli, you'll lose some of these healthy compounds in the cooking water. Quickly steaming and quickly sautéeing broccoli—and other cruciferous vegetables—are the best cooking methods to retain nutrients and phytochemicals.

QUICK TIPS TO ADD BROCCOLI TO YOUR DIET
- For a healthy side dish, serve lightly steamed broccoli sprinkled with fresh lemon juice and sesame seeds.
- Add sautéed broccoli florets to whole-wheat pasta and toss with extra-virgin olive oil, toasted pine nuts and sun-dried tomatoes.
- Make your own puréed broccoli soup. Sauté onion and garlic in a large saucepan. Add 4 to 6 cups (1 to 1.5 L) of low-sodium chicken broth and one bunch of chopped broccoli (stems and florets). Bring to a boil then simmer, covered for 15 minutes. Purée in batches, add seasonings and enjoy.

- Top a baked potato with chopped, steamed broccoli florets.
- Top a homemade pizza with chopped, steamed broccoli florets.
- Add chopped broccoli florets to tomato-based pasta sauces, stir-fries and egg-white omelets.
- Grate raw broccoli and use in your favourite coleslaw recipe.
- Snack on raw broccoli florets with hummus (chickpea) or black bean dip.

Recipes
Broccoli with Sesame Thai Dressing, page 243
Crunchy Broccoli Salad with Apple Dijon Dressing, page 245
Roasted Broccoli, page 267

Cabbage

This vegetable is another member of the cruciferous family and, like broccoli, it's well worth adding to your diet. As a cruciferous vegetable, cabbage is an excellent source of cancer-fighting glucosinolates that mop up harmful free radicals and help rid the body of carcinogens. In fact, studies suggest that eating cabbage on a regular basis can help reduce a woman's risk of breast cancer.

Recently, when researchers noticed that the breast cancer risk of Polish women rose threefold after they immigrated to the United States, they decided to evaluate the diets of Polish immigrant women living in Chicago and Detroit to find out if a food might be responsible. Their findings revealed that women who ate raw or lightly cooked cabbage at least three times per week had a significantly lower risk of breast cancer compared to their peers who ate only one serving per week. Interestingly, cabbage cooked for a long time had no bearing on breast cancer risk.

Eating plenty of cruciferous vegetables like cabbage has also been shown to prevent ischemic stroke. (An ischemic stroke occurs when an artery carrying oxygen-rich blood to the brain is blocked. If the artery remains blocked for more than a few minutes, the brain cells may die.) It's thought that cabbage and other cruciferous vegetables reduce markers of inflammation in the body; elevated inflammation markers signal a greater risk of cardiovascular disease, and as you already learned, a shorter life expectancy.

What is Chinese cabbage? Even though the name might not sound familiar, I am sure you've enjoyed Chinese cabbage—also known as bok choy—on many occasions. Bok choy has dark green ruffled leaves and white celery-like stalks that have a mild, peppery flavour. Both the greens and the stalks are used in salads and stir-fry recipes. As you'll see in Chapter 9, bok choy ranks among the top 25 foods for many nutrients!

NOTABLE NUTRIENTS IN CABBAGE
(PER 1/2 CUP/125 ML RAW)
9 calories, 0.4 g fat, 2 g carbohydrate, 1 g fibre, 13 mg vitamin C, 27 mcg vitamin K

QUICK TIPS TO ADD CABBAGE TO YOUR DIET

- Stuff cabbage leaves with a savoury ground turkey and herb filling for homemade cabbage rolls.
- Braise red cabbage with chopped apple and red wine. (The alcohol evaporates during cooking so kids can eat this dish too!)
- Use cabbage leaves to wrap your next taco or burrito. Or added shredded cabbage to fish tacos.
- Wrap up your leftovers—rice, chopped meat or chicken and veggies—in cabbage leaves and roll into small packages. Bake at 350°F (180°C) for 15 minutes, or until hot.
- Add shredded cabbage to sandwiches as a change from lettuce.
- Mix shredded red cabbage into your next green salad for added colour.
- Add chopped or shredded cabbage to soup, homemade or store-bought.
- Create your own version of coleslaw. For an Indian-inspired slaw, combine shredded cabbage with fresh lemon juice, olive oil, chopped scallions, and turmeric, cumin and chopped fresh coriander.

Recipes
Cabbage and Carrot Coleslaw, page 244
Kasha Cabbage Rolls, page 284
Nasi Goreng, page 273
Sesame Ginger Stir-Fried Tofu and Bok Choy with Brown Rice, page 301

Dark chocolate

You might be surprised to see chocolate on my list of anti-aging foods. Believe it or not, dark chocolate—not milk chocolate—is a rich source of antioxidants called flavonoids. These phytochemicals have antioxidant, anti-inflammatory and anti-clotting properties, all of which are thought to protect the heart. Flavonoids also help maintain the normal functioning of blood vessels as you age by helping them dilate and relax.

A number of studies have connected dark chocolate to better health. For example, researchers have found that eating a small serving—6 grams or 30 calories' worth—of dark chocolate lowers blood pressure in both healthy people and those with risk factors for heart disease.[5,6] The theory is that flavonoids in dark chocolate reduce blood pressure by increasing the production of nitric oxide in the lining of blood vessels, which causes the vessels to dilate. Italian researchers also demonstrated the ability of dark chocolate to lower blood pressure, reduce bad LDL cholesterol, and improve insulin sensitivity in 20 patients with never-treated hypertension.[7] Dark chocolate is a fair source of magnesium, too, a mineral that helps keep blood pressure and blood-sugar levels in check.

Chocolate is actually a plant food—it's made from cocoa beans. But the more chocolate is processed and the less cocoa mass it contains, the fewer the flavonoids it contains. White chocolate doesn't contain any flavonoids and milk chocolate has very few of them. Dark chocolate with 70 percent or greater cocoa solids has the most flavonoids.

Of course, there is a downside to adding dark chocolate to your diet: its high calorie count. Eating too much of even the finest dark chocolate will lead to weight gain if you don't make a trade-off somewhere else in your diet. Eat a 100-gram bar and you'll also consume 30 grams of fat and 400 calories. If you read the nutrition label on the wrapper of your chocolate bar, you'll notice that the fat in dark chocolate is mostly saturated fat, the type that's associated with increasing LDL (bad) cholesterol levels. Well, great news! The type of saturated fat in dark chocolate, called stearic acid, has no effect on blood cholesterol. When it comes to blood cholesterol, stearic acid is considered neutral.

My advice: Keep your portion size small (no more than 1 ounce/28 grams) and make room for other flavonoid-rich foods that come with fewer calories, such as berries, red grapes, apples, onions and green tea. Even then, you'll need to account for these calories in your diet by downsizing your portion of something else.

NOTABLE NUTRIENTS IN DARK CHOCOLATE

(PER 1 OUNCE/28 G SERVING)

167 calories, 11.9 g fat, 12.8 g carbohydrate (6.8 g saturated fat), 64 mg magnesium, 200 mg potassium, 22 mg caffeine

QUICK TIPS TO ADD DARK CHOCOLATE (IN SMALL PORTIONS!) TO YOUR DIET

• Read labels. Look for dark chocolate that contains at least 70 percent cocoa solids. The greater the percentage of cocoa solids, the more flavonoids.

• Enjoy a small square of dark chocolate after lunch to help curb sweet cravings later in the afternoon.

• Sip on a mug of homemade hot dark chocolate by mixing cocoa powder with skim milk. Add a teaspoon of sugar for sweetness if desired.

• For a healthy dessert when entertaining, dip strawberries in melted dark chocolate.

• Bake with unsweetened, dark chocolate. Add a little chopped dark chocolate to muffins, loaves and cookies.

• For a breakfast treat, add small pieces of dark chocolate to pancake and waffle batters.

Recipes

Chocolate Fruit Fondue, page 313
Chocolate Zucchini Muffins, page 307

Flaxseed

These tiny seeds, just slightly larger than sesame seeds, range in colour from golden to reddish brown. They come from flax, a blue-flowering crop grown on the Canadian prairies. From a nutrition and health standpoint, flaxseeds have plenty to offer. For one, they're rich in an omega-3 fatty acid called alpha-linolenic acid, or ALA for short, which possesses anti-inflammatory properties. ALA is used by the body to produce prostaglandins, hormone-like compounds that have far-reaching effects on your health. ALA is needed to make two types of prostaglandins, series 1 and series 3, both of which reduce inflammation. (Series 2 prostaglandins, on the other hand, are pro-inflammatory; they're produced from omega-6 fatty acids found in animal fat, margarine and many vegetable oils.)

A diet rich in ALA can help keep your heart younger as you age. A large Harvard study found that women who consumed the most ALA from their diet were half as likely to die from heart disease compared to their peers who consumed the least.[8] As well, the women who consumed 1.16 grams of ALA per day—the amount in roughly 1 tablespoon (15 ml) of ground flaxseed— were 40 percent less likely to suddenly die of cardiac arrest than women whose diets provided only 0.66 grams each day.[8] (Sudden cardiac death is unexpected death resulting from an abrupt loss of heart function. Death occurs within minutes after symptoms appear. People who suffer sudden cardiac death may or may not have diagnosed heart disease. However, the most common underlying reason for individuals to die suddenly from cardiac arrest is coronary heart disease.) A diet high in ALA has also been linked with significantly less plaque buildup in the coronary arteries.[9]

There are a number of ways in which ALA in flaxseed can guard against heart disease. Scientists believe ALA can help prevent abnormal heart rhythms that can cause a heart attack. As well, ALA's anti-inflammatory actions inhibit the production of C-reactive protein, an inflammatory chemical linked to a greater risk of heart disease. Flaxseed is also packed with soluble fibre, the type that lowers blood cholesterol, helping guard against heart disease.

A steady intake of flaxseed may also help lower the risk of certain cancers, including breast cancer. Animal studies have shown that a flax-rich diet reduced the size of breast tumours.[11,12] And a recent review of twenty-one studies concluded that a daily intake of flaxseed reduced the risk of breast cancer in postmenopausal women by 14 percent.[13] Flaxseed is a rich source of lignans, phytochemicals thought to protect from breast cancer by altering estrogen metabolism in the body.

Lignans have a similar chemical structure to human estrogen, so they're able to bind to estrogen receptors on breast cells. In so doing, they block the body's own potent estrogen from taking that spot. (A common thread in many of the identified risk factors for breast cancer is the length of time a woman's breast tissue is exposed to her body's circulating estrogen; the longer the exposure, the greater the risk of breast cancer. The female hormone estrogen may promote mutations in breast cells that could potentially lead to cancer.)

It's not only women who can benefit from the anti-cancer properties of flaxseed. In a study of 161 men with prostate cancer, those who supplemented their diet with 30 grams—2 tablespoons' worth—of ground flaxseed for one month pre-surgery had significantly slower growth of prostate tumours.[14] Scientists believe that omega-3s in flaxseed alter how cancer cells lump together while flaxseed's lignans choke off the tumour's blood supply. Both actions halt the growth of cancer cells.

It's important to add *ground* flaxseed to your diet instead of whole seeds. That's because whole flaxseed may pass through your intestine undigested, which means you won't reap their health benefits. Aim for 2 tablespoons (25 ml) of ground flaxseed per day. You can purchase ground flaxseed in vacuum-sealed packages at many grocery stores and health food stores. Ground flaxseed can be stored in an airtight container for several months.

NOTABLE NUTRIENTS IN GROUND FLAXSEED

(PER 2 TABLESPOONS/25 ML)
60 calories, 6 g fat (4 g polyunsaturated fat), 4 g fibre, 2.4 g ALA (women need 1.1 g of ALA per day; men require 1.6 g.)

QUICK TIPS TO ADD GROUND FLAXSEED TO YOUR DIET

• Blend ground flaxseed with skim milk or soy milk and frozen fruit for a nutritious smoothie.
• Add ground flaxseed to cookie, muffin, pancake or waffle batters.
• Sprinkle ground flaxseed over hot and cold breakfast cereals.
• Stir ground flaxseed into yogurt or applesauce for a quick dessert or snack.
• Mix a little ground flaxseed into mustard or mayonnaise for a healthy sandwich spread.
• Add ground flaxseed to lean ground beef or turkey when making burgers, meatballs or meat loaf.
• Sprinkle ground flaxseed over salads and soups.
• Make a healthy breading with egg whites, ground flaxseed and seasonings.

Recipes
Baked Lentils with Cumin Yogurt Sauce, page 293
Balsamic Glazed Mushroom and Soy Burgers, page 295
Rye Breakfast Bars with Flaxseed and Cranberries, page 230

Garlic

Garlic's health and medicinal properties have been known for thousands of years. In Biblical times, garlic was thought to preserve strength and was given to slaves to increase their fitness. In ancient Greece, athletes took garlic before competing in the Olympic Games to enhance strength and vigour. In 1858 Louis Pasteur—the scientist renowned for inventing the pasteurization process—noted garlic's antibacterial activity, and it was used as an antiseptic to prevent gangrene during World War I and World War II. Today scientists are praising garlic's potential to help treat or protect against certain cancers, heart disease, arthritis, even diabetes.

The disease-fighting properties of garlic are attributed to a variety of powerful sulfur-containing chemicals, in particular ones called allyl sulfides. (These are the same chemicals responsible for garlic's distinctive smell and onion's ability to make your eyes water!) Garlic also contains flavonoids, phytochemicals linked to disease prevention. In addition to phytochemicals, garlic offers essential nutrients, especially vitamin C, vitamin B6, manganese and selenium.

There's mounting evidence that garlic and its sulfur compounds inhibit the cancer process. Out of 37 observational studies conducted in humans using garlic and its sulfur compounds, 28 showed anti-cancer effects, most notably for digestive tract cancers. A combined analysis of 18 scientific papers concluded that people who ate raw or cooked garlic regularly faced about half the risk of stomach cancer and two-thirds the risk of colorectal cancer than people who ate little or none.[15] Another study revealed that among the 10,000 subjects studied, the more garlic (and onions) consumed the lower their risk for a wide range of cancers, including cancers of the oral cavity, larynx, esophagus, colon, ovaries and kidneys.[16]

Garlic also plays a role in keeping your heart fit as you age. It has potential cholesterol-lowering properties and can significantly impede the ability of platelets in the blood to clump together (aggregate). Platelet aggregation is one of the first steps in the formation of a blood clot that could lead to a heart attack or stroke. (A heart attack happens when a blood clot blocks the flow of blood through a coronary artery.) Some, but not all, studies also suggest that garlic might help lower blood pressure.

When it comes to adding garlic to your diet, more is not better. Eating too much garlic, especially raw garlic, can have side effects, the most common being breath and body odour. More uncomfortable and potentially serious adverse effects include an irritated digestive tract, heartburn, flatulence, nausea, vomiting and diarrhea. A hefty dose of garlic could also increase the risk of bleeding. If you're planning to have surgery, avoid using fresh garlic (and garlic supplements) seven days prior to the procedure.

NOTABLE NUTRIENTS IN GARLIC
(PER 1 CLOVE)
4 calories, 0 g fat, 1 mg vitamin C, 0.04 mg vitamin B6, 0.4 mcg selenium, 0.05 mg manganese

QUICK TIPS TO ADD GARLIC TO YOUR DIET

- Sauté steamed spinach with minced or crushed garlic and sprinkle with fresh lemon juice.
- Add minced garlic to soups and pasta sauces.
- Add chopped raw garlic to marinades for meat, chicken or seafood.
- Use crushed garlic as part of a spice rub for grilled meat.
- Make your own tzatziki with non-fat plain yogurt, garlic and cucumber (check your cookbooks for a recipe). Serve as a condiment with grilled chicken or use as a dip with whole-wheat pita bread.
- Make garlic mashed potatoes. Mash roasted garlic, boiled Yukon Gold potatoes and olive oil for a delicious and filling side dish.
- Spread roasted garlic on whole-grain crackers as an appetizer.

Green tea

Drinking green tea regularly has been linked with lower rates of some cancers as well as of heart disease. While the evidence is not as strong, study findings also hint that green tea can prevent arthritis. Studies that track the diets of people over several years have associated regular green tea consumption with a lower risk of cancer of the bladder, colon, stomach, esophagus and pancreas. Green tea drinkers might also be protected from breast cancer. A review of studies examining the link between green tea and breast cancer—three from Japan and one from Los Angeles—found that compared to women who consumed less than 1 cup (250 ml) of green tea per day, those who drank at least 5 cups (1250 ml) daily were 22 percent less likely to develop breast cancer.[17] Studies also suggest that regularly drinking green tea can reduce the risk of developing ovarian cancer.

Green tea is good for your heart too. Studies conducted in men and women have linked green tea consumption with a lower risk of heart attack and death from heart disease. Drinking green tea on a daily basis has been shown to lower LDL blood cholesterol and triglycerides (a type of blood fat) and reduce free radicals that damage LDL cholesterol particles, making LDL more likely to stick to artery walls. What's more, drinking at least 1/2 cup (125 ml) of green tea each day has also been shown to keep blood pressure down. Green tea may also help thin the blood and prevent blood clots from forming.

Green tea owes its disease-fighting properties to powerful antioxidants called *catechins* (a class of flavonoids). According to researchers from the United Kingdom, the antioxidant activity of two cups of tea is equal to one glass of red wine, seven glasses of orange juice or twenty glasses of apple juice.[18] What's more, test-tube studies have shown that tea catechins are more powerful antioxidants than vitamins C and E.

The primary catechin found in green tea is called epigallocatechin gallate (EGCG), a potent antioxidant. Because green tea leaves are produced differently from black tea leaves—they are not fermented before they are heated and dried—they contain three times more catechins than black tea. Green tea also contains other flavonoids called flavonols, including kaempferol, quercitin and myricitin.

Is it better to brew green tea from loose tea or from tea bags? Loose-leaf teas are made up of whole or broken leaves while tea bags are filled with fannings or dust, the waste product produced from sorting higher quality loose-leaf tea. In my opinion, a cup of brewed loose-leaf tea is much better-tasting than one brewed from bags, and it also contains more antioxidants. A whole tea leaf has more surface area, which means the hot water can extract from it more flavour and antioxidants. Tea bags containing fannings and dust, on the other hand, don't have as much surface area for this extraction.

QUICK TIPS TO ADD GREEN TEA TO YOUR DIET

It's important to brew green tea properly for the best tasting cup of tea. Water for green tea should be slightly less than boiling, around 80°C to 85°C (176°F to 185°F); the higher the quality of the leaves, the lower the temperature. (Hotter water will burn green tea leaves, producing a bitter taste.) First warm the cup or pot you're going to use with hot water. Use 1 teaspoon (5 ml) of loose green tea leaves per 6 to 8 ounce (175 to 250 ml) cup. Once the kettle boils, let it cool for one minute before pouring the hot water over the tea leaves. Green tea should be steeped for one to two minutes. Use a strainer or infuser in your cup or teapot. Infusers can be purchased at tea shops and kitchen stores.

- Start your day with a cup of freshly brewed green tea.
- Brew green tea in cold water for 20 minutes and use as a braising liquid or a liquid in marinades, sauces and gravies.
- Use brewed green tea to sauté or stir-fry vegetables.
- As a change from water, serve freshly brewed green iced tea with lunch or dinner. Garnish with slices of lemon and sweeten to taste. (When making iced tea, double the strength of hot tea, since it will be poured over ice.)
- If you drink soft drinks with meals, replace them with a cup of green tea.

Recipes
Ginger Green Tea Marinade, page 304
Lemon Iced Green Tea, page 234

Kale

When it comes to leafy green vegetables, it's hard to beat the nutritional value and health benefits of kale. This is one vegetable that should definitely become a regular part of your anti-aging diet. Kale is low in calories, fat free, high in fibre and a good source of vitamins A, C and K, folate (a B vitamin), iron, calcium and potassium. What's more, kale is an exceptional source of phytochemicals that promote longevity.

This leafy green vegetable belongs to the cruciferous family of vegetables. Like broccoli and cabbage, kale is an excellent source of cancer-fighting glucosinolates that boost the body's detoxification enzymes, thus helping clear potential carcinogens away. A diet rich in leafy greens, including kale, is linked with protection from stomach and ovarian cancer. These vegetables seem to work best at fighting cancers that involve *epithelial cells*, the cells that line the body's organs. The vitamin A in kale maintains healthy body tissues, especially epithelial and mucous tissues, the body's first line of defence against invading organisms and toxins. When our vitamin A levels are low, we're much more susceptible to infection. Kale's vitamin C content helps to build a strong immune system and quench harmful free radicals.

One of kale's impressive anti-aging effects is its ability to help keep your vision sharp as you age. Kale tops the list of vegetables when it comes to lutein and zeaxanthin, two phytochemicals that help prevent the age-related changes in the eye that cause cataracts. Lutein and zeaxanthin are found in large amounts in the lens and retina, where they act as antioxidants protecting from free radical damage. Other antioxidants in kale such as vitamin C and beta carotene also fend off free radicals in the eye. Studies have found that people who get the most lutein from their diet have a 20 percent to 50 percent lower risk of cataract or having cataract extraction surgery compared to people who consume the least.[19]

Cataracts occur when some of the proteins in the lens clump together and start to cloud a small area of the lens. In a normal eye, light passes through the transparent lens to the retina. Once it reaches the retina, light is transformed into nerve signals that are sent to the brain. In order for the retina to receive a sharp image, the lens must be clear. If the lens is cloudy from a cataract, the image you see will be blurred. Your risk for developing a cataract rises as you get older but other risk factors include cigarette smoking, diabetes and a diet low in antioxidants.

Eating kale on a regular basis can also forestall age-related macular degeneration (AMD), the leading cause of blindness in adults over 50. AMD attacks the central part of the retina called the macula, which controls fine, detailed vision. The condition results in progressive loss of visual sharpness, making it difficult to drive a car, read a book and recognize faces. In the macula, lutein acts as a filter, protecting structures of the eye from the damaging effects of the sun's ultraviolet light. Lutein contributes to the density, or thickness, of the macula—the denser the macula, the better it can absorb incoming light.

Eating kale on a regular basis can benefit your brain too. Mental performance normally declines with age, but the results of one large study suggest that eating vegetables daily—especially kale—can dramatically slow the rate of cognitive decline. Among 3718 men and women aged 65 and older, those who ate at least two servings of vegetables each day had 40 percent less cognitive decline than those who ate less than one full serving per day—results expected of people five years younger. The study found all types of vegetables protective, especially zucchini, eggplant, broccoli, lettuce, tossed salad and leafy greens such as kale and collards.[20] Vegetables, kale in particular, contain vitamin E, which shields brain cell membranes from free radical damage. The brain is especially vulnerable to free radical damage because of its high demand for oxygen, its abundance of easily oxidized cell membranes and its weak antioxidant defences.

Kale is also a good source of manganese, a trace mineral that's a critical component of superoxide dismultase, an antioxidant enzyme. Superoxide dismultase is found exclusively inside the mitochondria, or energy factory, of body cells, where it protects against damage from free radicals formed during energy production. Kale is also loaded with vitamin K, a nutrient that helps maintain bone density as we age.

NOTABLE NUTRIENTS IN KALE
(PER 1/2 CUP/125 ML, COOKED)
18 calories, 0.2 g fat, 1.3 g fibre, 27 mg vitamin C, 0.5 mg vitamin E, 531 mcg vitamin K, 5.3 mg beta carotene,* 12 mg lutein plus zeaxanthin,* 47 mg calcium, 0.27 mg manganese

*There are no official daily requirements for beta carotene or lutein plus zeaxanthin. However, a daily intake of 6 to 15 milligrams of lutein plus zeaxanthin per day is thought to be optimal for eye health. An intake of 3 to 6 milligrams of beta carotene per day is enough to maintain blood levels of beta carotene in the range that's associated with a lower risk of chronic disease.

QUICK TIPS TO ADD KALE TO YOUR DIET
- Sauté kale with fresh garlic and chili peppers and drizzle with roasted sesame oil just before serving.
- Braise chopped kale and apples. Before serving, sprinkle with balsamic vinegar and chopped walnuts.
- Combine chopped kale (blanched or steamed), pine nuts, sun-dried tomatoes and feta cheese with whole-wheat pasta. Drizzle with extra-virgin olive oil.
- Stir cooked kale into a pot of garlic mashed potatoes.
- Add raw kale leaves to any soup and simmer until leaves are tender. Kale leaves are sturdy and hold up well in soups, sauces and stir-fries.
- Toss tender young kale leaves into a salad of mixed greens.
- Add cooked kale to your favourite pasta salad recipe.

Recipes
Kale "Chips" with Sea Salt, page 238
Spicy Sautéed Kale, page 271

Lentils

Eating legumes more often—including lentils and black beans—is an excellent way to cut back on animal protein and adopt a plant-based diet that's associated with longevity. Earlier I discussed the nutritional merits of black beans, especially in terms of their high antioxidant content. But lentils, too, should become a regular part of your diet if they aren't right now. Like black beans, they're an excellent source of protein. In fact, with the exception of soybeans, lentils deliver more protein per serving than any other bean. Lentils also contain slow-burning, low-glycemic carbohydrate that helps keep your insulin level low. And they're a great source of soluble fibre, the type that keeps LDL blood cholesterol in check. Lentils also provide magnesium and potassium, two minerals needed for healthy blood pressure.

But it's their folate content that makes lentils really shine. Meeting your daily requirements for the B vitamin folate (400 micrograms) is essential to help forestall the effects of aging on your cells. With each passing year, the DNA in our cells becomes more vulnerable to damage from free radicals, cigarette smoke, environmental toxins and radiation. This injury can cause mutations in DNA that affect how body proteins function and, ultimately, how our body performs. DNA mutations can also lead to the development of cancer.

Folate is critical both for making DNA and for preventing harmful changes to DNA. Think of folate as the guardian of your genetic material—it maintains the health and stability of your DNA as you age. Folate can also help keep your arteries youthful. This B vitamin—along with B6 and B12—is necessary for the breakdown of homocysteine, an amino acid produced normally in your body. Without folate, homocysteine builds up in the bloodstream and causes damage to artery walls. Over time, this blood vessel damage can lead to heart disease and dementia.

NOTABLE NUTRIENTS IN LENTILS
(PER 1/2 CUP/125 ML, COOKED)
115 calories, 9 g protein, 20 g carbohydrate, 8 g fibre, 179 mcg folate, 3.3 mg iron, 36 mg magnesium, 365 mg potassium

QUICK TIPS TO ADD LENTILS TO YOUR DIET

The most common types of dried lentils are green or brown, but they're also available in yellow, red and orange colours. Brown and green lentils retain their shape after cooking, while the others tend to become soft and mushy.

- Add cooked lentils to your favourite tomato-based pasta sauce instead of ground meat.
- Toss cooked lentils, chopped bell pepper and chopped red onion with a red-wine vinaigrette to make a cold salad. Add fresh herbs like parsley or cilantro.
- Add canned lentils, drained and rinsed, to any soup or stew to boost your fibre and folate intake.
- Cook dried lentils in a sodium-reduced chicken or vegetable broth to make a Moroccan lentil soup. Add vegetables of your choice and season with dried coriander, cumin, turmeric and cayenne.
- Try making dal, a delicious Indian lentil curry made with red lentils, coconut milk and spices. You'll find many recipes online—check out www.epicurious.com and www.cookinglight.com. To reduce the calorie and fat content, use "lite" coconut milk.

Recipes

Baked Lentils with Cumin Yogurt Sauce, page 293
Garlic and Rosemary Lentil Burgers with Warm Mushroom Gravy, page 299
Lentil Salad with Citrus Yogurt Dressing, page 249
Red Lentil Soup, page 260
Red Rice and Leek Casserole with White Wine and Lemon, page 275

Oats

Most of us know that whole grains, such as oats, are good for us. People who eat whole grains more often than refined (white) grains are less likely to develop heart disease, stroke, type 2 diabetes and certain cancers. Whole grains like whole wheat, rye meal, quinoa, barley, flaxseed and oats contain a bundle of nutrients and phytochemicals that work together to keep you healthy as you age. But oats have a few health-promoting ingredients that distinguish them from other whole grains. As you'll read, they're one of the best grains to eat to keep your heart youthful and fit as you grow older.

Oats contain a certain type of soluble fibre called beta-glucan. Study after study has demonstrated the ability of beta-glucan to lower blood-cholesterol levels in people with high cholesterol. Once consumed, beta-glucan binds to cholesterol in the digestive tract, preventing it from ending up in the bloodstream. All it takes is 3 grams of oat fibre per day—the amount in 1.5 cups (375 ml) of cooked oatmeal—to bring down blood cholesterol by as much as 23 percent. That's impressive when you consider that every 1 percent drop in blood cholesterol translates into a 2 percent reduction in the risk of heart disease.

Oats also have unique antioxidants called avenanthramides, which prevent free radicals from oxidizing LDL cholesterol particles. (If you'll recall, I told you earlier that once LDL cholesterol particles become oxidized, they stick to artery walls much easier.) Research in the lab has also demonstrated the ability of these antioxidants to block the production of molecules involved in the attachment of immune cells to artery walls, the first step in the development of heart disease.

And that's not all. A regular intake of oats can add years to your life by guarding against type 2 diabetes. For starters, oats are a good source of magnesium, a mineral used to make enzymes involved in the body's use of glucose and insulin. Oats are also a low-glycemic food thanks to their beta-glucan content. That means that after you eat a bowl of oatmeal, your blood sugar rises gradually, not quickly as it would if you ate a refined cereal such as Rice Krispies. A slow rise in blood sugar means your insulin level doesn't spike. And remember, keeping your insulin level low is linked with longevity.

There's one more reason to make oats a regular part of your diet. They're a great source of selenium, an important antioxidant and a key component of glutathione peroxidase, one of the body's antioxidant enzymes. Selenium works with vitamin E throughout the body to neutralize free radicals before they harm cells. Selenium is also needed to repair the DNA in our cells.

Are instant oats as good for you as old-fashioned rolled oats? Instant oats may be convenient, but they're not as good for you as large flake rolled oats or steel-cut oats. Instant oats, which start out as rolled oats, are processed into a powder to speed cooking time. As a result, instant oats are digested more quickly than large flake oats and cause a faster rise in blood glucose. In other words, they're higher on the glycemic-index scale. As well, most brands of instant oats have added sodium and many have added sugar—as much as 4 teaspoons' worth (20 ml) per package.

My advice: Choose large flake (old-fashioned) rolled oats or steel-cut oats. They both have a low glycemic-index value and they're salt- and sugar-free. Rolled oats are oat kernels that have been steamed, rolled and flaked for easier cooking. Steel-cut oats are oat kernels that have been chopped into two or three pieces. Steel-cut oats require more cooking time than other oats and remain very chewy. (Quick cooking oats are rolled oats that have been chopped into small flakes and take only three to four minutes to cook.)

NOTABLE NUTRIENTS IN OATS

(PER 1 CUP/250 ML, COOKED)

166 calories, 6 g protein, 28 g carbohydrate, 4 g fibre, 66 mg magnesium, 12.6 mcg selenium

QUICK TIPS TO ADD OATS TO YOUR DIET

- Start the day with a bowl of cooked oatmeal. Top with slivered almonds, berries and a spoonful of low-fat yogurt.
- Stir raw oats into muffin, pancake or waffle batters.
- Mix oats—cooked or raw—into lean ground beef or turkey when making burgers, meatballs or meat loaf.
- For a concentrated source of fibre, sprinkle oat bran over a bowl of hot or cold breakfast cereal.

Recipes

Almond Orange Granola Parfait, page 225
Baked Lentils with Cumin Yogurt Sauce, page 293
Balsamic Glazed Mushroom and Soy Burgers, page 295
Cinnamon Stovetop Oatmeal with Fresh Berries, page 227
Field Berry Almond Pancakes, page 228

Olive oil (extra-virgin)

This rich, dark green oil is a staple food in the Mediterranean diet, a pattern of eating renowned for its numerous health benefits, including protection from arthritis, high blood pressure, heart disease, type 2 diabetes, cancers and Alzheimer's disease. The olive oil–rich Mediterranean diet has even been shown to increase longevity. Over a ten-year period, elderly Europeans who adhered most closely to the diet had half the risk of dying from any cause compared to their peers who didn't follow a Mediterranean-style diet.[21,22] The reduced chance of death was due mainly to a lower risk of developing or succumbing to heart disease or cancer.

To be fair, the health benefits of the Mediterranean diet can't be attributed only to olive oil. The diet is high in vegetables, fruit, legumes and grains, and also contains moderate amounts of white meat and fish. And it's sparse in red meat, a central theme in the diets of the long-lived Blue Zone residents. But the fact that the majority of fat in the Mediterranean diet comes from olive oil has received plenty of attention from scientists.

Olive oil is unique from other cooking oils in that 77 percent of its fat content is heart-healthy monounsaturated fat. When used in place of saturated (animal) fat, monounsaturated fat lowers LDL (bad) cholesterol and can even raise HDL (good) cholesterol, thereby guarding against heart attack and stroke. As well, olive oil contains vitamin E and phytochemicals that function as antioxidants to protect LDL cholesterol particles from free radical damage. Olive oil also contains olecanthal, a phytochemical with anti-inflammatory effects similar to those of Aspirin or ibuprofen. Other phytochemicals in olive oil have anticoagulant effects, reducing the likelihood of a life-threatening blood clot from forming.

There's more to olive oil than heart health. It's known now that monounsaturated fat improves how the body uses insulin in people with diabetes. Studies, too, have found a link between anti-inflammatory compounds in olive oil and lower rates of rheumatoid arthritis. And it's thought that olive oil's phytochemicals prevent bone loss and protect DNA from free radical damage.

Does the grade of olive oil matter? Yes, it does! Olive oil is available in a variety of grades that reflect the extent that it's been processed. Extra-virgin and virgin olive oils are not refined in any way. Olives of these grades were pressed using minimal heat and no chemicals. Because extra-virgin and virgin olive oils are minimally processed, they contain the highest amount of phytochemicals and nutrients. Don't be fooled: Olive oil labelled "pure olive oil" or simply "olive oil" is usually *refined* olive oil with just a little extra-virgin or virgin olive oil added to provide some flavour, aroma and colour.

NOTABLE NUTRIENTS
IN EXTRA-VIRGIN OLIVE OIL
(PER 1 TABLESPOON/15 ML)
119 calories, 13.5 g fat (9.8 g monounsaturated fat), 0 mg cholesterol, 2.9 IU vitamin E

QUICK TIPS TO ADD OLIVE OIL TO YOUR DIET

- Make homemade salad dressings with extra-virgin olive oil and a red wine or balsamic vinaigrette.
- Drizzle a little extra-virgin olive oil over grilled vegetables or brush over baked or grilled fish before serving.
- Drizzle extra-virgin olive oil over crusty whole-grain bread or an open-faced sandwich.
- Add extra-virgin olive oil to garlic mashed potatoes instead of butter.

Oranges

Oranges are famous for their vitamin C, a powerful antioxidant, but there are many more reasons why you should make a point of including this juicy, sweet fruit in your diet. A diet rich in citrus fruit offers protection from heart disease, stroke, digestive tract cancers, lung cancer, colon cancer and pancreatic cancer. What's more, oranges may also help ward off other health problems associated with aging, including arthritis, cataracts, macular degeneration and cognitive impairment.

Certainly, vitamin C is one reason oranges are associated with a lower risk of age-related diseases. One large orange supplies more than a day's worth of the nutrient, which is critical for maintaining a healthy immune system as you age. Vitamin C helps keep the cartilage in your joints strong, which reduces the likelihood of osteoarthritis developing. And vitamin C has strong antioxidant effects that protect cells and body tissues. Oranges also contain generous amounts of folate and potassium, nutrients that keep your blood vessels healthy.

Oranges also contain unique phytochemicals that scientists believe play a large role in the fruit's ability to fight disease. In fact, one orange contains almost two hundred different phytochemicals. Of particular interest are compounds called limonoids and flavanones, which have been the focus of many studies. Limonoids, which are found in orange peel and are readily absorbed and utilized by the body, have been shown to fight cancers of the mouth, breast, stomach and colon. Studies have also demonstrated that phytochemicals in oranges block tumour growth by acting directly on cancer cells, impeding their ability to multiply.

The most important flavanone in oranges is called hesperidin. Animal studies have shown that a diet enriched with hesperidin is able to lower high blood pressure and cholesterol. Hesperidin also has strong anti-inflammatory properties and acts to strengthen and tone blood vessel walls. Most of the hesperidin in oranges is found in the peel and inner white pulp rather than in the juicy flesh. That means you will likely get more of this disease-fighting compound by eating citrus fruit whole (but peeled, of course) than you will by processing fruit into juice.

NOTABLE NUTRIENTS IN 1 MEDIUM-SIZED ORANGE

62 calories, 0 g fat, 3.1 g fibre, 70 mg vitamin C, 39 mcg folate, 52 mg calcium, 237 mg potassium

QUICK TIPS TO ADD ORANGES TO YOUR DIET

- Add orange segments to your favourite fruit salad recipe.
- Blend orange segments into a banana smoothie for extra flavour and fibre.
- Add a teaspoon of orange zest (peel) to black or herbal tea for an infusion of limonoids.
- Toss orange segments into a spinach salad—the vitamin C will help your body absorb the iron in the spinach more readily.
- Add orange segments to a mixed bean salad for a dash of colour and flavour.
- Use freshly squeezed orange juice in vinaigrettes and marinades, and add a little finely grated orange peel.

Recipes

Lentil Salad with Citrus Yogurt Dressing, page 249
Pumpkin Orange Banana Smoothie, page 235

Pomegranate

The pomegranate has been valued for its medicinal properties since ancient times but only recently has it gained "super food" status in North America. It's the seeds of the pomegranate that have attracted the attention of nutrition and health researchers.

Inside a pomegranate's rosy red shell you'll find individual cells, separated by membranes, containing glistening red seeds. Each seed is surrounded by a juice-filled sac (called an aril), which is pressed out during processing. Pomegranate seeds contain potent antioxidants, in particular some called polyphenols. Research tells us that the antioxidant level in pomegranate juice is higher than that in other fruit juices—including blueberry, cranberry and orange—and even higher than the level in red wine.

Pomegranate's polyphenols are thought to benefit the heart. Studies have found that drinking 100 percent pure pomegranate juice improved blood flow, reduced blood pressure and delayed the oxidation of LDL (bad) cholesterol in patients with heart disease. The juice has even been shown to lower LDL cholesterol and increase HDL (good) cholesterol levels in people with type 2 diabetes. Pomegranate juice appears to stimulate the production of nitric oxide, a chemical that helps blood vessels relax.

Other studies suggest that pomegranate polyphenols might guard against prostate and lung cancer.

While it's too soon to say that drinking pomegranate juice prevents disease, it's clearly a healthy and nutritious addition to your diet, especially since it is also a good source of potassium and provides some vitamin C.

If you want to add pomegranate juice to your diet, you'll need to factor in a few extra calories on your Longevity Diet meal plan. One cup (250 ml) of pomegranate juice supplies roughly 160 calories whereas the same serving of orange juice has 110 calories. One-half of a whole pomegranate—a food guide serving—has 53 calories.

What's the easiest way to remove the seeds from a pomegranate? Before you can enjoy pomegranate seeds you have to get inside the thick outer shell. Start by cutting off the "crown," then score the outer layer of skin into sections. In a large bowl of water, break apart the sections along the score lines. Roll out the arils with your fingers. The arils will sink to the bottom while the white membrane floats to the top of the water.

After skimming off the membrane, drain the water from the bowl or pour it through a sieve. You can eat the arils whole, seeds and all, or you can add them to salads, cereals, smoothies and other recipes. To get the juice, push the arils through a sieve.

NOTABLE NUTRIENTS IN POMEGRANATE
(PER 1/2 CUP/125 ML OF SEEDS)
72 calories, 1 g fat, 16 g carbohydrate, 9 mg vitamin C, 33 mcg folate, 205 mg potassium

QUICK TIPS TO ADD POMEGRANATE TO YOUR DIET

- Make a breakfast smoothie with pomegranate seeds, banana, ground flaxseed and low-fat milk or soy milk.
- Sprinkle pomegranate seeds over cold breakfast cereal or stir them into a bowl of whole grain oatmeal.
- Toss pomegranate seeds into a green salad for an infusion of antioxidants and vibrant colour.
- Top a bowl of yogurt with pomegranate seeds for a healthy dessert or snack.
- Add pomegranate seeds to muffin, pancake and waffle batters.
- Garnish steamed brown rice and other whole grains with pomegranate seeds.
- Mix pomegranate seeds with plain yogurt to make a tasty dipping sauce for skewers of grilled chicken, pork or lamb.

Recipes
Açaí Pomegranate Smoothie, page 232
Wheat Berry and Pomegranate Salad with Maple Dijon Dressing, page 253

Red bell peppers

This sweet, crunchy vegetable is one of the very best sources of vitamin C, an antioxidant that keeps cells healthy as you age. In fact, one red bell pepper has twice as much of the nutrient as an orange! You've already heard about the many ways vitamin C helps boost your immune system and protects your cells and tissues from the wrath of free radicals. But red peppers have another antioxidant that oranges don't: beta carotene, a phytochemical that can help guard against heart disease and certain cancers.

While sweet potatoes (which you'll read about later) and carrots are most famous for beta carotene, red peppers also contribute to your daily intake of this nutrient. What's more, they're also a source of folate and B6, vitamins that help reduce high levels of homocysteine in the blood. Having too much homocysteine has been shown to cause damage to blood vessels and is linked with a greater risk of heart attack, stroke and Alzheimer's disease.

Adding red peppers to your diet may also keep your eyes younger as you age. Italian researchers found that people who had the most versus the least vegetables in their diet—including red peppers—were significantly less likely to require an operation to remove cataracts. Red pepper's outstanding vitamin C content protects the lens of the eye from oxidative damage. But, unlike green peppers, red peppers are also a source of lutein and zeaxanthin, two protective phytochemicals concentrated in the retina.

Even better, red peppers deliver plenty of anti-aging nutrients for only a few calories. One whole bell pepper has only 36 calories.

NOTABLE NUTRIENTS IN RED BELL PEPPERS

(PER 1/2 MEDIUM-SIZED RED PEPPER, RAW)

18 calories, 0.2 g fat, 3.5 g carbohydrate, 1.2 g fibre, 76 mg vitamin C, 27 mcg folate, 0.2 mg vitamin B6, 1 mg beta carotene, 126 mg potassium

QUICK TIPS TO ADD RED BELL PEPPERS TO YOUR DIET

- Toss chopped red bell pepper into tuna or chicken salad for added crunch and colour.
- Sauté strips of red pepper with broccoli, mushrooms and garlic for a nutrient-rich vegetable side dish.
- Grill red peppers on the barbecue, then drizzle them with a balsamic vinaigrette and chopped fresh basil. Serve with dinner and add the leftovers to a sandwich or salad.
- Purée roasted and peeled red peppers with sautéed onions and zucchini. Add to a sodium-reduced chicken or vegetable stock to make a delicious soup.
- Enjoy raw red pepper sticks dipped in hummus (chickpea dip) for a healthy, low-calorie afternoon snack.

Recipes

Balsamic Grilled Bell Peppers, page 265
Red Pepper and Asparagus Omelet, page 222

Red grapes

Along with their crunchy texture and sweet, tart flavour, red grapes deliver a handful of phytochemicals linked with health and longevity. These compounds are concentrated in the skin and seeds, at about one hundred times the level of their concentration in the juicy middle section of the grape. Three types of phytochemicals in red grapes are most important when it comes to health: anthocyanins, proanthocyanidins and resveratrol. Like berries, grapes are also rich in ellagic acid, a potent flavonoid that helps fight cancer.

Plenty of research has confirmed the protective effects on the heart of red or purple grapes and grape juice. Phytochemicals in grapes help prevent harmful blood clots from forming, act as antioxidants to shield LDL cholesterol from free radical damage, reduce homocysteine in the blood and inhibit the buildup of plaque on artery walls. Grapes have also been shown to stimulate the production of nitric oxide in blood vessel walls, which relaxes blood vessels and lowers blood pressure. Scientists also demonstrated the ability of a Concord grape extract to lower LDL cholesterol, raise HDL cholesterol and reduce inflammation.

Resveratrol, an antioxidant in red grapes, exerts many different beneficial effects in the body and continues to be the focus of many studies. The phytochemical has been shown to block many steps in the cancer development process. In the lab, resveratrol has been shown to inhibit prostate cancer cell growth and kill cancer cells. It's also thought to have anti-inflammatory effects in the body.

Anthocyanins and proanthocyanidins, too, have been shown to have anti-cancer and immune-boosting properties and can detoxify the activity of some cancer-causing substances. In experimental studies, Concord grape juice was able to protect healthy breast cells from DNA damage caused by a chemical carcinogen. Grape juice also seems to suppress the growth and development of breast cancer cells in lab animals given chemically induced tumours. Animals receiving grape juice had smaller and fewer tumours than did the control animals.

Promising data hints that drinking grape juice can help to keep your brain healthy and delay neurodegenerative diseases. In one study, participants that drank purple grape juice and similar fruit juices three times a week were about 7 percent less likely to develop Alzheimer's disease than people who drank juice less than once per week.[23] What's more, lab animals fed purple grape juice showed significantly improved scores on memory and coordination tests. Compared to other juices, purple grape juice has the highest concentration of antioxidants.[24]

Even more exciting is the potential for resveratrol to dramatically extend lifespan. Scientists have learned that this phytochemical is a potent activator of SIR-2, an enzyme that is responsible for the extension of lifespan in many species when they are placed on calorie-restricted diets. When confronted with a shortage of calories, SIR-2 turns off many age-promoting activities in cells and enables cells to use other sources of energy. Researchers have learned that resveratrol can directly activate SIR-2, and in so doing can prolong the lifespan of yeast by 70 percent! Resveratrol has also been shown to increase the lifespan of worms, fruit flies, fish and mice. It's not yet known, however, whether the compound can buy humans more time.

Are red grapes, purple grape juice and red wine equally beneficial? Although all three contain anthocyanins, proanthocyanidins and resveratrol, grape juice and red wine have a higher concentration than fresh grapes. But if you drink too much juice, you'll add excess calories and sugar to your diet, which can be bad news for your weight and blood sugar. If you drink too much red wine, the excess alcohol can increase the risk of certain cancers, not to mention increase your blood pressure. If you opt for juice, keep your serving size to 3/4 cup (175 ml). When it comes to red wine, limit your intake to one 5 ounce glass per day and avoid products labelled grape "drink." Choose products that are 100 percent pure grape juice. Include a serving of red grapes (20 grapes) in your diet on a regular basis.

NOTABLE NUTRIENTS IN RED GRAPES
(20 GRAPES)
68 calories, 0 g fat, 18 g carbohydrate, 1 g fibre, 10 mg vitamin C, 187 mg potassium

QUICK TIPS TO ADD RED GRAPES TO YOUR DIET

- Toss sliced red grapes into a mixed green salad.
- Serve stewed red grapes with poached chicken breast for a light entrée.
- Keep a small bowl of red grapes on your desk to eat as a healthy snack during the workday.
- Add sliced or whole red grapes to any fruit salad or mix into low-fat yogurt for a healthy snack or dessert.

- Freeze red grapes and reach for them instead of cookies or candy when you have a craving for something sweet.

Recipes
Arugula, Red Grape and Toasted Walnut Salad, page 241
Crunchy Broccoli Salad with Apple Dijon Dressing, page 245
Spicy Grape and Ginger Chutney, page 306

Salmon and other omega-3-rich fish

I'd be remiss if I didn't include salmon on my list of longevity foods. It's an excellent source of protein that's low in cholesterol-raising saturated fat. Its real claim to fame, though, is its exceptionally high level of two omega-3 fatty acids, called DHA (docosahexaenoic acid) and EPA (eicosapentaenoic acid). A steady intake of these fats is associated with longevity and a reduced risk of heart disease, macular degeneration, Alzheimer's disease and cancer. The benefits of eating fish are so clear that Health Canada and the Heart and Stroke Foundation of Canada advise people to consume fish, especially fatty fish, at least two times per week.

After reviewing hundreds of studies on fish and health, researchers from the Harvard School of Public Health and Harvard Medical School concluded that eating one to two servings of fish per week was enough to reduce the risk of dying from heart disease by 36 percent. Studies have demonstrated the ability of these omega-3s to make the blood less likely to form clots and to protect against irregular heartbeats that cause sudden cardiac death. Omega-3s in fish oil can also reduce elevated blood fats—triglycerides—which contribute to hardening of the arteries and the risk of stroke and heart attack.

SALMON PREVENTS TELOMERE SHRINKAGE Exciting new research suggests that eating salmon regularly can turn back the biological clock by slowing down telomere shortening, a marker of aging. That's what researchers from the University of California, San Francisco, found when they studied men and women with stable coronary artery disease. Those with the highest levels of omega-3 fats in the blood had a slower rate of telomere shortening.[25] (The only way to increase the level of omega-3 fats in your bloodstream is to eat oily fish, especially salmon, or to take a fish oil capsule.)

Remember telomeres from Chapter 1? They're sequences of DNA that bookend chromosomes and protect the ends from damage. Telomeres allow cells to divide while holding the important genetic material intact. But every time a cell divides, telomeres get progressively shorter until, eventually, the cell dies. Telomere shortening has been linked to the aging process, cancer and a higher risk of early death. Anti-aging scientists speculate that counteracting telomere shortening can allow people to live longer—and in better health.

Eating salmon may also keep your brain healthy as you age. A study that followed 815 adults, aged 65 to 94 years, revealed that those who ate fish at least once per week were 60 percent less likely to develop Alzheimer's disease during the four years of the study than the people who rarely or never ate fish.[26] Another study linked regular fish consumption to a 60 percent lower risk of dementia, in particular Alzheimer's.[27] Omega-3 fatty acids, especially DHA, make up 60 percent of the communicating membranes of the brain, where they keep the lining of brain cells flexible so that memory messages can pass easily between cells.

A number of studies also suggest that eating fish, especially fatty fish, one to four times per week guards against age-related macular degeneration and reduces the risk of the disease progressing to an advanced form. DHA is a key fatty acid found in the retina. Here it exerts anti-inflammatory, anti-blood clotting and triglyceride-lowering effects that help prevent hardening of the blood vessels in the eye.

In addition to omega-3s, salmon delivers other nutrients important for healthy aging. One 3 ounce (90 gram) serving has a full day's worth of B12, a vitamin essential for maintaining healthy DNA and nerves. The same-sized serving supplies two-thirds of your daily selenium requirement, an antioxidant that attacks free radicals. As well, salmon is one of the very few foods that contain an appreciable amount of vitamin D, a nutrient that boosts the immune system, reduces inflammation and is associated with a lower risk of certain cancers and heart disease.

Getting enough vitamin D may also increase lifespan by preventing the age-related decline in telomere length. In one study from the United Kingdom, women with the highest versus the lowest level of vitamin D in their bloodstream had the longest telomeres, whose length correlated to roughly five additional years of life. Women with the lowest vitamin D level had the highest level of C-reactive protein (CRP), an indication of chronic inflammation in the body.[28]

Other omega-3 fish worth adding to your diet include trout, Arctic char, sardines and herring. Below you'll also find a recipe for a delicious trout dish.

Some people are concerned about harmful chemicals in fish. It's true that women of childbearing age and young children should not eat fish high in mercury. These species include fresh and frozen tuna, shark, swordfish, marlin, orange roughy, escolar and canned albacore (white) tuna. (Albacore tuna is generally from larger, older fish that have accumulated more mercury. Light canned tuna contains smaller species of tuna such as skipjack, yellowfin and tongol, which are lower in mercury.)

The concern is that mercury can accumulate in the body and affect the developing nervous system, especially the brain, of infants and young children. If women consume too much mercury before and during their pregnancy, it may increase the risk of birth defects and learning disabilities in children.

The good news is that salmon—along with other omega-3-rich fish like trout, sardines, Arctic char and herring—is low in mercury.

NOTABLE NUTRIENTS IN SALMON
(PER 3 OUNCES/90 GRAMS, COOKED)
175 calories, 19 g protein, 10.5 g fat (2 g saturated fat), 6.8 mg niacin, 2.38 mcg vitamin B12, 310 IU vitamin D, 35 mcg selenium

QUICK TIPS TO ADD SALMON TO YOUR DIET
- For a twist on scrambled eggs, combine egg whites with smoked trout and chopped onion and red bell pepper.
- Enjoy a slice of whole-grain pumpernickel bread topped with smoked salmon, light cream cheese and a few capers.
- Skewer marinated chunks of fresh salmon, red pepper, zucchini, eggplant and red onion, and broil or grill on the barbecue.
- Grill or bake an extra salmon filet or steak and save it to serve over a bed of spinach for lunch the next day.
- Make your own version of salad niçoise by combining canned salmon with chilled cooked green peas, halved cooked new potatoes, a sliced hard-cooked egg, capers and olives. Season to taste and drizzle with a lemon vinaigrette.

Recipes

Salmon Quinoa Salad with Spicy Ginger Dressing, page 251
Salmon with White Wine, Lemon and Garlic, page 288
Sesame Salmon Wrap, page 289
Thai Roasted Trout with Fresh Lime, page 291
Wasabi and Ginger Baked Salmon, page 292

Soybeans

These tiny little beans are a staple food for some of the longest-lived people in the world. Residents of Okinawa regularly eat tofu made from soybeans, as do vegetarian Seventh-day Adventists living in Loma Linda, California. The fact that soybeans are jam-packed with vitamins, minerals and many unique phytochemicals may explain their role in longevity.

Like black beans and lentils, soybeans are nutrient rich. They're an exceptional source of many vitamins and minerals that keep us healthy as we age, such as folate, calcium and magnesium. And they are an incredible source of protein, which we need to maintain muscle mass. One 3/4 cup (175 ml) serving of cooked soybeans has 21 grams of protein, the amount that's found in a similar sized serving of poultry and meat. What's more, soybeans are the only plant food considered a "complete" protein. That means that like animal foods, soybeans supply the right proportions of all essential amino acids needed by the human body.

It is soy's anti-cancer potential that has researchers excited. Research conducted in more than 12,000 Californian Seventh-day Adventist men found that those who drank soy milk once daily, compared to those who never drank it, were 70 percent less likely to develop prostate cancer.[29] Epidemiological studies have also linked a high soy intake (soybeans, tofu, miso) among Asian women with a lower risk of breast cancer. And there's some evidence that soy can reduce the risk of breast cancer in non-Asian women. Researchers from Johns Hopkins School of Medicine combined the results of 18 studies that examined soy intake and breast cancer risk. Among all women, a high soy intake (tofu and soy foods) was associated with a modest protective effect. Women who consumed the most soy had a 14 percent lower risk of breast cancer. Soy's protective effect was stronger in premenopausal women than in postmenopausal women. Premenopausal women with high soy intakes were 30 percent less likely to develop breast cancer, compared to premenopausal women who consumed the least.[30]

Scientists have shown the ability of phytochemicals in legumes—known as saponins, protease inhibitors and phytic acid—to block the reproduction of cancer cells and slow the growth of several types of tumours. Compounds called isoflavones in soybeans can keep testosterone levels in check, thereby reducing the risk and progression of prostate cancer. (Prostate cancer cells feed off testosterone.) Isoflavones also behave like weak forms of the body's own estrogen. That means that isoflavones compete for the same place on breast cells that estrogen does. (Estrogen can trigger the growth of breast cancer.) When isoflavones attach to breast cell receptors they elbow out estrogen. By counteracting the action of estrogen, it's thought that soybeans and soy foods can reduce a woman's risk of breast cancer.

NOTABLE NUTRIENTS IN SOYBEANS AND TOFU

Soybeans (1/2 cup/125 ml, cooked)
149 calories, 14 g protein, 8.5 g carbohydrate, 5.2 g fibre, 46 mcg folate, 88 mg calcium, 4.4 mg iron, 74 mg magnesium, 443 mg potassium
Tofu, firm, made with calcium sulfate (1/2 cup/125 ml)
183 calories, 20 g protein, 5.4 g carbohydrate, 3 g fibre, 37 mcg folate, 861 mg calcium, 3.4 mg iron, 73 mg magnesium, 299 mg potassium
*Soy milk, plain** (1 cup/250 ml)
100 calories, 7 g protein, 4 g fat, 8 g carbohydrate, 3 mcg vitamin B12, 100 IU vitamin D, 300 mg calcium, 299 mg potassium

*Plain *unsweetened* soy milk has no added sugar and 80 calories per cup (250 ml).

QUICK TIPS TO ADD SOY TO YOUR DIET

- At breakfast, replace bacon with a soy-based breakfast meat to reduce saturated fat.
- Enjoy a fruit smoothie made with an unflavoured soy beverage for a healthy breakfast or snack.
- When making muffins, replace up to one-half the wheat flour with soy flour.
- Add cooked soybeans to salads, soups and chili. Buy them canned for convenience—simply drain and rinse the beans under running water in a colander to remove excess sodium.
- Replace poultry or meat with cubes of extra-firm tofu in your next stir-fry.

Recipes
Balsamic Glazed Mushroom and Soy Burgers, page 295
Sesame Ginger Stir-Fried Tofu and Bok Choy with Brown Rice, page 301

Spinach

Here's another leafy green vegetable that should be a regular part of your menu. Like kale, spinach is an outstanding source of lutein that keeps your eyes healthy as you age. (One half-cup/125 ml of cooked spinach delivers 10 milligrams of lutein; experts contend we need to consume 6 to 15 milligrams per day for optimal eye health.) Spinach is also a good source of anti-cancer compounds including flavonoids, beta carotene and vitamins A and C. That's not all. Eating spinach more often can also help preserve your memory as you get older; its vitamin E content defends brain cells from harmful free radicals.

But there are other reasons why spinach is among my top 25 longevity foods. For starters, it's one of the very best food sources of folate—a half-cup (125 ml) of cooked spinach supplies one-third of your daily folate requirements. You have already read about the importance of folate in the creation and repair of DNA. The B vitamin is also needed to break down a potentially dangerous chemical in the bloodstream called homocysteine that can lead to heart attack or stroke if levels get too high.

Another consequence of growing old is thinning bones. We're all aware that losing too much bone mass over the years can lead to osteoporosis, a condition of thin, weak bones that are more susceptible to fracture. Turns out, spinach can help maintain your bone density, because it is an exceptional source of vitamin K. A number of studies have revealed that men and women who get the most vitamin K in their diet—versus the least—have stronger bones and a lower risk of hip fracture. Scientists estimate it takes about 200 micrograms per day to protect bones from thinning. As you'll see in the Notable Nutrients below, one serving (1/2 cup/125 ml) of cooked spinach has twice as much.

As vegetables go, spinach is a pretty good source of iron, an integral component of hemoglobin, which transports oxygen from your lungs to all body cells, and part of key enzyme systems for energy production and metabolism. If your body lacks iron, you will feel drained and lethargic.

Which is healthier, raw or cooked spinach? Both are healthy ways to enjoy spinach. But cooked spinach packs a much stronger nutritional punch.

Cooked spinach has a higher antioxidant content (e.g., lutein, beta carotene) since heating releases these antioxidants by breaking down cell walls. When it comes to calcium, magnesium and iron, high levels of a compound in raw spinach called oxalic acid bind these minerals and reduce their absorption. Cooking releases some of the minerals bound to oxalic acid. Three cups (750 ml) of raw spinach, for example, has 90 milligrams of calcium, whereas 1 cup (250 ml) of cooked has 244 milligrams, nearly triple the amount.

NOTABLE NUTRIENTS IN SPINACH
(PER 1/2 CUP/125 ML, COOKED)
22 calories, 0 g fat, 3.4 g carbohydrate, 2.2 g fibre, 131 mcg folate, 1.9 mg vitamin E, 444 mcg vitamin K, 122 mg calcium, 3.2 mg iron, 78 mg magnesium, 5.6 mg beta carotene,* 10.2 mg lutein plus zeaxanthin*

*There are no official recommended daily intakes for beta carotene or lutein plus zeaxanthin. However, 6 to 15 milligrams of lutein plus zeaxanthin per day is thought to be optimal for eye health. An intake of 3 to 6 milligrams of beta carotene per day is enough to maintain blood levels of beta carotene in the range that's associated with a lower risk of chronic disease.

QUICK TIPS TO ADD SPINACH TO YOUR DIET
- Toss steamed spinach with pressed garlic, fresh lemon juice and a drizzle of extra-virgin olive oil.
- Splash a little raspberry or champagne vinegar over a side of steamed spinach.
- Add layers of steamed spinach to your favourite lasagna recipe.
- Stir 4 cups (1 L) of baby spinach leaves into a tomato-based pasta sauce at the end of cooking.
- Add baby spinach to your next egg-white omelet.
- Use spinach leaves instead of lettuce in sandwiches and wraps.

Recipes
Baked Pita Pizza with Chicken, Spinach and Fresh Basil, page 277
Fig and Roasted Walnut Salad, page 246
Salmon Quinoa Salad with Spicy Ginger Dressing, page 251
Sesame Salmon Wrap, page 289
Simple Sautéed Spinach, page 270

Sweet potato

If you aren't already eating one bright-orange coloured vegetable each day, it's time to start. Since 2007, Health Canada has advised all Canadians to include one of these antioxidant-rich vegetables in their daily diet. That's because they are an exceptional source of beta carotene, an antioxidant that's linked with protection from heart disease and cancer.

Beta carotene not only protects cells in the body from damage caused by free radicals, it also stimulates communication between cells, which is thought to play a role in cancer prevention. Cancerous cells are a good example of cell communication gone awry. In cancer, instead of cells having clearly assigned functions, they grow out of control and form tumours. Normally, when a healthy cell senses there's something wrong with its neighbour, it sends a message to that cell, instructing it to self-destruct. But when cell communication is impaired, this does not occur, and cancerous cells may grow.

Beta carotene also protects your LDL cholesterol particles from becoming oxidized, or damaged, by free radicals. That protection is important, as we've seen, since oxidized LDL cholesterol readily sticks to artery walls, making it more dangerous to heart health.

But there's more to sweet potatoes than their high beta carotene content. They're also a good source of fibre and potassium and, unlike white baking potatoes, they provide low-glycemic carbohydrate that won't spike your blood sugar and insulin levels.

What's the difference between sweet potatoes and yams? Sweet potatoes are often confused with yams. In most cases, the "yams" sold in grocery stores are actually orange-coloured sweet potatoes. The sweet potato has orange flesh and its skin may be white, yellow, orange or purple. Sometimes it's shaped like a potato and sometimes it's longer and tapered at both ends.

Yams, on the other hand, have a flesh colour that varies from white to ivory to yellow to purple. Their shape is long and cylindrical and their skin has a rough and scaly texture. Unlike sweet potatoes, yams are not an exceptional source of beta carotene. (They are, however, excellent sources of dietary fibre, vitamin C, potassium and vitamin B6.)

NOTABLE NUTRIENTS IN SWEET POTATO
(PER 1/2 MEDIUM POTATO, BAKED, WITH SKIN)
52 calories, 0 g fat, 12 g carbohydrate, 2 g fibre, 6.6 mg beta carotene, 271 mg potassium

QUICK TIPS TO ADD SWEET POTATO TO YOUR DIET

- Add cooked, puréed sweet potato to muffin, quick bread and pancake recipes.
- Purée cooked sweet potato with bananas, maple syrup and cinnamon, and top with chopped pecans for a delicious side dish or dessert.
- Add diced cooked sweet potato to your favourite fruit salad recipe. Try it with pineapple, banana, apples or pears.
- Add diced sweet potato to any soup—homemade or store-bought.
- Toss cooked sweet potato with whole-grain pasta. Toss with extra-virgin olive oil, fresh herbs and a little grated Parmesan cheese.
- Mix steamed sweet potato cubes with tofu and broccoli. Top with raisins and serve with a vinaigrette dressing.
- Make sweet potato chips. Thinly slice sweet potato, brush with olive oil and sprinkle with a little salt, pepper and spices. Roast in 400°F (200°C) oven until golden and crisp.
- Bake a sweet potato and top it with a dash of cinnamon and brown sugar.

Recipes
Sweet Potato Cranberry Drop Biscuits, page 239
Sweet Potato Soup with Maple Glazed Walnuts, page 263
Zesty Sweet Potato Wedges, page 272

Tomatoes

Most people are only too happy to include tomatoes as part of their healthy diet. Who doesn't like a fresh tomato sandwich in the summer or a plate of spaghetti and tomato sauce on a cold winter's day? Low in fat and calories, tomatoes are an excellent source of vitamins A and C and they're a good source of B vitamins and potassium, a mineral that helps regulate blood pressure. Tomatoes also contain vitamin K, a vitamin important for maintaining healthy bones as we age. But it's their lycopene content that's positioned tomatoes as an anti-aging food. Lycopene, a phytochemical that gives tomatoes their bright red colour, is a powerful antioxidant that neutralizes harmful free radicals that accelerate aging in cells.

If you want to get the most lycopene from your tomatoes, there are a few things you need to know. For starters, cooking tomatoes increases the amount of lycopene that's available for absorption in the body. Lycopene is tightly bound in the cell walls of foods; processing breaks down the cells walls and releases lycopene. That's why heat-processed tomato products—such as tomato paste, tomato juice, tomato sauce, even ketchup—contain the highest concentrations of bioavailable lycopene (that is, lycopene that is available for the body to absorb).

Lycopene's claim to fame is its potential protective effect against prostate cancer, a disease of aging that affects more men than any other cancer. Over the past decade, numerous studies have shown that men who eat tomato-based foods frequently are less likely to develop prostate cancer than those who seldom eat these foods. Lycopene shields DNA in prostate cells from free radical damage but it also has anti-inflammatory and immunity-enhancing effects. What's more, in the lab it's been shown to stop the growth of cancer cells.

There's no official recommended daily intake for lycopene, but studies suggest that 6 to 15 milligrams daily offers cancer protection. It's not hard to get this much lycopene in your diet when you consider that 1 cup (250 ml) of tomato juice packs 22 milligrams! In contrast, one medium-sized raw tomato has 3 milligrams of lycopene. Because tomato sauce offers a particularly concentrated source of lycopene, I've listed its nutrient content below.

NOTABLE NUTRIENTS IN TOMATO SAUCE
(PER 1/2 CUP/125 ML)
29 calories, 0.2 g fat, 6.5 g carbohydrate, 9 mg vitamin C, 17 mg lycopene, 405 mg potassium, 642 mg sodium (choose reduced-sodium products if available)

QUICK TIPS TO ADD TOMATOES TO YOUR DIET
- Enjoy broiled fresh tomatoes as a side dish. Remove tomato core and halve crosswise. Drizzle with olive oil, sprinkle with salt, pepper and herbs of your choice. Broil until tomatoes are tender and topping is lightly

browned. Or bake in a hot oven (425°F/220°C) for 10 to 15 minutes or until tender.

- Add chopped fresh tomatoes to egg-white omelets and frittatas. (Roma tomatoes hold their shape best because they contain less water.)
- Toss diced fresh tomatoes with a homemade three-bean salad and serve on crisp lettuce leaves.
- Stuff whole-tomato cups with your favourite seafood salad for a quick, cold lunch.
- Add canned tomatoes (chopped, puréed or whole) to pasta sauces, canned soups, chili, stews or casseroles. Choose reduced-sodium or salt-free brands.
- Enjoy a bowl of gazpacho soup. Purée tomatoes, cucumbers, bell peppers and green onions and a drizzle of olive oil together in the food processor. Season with your favourite herbs and spices.
- Add diced tomatoes to guacamole or hummus dip for extra colour and nutrition.
- Eat a fresh in-season tomato out of hand, just as you would an apple.
- Drink a glass of lycopene-rich tomato juice or vegetable cocktail with lunch or dinner or as a snack. Look for a sodium-reduced brand.

Recipes

Braised Tilapia with Tomato Fennel Sauce, page 286
Fresh Tomato Soup with Garlic and Basil, page 258
Ginger Tomato Chicken Pasta, page 280
Grilled Chicken with Tomato Cilantro Citrus Salsa, page 282
Roasted Tomatoes with Herbes de Provence, page 268
Sautéed Cherry Tomatoes with Garlic and Fresh Basil, page 269

Walnuts

Eating a handful of walnuts each day can lower elevated LDL cholesterol and blood pressure. Like almonds, walnuts are an important source of heart-healthy monounsaturated fat. But walnuts differ from other nuts in that they contain alpha-linolenic acid (ALA), an omega-3 fatty acid. In fact, a 1 ounce serving of walnuts (14 halves) has 2.6 grams of ALA—more than a day's worth! (Women require 1.1 grams per day; men need 1.6.) ALA can defend against heart disease and heart attack by helping prevent erratic heart rhythms, by making the blood less likely to clot inside arteries and by reducing inflammation that could otherwise turn cholesterol into artery-clogging plaques.

Walnuts are also a good source of arginine, an amino acid that plays a role in lowering high blood pressure. The body converts arginine to nitric oxide, a chemical that helps keep blood vessel walls smooth and allows them to relax. And walnuts deliver antioxidants; along with pecans and chestnuts, they have more antioxidants than other nuts. Two of these antioxidants, ellagic acid and gallic acid, fend off free radical damage to LDL cholesterol.

Antioxidants in walnuts may promote healthy longevity in another important way: by keeping the brain healthy. New animal research has found that a diet containing 6 percent walnuts (about 1 ounce/30 g of walnuts a day, for humans) was able to reverse age-related motor and cognitive deficits in aged rats.[31] The researchers think that walnuts may have the ability to protect the brain by quenching free radicals, which we become more susceptible to with age, as well as by promoting communication between brain cells and the growth of new brain cells. In other words, adding walnuts to your diet may delay—or prevent—the onset of neurodegenerative diseases such as Alzheimer's.

NOTABLE NUTRIENTS IN WALNUTS
(PER 1 OUNCE/30 G OR 14 HALVES)
185 calories, 18.5 g fat (1.7 g saturated fat), 4.3 g protein, 4 g carbohydrate, 2 g fibre, 28 mcg folate, 2.6 g ALA

QUICK TIPS TO ADD WALNUTS TO YOUR DIET
* Mix chopped walnuts into yogurt or sprinkle over a bowl of hot whole-grain cereal.
* Stir chopped walnuts into muffin, pancake and waffle batters.
* Add walnuts to sautéed vegetables such as green beans or Brussels sprouts.
* Toss a handful of toasted walnuts into a green salad or an arugula salad.
* Add walnuts to brown rice pilafs and grain salads.

Recipes
Arugula, Red Grape and Toasted Walnut Salad, page 241
Fig and Roasted Walnut Salad, page 246
Sweet Potato Soup with Maple-Glazed Walnuts, page 263

6

Vitamins, minerals and supplements for longevity

By now I hope you're eager to start adding to your diet at least a few of the 25 amazingly healthy foods I discussed in the previous chapter. You might even be keen to try a few of my recipes that feature these foods (in Part 4). Not only do these longevity foods and beverages (in the case of green tea!) taste delicious, they're brimming—as we've learned—with protective phytochemicals that fight disease. Many of these foods owe some of their anti-aging properties to a specific vitamin or mineral, micronutrients needed by the body in very small amounts for normal growth, function and maintenance of healthy tissues. (The body needs macronutrients, on the other hand, in larger quantities; they include carbohydrate, protein and fat.) For example, you may remember that vitamin E, plentiful in kale and other leafy green vegetables, helps delay cognitive decline by shielding our brain cells from damaging free radicals. And the B vitamin folate, found in lentils, is needed to repair our cells' DNA as we age.

There are a few nutrients, however, that deserve special attention when it comes to longevity. That's because they've been shown, in well-controlled scientific studies, to increase life expectancy or influence the aging process in cells. We've already talked about a few of these, but I want to tell you now about some other foods that can help increase your intake of these life-enhancing nutrients. Because these nutrients are so critical for healthy aging, it's important to know other exceptional food sources to incorporate into your diet. And in some cases, you'll need to rely on a supplement to get what you need—I'll tell you what to look for, and how to supplement safely.

Vitamin C

We've all heard that vitamin C is good for us—it bolsters the immune system, strengthens blood vessels, supports collagen synthesis in our joints and promotes wound healing. Vitamin C also acts as a potent antioxidant and, as such, can help keep you healthier longer. Studies suggest that consuming enough vitamin C in your daily diet can protect against age-related diseases such as heart disease, stroke, cataract and macular degeneration. What's more, vitamin C can help regenerate another key antioxidant, vitamin E. When vitamin E neutralizes harmful free radicals, it becomes oxidized in the process. Vitamin C is able to regenerate vitamin E from its oxidized state so it can continue defending your cells from free radicals.

But the antioxidant powers of vitamin C can protect your genes too. You've already learned that telomeres are sequences of DNA located at the ends of chromosomes that shrink with aging, cell division, oxidative stress and inflammation. When telomeres become too short, the cell can no longer divide and it dies. A number of studies have linked longer telomeres with an increased life expectancy. Turns out, a number of studies have also linked higher intakes of vitamin C to longer telomeres! You'll read about one such study later in this chapter.

Sounds good so far. The problem is that many people don't get enough vitamin C to slow aging and guard against the illnesses associated with it. Vitamin C is found in fruits and vegetables, healthy foods that busy people tend to neglect. It's not often that I meet a client who is consuming 7 to 10 servings of fruits and vegetables combined. That's right: You need 7 to 10 servings per day! (A serving is one medium-sized fruit, 1/2 cup/125 ml of cooked or raw vegetables or 1 cup/250 ml of salad greens.)

HOW MUCH VITAMIN C DO YOU NEED? Men need 90 milligrams of vitamin C per day and women require 75 milligrams. If you smoke, you need to boost your daily intake by 35 milligrams to help fight off the free radicals formed from cigarette smoke. Health Canada's official recommended daily intakes for vitamin C are based on what's needed to prevent a deficiency disease like scurvy, not what's required to prevent age-related illness. Based on large observational studies, the amount of vitamin C that's needed to reduce your risk of chronic disease is higher than our current recommended daily intakes.

The Linus Pauling Institute, a micronutrient research centre at Oregon State University, recommends that healthy men and women get at least 400 milligrams of vitamin C per day. This is the amount that's been shown to maximize the level of vitamin C in the blood and in the cells of young, healthy non-smokers. If you consume 7 servings of fruits and vegetables each day—about 3 1/2 cups' (875 ml) worth, roughly enough to fill a small pie plate or loaf pan—you'll get close to 280 milligrams of vitamin C. Of course, if you add more vitamin C–rich vegetables to your diet, you'll get even more vitamin C. You'll also get some from a multivitamin, typically 75 to 100 milligrams, although some brands contain as much as 500 milligrams.

If you want to be certain you're getting at least 400 milligrams of vitamin C each day, you can take a separate 200 to 250 milligram vitamin C supplement. There's some evidence to suggest that adults aged 65 and older may need more than 400 milligrams of vitamin C to fully saturate their cells. It's thought that one of the mechanisms by which cells uptake vitamin C declines with age. My advice: Be sure to get *all* your fruits and vegetables every day, then take a supplement with 200 to 250 milligrams of vitamin C once or twice per day.

Vitamin C content of selected foods

Food	Vitamin C (milligrams)
Cantaloupe, cut up, 1 cup (250 ml)	60
Grapefruit, red or pink, 1/2	47
Kiwi, 1 medium	70
Mango, 1	49
Orange, 1 medium	70
Orange juice, fresh, 1 cup (250 ml)	131
Papaya, 1/2	95
Pineapple, cut up, 1 cup (250 ml)	74

Food	Vitamin C (milligrams)
Raspberries, 1 cup (250 ml)	32
Strawberries, raw, 1 cup (250 ml)	89
Broccoli, raw, 1 spear	141
Brussels sprouts, cooked, 1/2 cup (125 ml)	50
Cabbage, raw, 1 cup (250 ml)	40
Cauliflower, raw, 1 cup (250 ml)	48
Green pepper, raw, 1/2 cup (125 ml)	60
Kale, cooked, 1 cup (250 ml)	53
Potato, baked with skin, 1	27
Red pepper, raw, 1/2 cup (125 ml)	85
Tomato juice, 1 cup (250 ml)	44
Vegetable cocktail, 1 cup (250 ml)	67

Source: U.S. Department of Agriculture, Agricultural Research Service. 2009. USDA National Nutrient Database for Standard Reference, Release 22. Nutrient Data Laboratory Home Page, www.ars.usda.gov/nutrientdata.

Vitamin D

It's found in salmon, other oily fish, egg yolks and butter. It's added to milk, plant-based beverages (soy, almond, rice) and some brands of orange juice. But I will tell you right now that you cannot rely on your diet to get what you need. Our main source of vitamin D is sunshine, since exposure to sunlight triggers vitamin D synthesis in our skin. But even that's often insufficient to prevent a vitamin D deficiency given the long, dark winters we endure in Canada.

In addition to its important role in supporting a healthy immune system, reducing inflammation and maintaining bone density as we age, vitamin D is also linked to a lower risk of certain cancers and of coronary heart disease. If we get enough vitamin D, it may even protect against multiple sclerosis and rheumatoid arthritis. But there's another way that vitamin D can slow aging and increase lifespan. If you've got enough of the vitamin in your bloodstream, it seems to prevent the age-related decline in telomere length, a marker of aging.

VITAMIN D FOR LONGER TELOMERES In a study of 2160 women aged 18 to 79 years, researchers found that those with the highest blood level of vitamin D had the longest telomeres, even after adjusting for age differences. The women taking vitamin D supplements had longer telomeres than those who didn't take vitamin D pills. Interestingly, the women with low levels of vitamin D had the highest blood level of C-reactive protein, a marker of chronic inflammation. Compared to the women with the lowest vitamin D levels, those with the highest levels had telomeres whose length correlated to five additional years of life.[1] The researchers think vitamin D's anti-inflammatory actions help protect telomeres from eroding.

HOW MUCH VITAMIN D? It's well accepted that the current recommended daily intakes of vitamin D are too low given what scientists know now and need to be revised. In June 2007, the Canadian Cancer Society advised Canadian adults to take a vitamin D supplement of 1000 IU (international units) in the fall and winter. Older adults, people with dark skin, those who don't go outdoors often, and those who wear clothing that covers most of their skin should take the supplement all year round. (After age 50 our skin becomes less efficient at producing vitamin D from sunlight. People with dark-coloured skin also synthesize less vitamin D from the sun. As well, keep in mind that always wearing sunscreen while in the sun—a wise thing to do—also limits the vitamin D we produce.)

How much vitamin D you need to consume each day depends on how much it takes to keep your blood level in the "sufficient" range (above 75 nmol/L). Some people will need more than 1000 IU per day. For example, research suggests that if you have dark-coloured skin and don't get out in the sun in the summer to build up vitamin D stores you will need 3100 IU in the winter and 2100 IU in the summer to maintain a healthy blood level. If you're fair-skinned and prudent about sun exposure, you need 2550 IU in the winter and 1000 IU in the summer.[2] People who are obese may need more too, since vitamin D tends to become isolated in fat cells, making it less available for other cells to use. If you are unsure about what you need, ask your doctor to measure the level of vitamin D in your blood (the test is called 25-hydroxy vitamin D).

Be sure to choose a supplement with vitamin D3, the form that's more active in the body. I recommend the following vitamin D intakes to my clients all year round.

Age	Daily vitamin D dose
Children	400 IU
Teenagers	1000 IU
Adults, aged 19–50, fair-skinned	1000 to 2000 IU
Adults, aged 19–50, dark-skinned	2000 to 3000 IU
Adults, aged 50+, fair-skinned	2000 IU
Adults, aged 50+, dark-skinned	3000 IU

Vitamin E (alpha-tocopherol)

This important antioxidant nutrient works hard to protect lipids, or fats, in your body from free radical damage. That makes vitamin E a primary antioxidant defence for your brain cell membranes, which are rich in lipids and extremely susceptible to oxidation. It's believed vitamin E's antioxidant action keeps your brain healthy as you age and even lowers the risk of Alzheimer's disease. In 2010, a study of 5395 men and women aged 55 and older found that over ten years, those who consumed the most vitamin E from foods were 25 percent less likely to develop Alzheimer's than folks whose diets provided the least.[3] Researchers speculate that vitamin E can also mitigate the toxic effects of beta-amyloid, a protein that accumulates and clumps in the brain causing the hallmark memory loss and dementia of Alzheimer's disease.

Vitamin E can also guard against heart disease. The vitamin acts as a buffer between LDL cholesterol particles and free radicals, preventing oxidization. As we know now, oxidized LDL cholesterol becomes sticky, easily depositing on the interior lining of artery walls. But vitamin E's beneficial effects don't stop here. Research has determined that women who get the most vitamin E from their diet—versus the least—have longer telomeres![4]

The recommended dietary allowance (RDA) for vitamin E (alpha-tocopherol) is 15 mg (22.5 IU) for adults and teenagers. Boys and girls aged

9 to 13 need 11 milligrams per day; kids aged 4 to 8 require 7 milligrams and younger children, aged 1 to 3, should consume 6 milligrams daily. The list below shows some of the very best food sources.

Vitamin E content of selected foods

Food	Vitamin E (mg)
Wheat germ oil, 1 tbsp (15 ml)	20.3
Sunflower seeds, dry roasted, 2 tbsp (25 ml)	6.5
Almonds, dry roasted, 1 ounce (28 g) or 23 nuts	7.3
Sunflower oil, 1 tbsp (15 ml)	5.6
Safflower oil, 1 tbsp (15 ml)	4.6
Hazelnuts, dry roasted, 1 ounce (28 g) or 24 nuts	4.3
Grapeseed oil, 1 tbsp (15 ml)	3.9
Soy beverage, 1 cup (250 ml)	3.3
Spinach, frozen, cooked, 1/2 cup (125 ml)	3.3
Mixed nuts (with peanuts), dry roasted, 1 ounce (28 g)	3.1
Tomato sauce, canned, 1/2 cup (125 ml)	2.5
Canola oil, 1 tbsp (15 ml)	2.4
Papaya, 1 medium	2.2
Olive oil, 1 tbsp (15 ml)	1.9
Spinach, cooked, 1/2 cup (125 ml)	1.9
Beet greens, cooked, 1/2 cup (125 ml)	1.3
Broccoli, cooked, 1/2 cup (125 ml)	1.1

Source: U.S. Department of Agriculture, Agricultural Research Service. 2009. USDA National Nutrient Database for Standard Reference, Release 22. Nutrient Data Laboratory Home Page, www.ars.usda.gov/nutrientdata.

SHOULD YOU TAKE A VITAMIN E SUPPLEMENT? My advice: Get your vitamin E by eating a variety of healthy foods. Findings from a few studies suggest that taking a high-dose vitamin E supplement may do more harm than good, especially if you have heart disease or diabetes. If you do decide to supplement, take no more than 200 IU per day. If you have been diagnosed with coronary heart disease or diabetes, take no more than 100 IU per day.

Calcium

No doubt you've heard over and over that calcium is good for your bones. It's true that meeting your daily calcium requirement is an important strategy to maintain bone density as you age and reduce your risk of osteoporosis. But calcium also plays an important role in keeping your blood pressure in the normal range. The mineral inhibits the production of hormones that make blood vessels constrict, so calcium-rich foods are key in diets designed to lower high blood pressure. By helping you manage your blood pressure, calcium guards against heart attack and stroke.

Researchers also think that getting enough of the mineral can protect against colon cancer. Some studies have shown that people who consume more calcium through their diet have a lower risk of developing the cancer. Calcium supplements have also been linked with protection against precancerous colon polyps. Calcium acts by binding with toxic bile acids that can irritate the bowel, which prevents inflammation that can lead to abnormal cell growth. As well, calcium promotes cells' ability to make sticky proteins called adhesion molecules. These proteins help cells to maintain tight borders and resist being overgrown by precancerous neighbouring cells.

CALCIUM ADDS YEARS TO YOUR LIFE It seems that a diet high in calcium can indeed help us live longer in a couple of ways. It can help lower blood pressure—important in maintaining heart health and preventing stroke—and it can also reduce inflammation in the body by increasing levels of anti-inflammatory chemicals. In a ten-year study, Swedish researchers found that among 23,366 men aged 45 to 79, those who consumed the most calcium from foods—versus the least—had a 25 percent lower risk of dying from any cause during the study period and a 23 percent lower risk of dying from heart disease specifically. The men consuming the most calcium were taking 2000 milligrams per day, compared to about 1000 milligrams for those taking the least. Their main sources of calcium were milk, milk products and cereal products. None of the men took calcium supplements.[5]

HOW MUCH CALCIUM DO YOU NEED? The top calcium consumers in the Swedish study had a daily calcium intake above the recommended intake. Men and women aged 19 to 50 are advised by Health Canada to get 1000 milligrams of calcium per day. Adults aged 51 and older require 1200 milligrams daily. Teenagers require 1300 milligrams of calcium daily, kids aged 4 to 8 need 800 milligrams and children aged 1 to 3 require 500 milligrams daily.

Calcium content of selected foods

	Calcium (milligrams)
Dairy foods	
Milk, skim, 1%, 2%, 1 cup (250 ml)	300
Chocolate milk, 1 cup (250 ml)	290
Cheese, cheddar, 1.5 oz (45 g)	300
Cheese, Swiss or Gruyère, 1.5 oz (45 g)	480
Cheese, mozzarella, 1.5 oz (45 g)	228
Cheese, cottage, 1/2 cup (125 ml)	75
Cheese, ricotta, 1/2 cup (125 ml)	255
Evaporated milk, 1/2 cup (125 ml)	350
Light sour cream, 1/4 cup (50 ml)	120
Skim milk powder, dry, 3 tbsp (50 ml)	155
Yogurt, plain, 3/4 cup (175 ml)	300
Yogurt, fruit flavoured, 3/4 cup (175 ml)	250
Non-dairy foods	
Soybeans, cooked, 1 cup (250 ml)	175
Soybeans, roasted, 1/4 cup (50 ml)	60
Soy beverage, fortified, 1 cup (250 ml)	330
Baked beans, 1 cup (250 ml)	150
Black beans, 1 cup (250 ml)	102
Kidney beans, 1 cup, cooked (250 ml)	69
Lentils, cooked, 1 cup (250 ml)	37
Tempeh, cooked, 1 cup (250 ml)	154
Tofu, raw, firm, with calcium sulfate, 4 oz (120 g)	260
Tofu, raw, regular, with calcium sulfate, 4 oz (120 g)	130
Sardines, 8 small (with bones)	165

	Calcium (milligrams)
Salmon, sockeye, half of one 213 g can; drained (with bones)	235
Broccoli, raw, 1 cup (250 ml)	42
Broccoli, cooked, 1 cup (250 ml)	94
Bok choy, cooked, 1 cup (250 ml)	158
Collard greens, cooked, 1 cup (250 ml)	357
Kale, cooked, 1 cup (250 ml)	179
Rutabaga, cooked, 1/2 cup (125 ml)	57
Swiss chard, raw, 1 cup (250 ml)	21
Swiss chard, cooked, 1 cup (250 ml)	102
Okra, cooked, 1 cup (250 ml)	176
Figs, 5 medium	135
Orange, 1 medium	50
Almonds, 1/4 cup (50 ml)	100
Brazil nuts, 1/4 cup (50 ml)	65
Hazelnuts, 1/4 cup (50 ml)	65
Blackstrap molasses, 2 tbsp (25 ml)	288
Fancy molasses, 2 tbsp (25ml)	70
Calcium-fortified orange juice, 1 cup (250 ml)	300 to 360

Source: U.S. Department of Agriculture, Agricultural Research Service. 2009. USDA National Nutrient Database for Standard Reference, Release 22. Nutrient Data Laboratory Home Page, www.ars.usda.gov/nutrientdata.

DO YOU NEED A CALCIUM SUPPLEMENT? The vast majority of clients I meet in my private practice don't get enough calcium in their diet. And when you are over 50 and need 1200 milligrams daily, it can be challenging to get it from foods alone. On my Longevity Diet, you will be consuming two to three Milk or Milk Alternative servings each day, which will give you 600 to 900 milligrams of calcium. I will also encourage you to add other calcium-rich foods to your daily diet, such as legumes, nuts and leafy greens. Even then, some of you will come up short and need to supplement. Here's what you should know before you select a calcium supplement.

CALCIUM CARBONATE VS. CALCIUM CITRATE The most common compounds used in calcium supplements are carbonate and citrate. Calcium carbonate supplements are generally the least expensive and most widely used. They also contain twice as much elemental calcium—usually 500 or 600 milligrams per tablet—as supplements made from calcium citrate. Supplements made from calcium citrate typically provide 300 to 350 milligrams of elemental calcium per tablet. Elemental calcium is the amount of calcium in a supplement that's available for your body to absorb—it's the amount that your daily calcium requirements are based upon. Most products list the amount of elemental calcium on the label. But some brands list only the total weight (milligrams) of the tablet. This is the weight of the calcium, plus the compound it's bound to—carbonate or citrate.

Let's say you're 52 years old and your diet provides two milk servings, roughly 600 milligrams of calcium. That means you need to make up the rest of your daily requirement—600 milligrams—from a calcium supplement. A calcium carbonate product may be more convenient. That's because you only have to take one calcium carbonate pill instead of two calcium citrate tablets. But there are advantages to taking calcium citrate supplements, especially if you have decreased stomach acid. Calcium citrate is readily absorbed in your intestine so it can be taken any time of day, even on an empty stomach. In contrast, calcium carbonate requires extra stomach acid for absorption, so it's best taken with food or immediately after eating.

HOW TO TAKE YOUR CALCIUM SUPPLEMENT Spread your calcium intake over the course of the day. Absorption from supplements is best in doses of 500 milligrams or less because the percentage of calcium your body absorbs decreases as the amount in the supplement increases. If you take medications, check with your pharmacist about possible interactions with calcium. Calcium can interfere with the body's ability to use certain drugs including tetracycline, bisphosphonates (Fosamax, Actonel), hypothyroid medication (Synthroid) and iron supplements. Finally, don't consume more than 2500 milligrams of calcium per day from food and supplements combined. Too much calcium can upset the stomach, elevate blood-calcium levels, impair kidney function and decrease your body's absorption of other minerals.

Magnesium

This is one mighty mineral. More than 300 biochemical reactions in the body involve magnesium. Among its many roles, magnesium helps to maintain normal muscle and nerve function, keeps heart rhythm steady, supports a healthy immune system and keeps bones strong. It also helps regulate blood-sugar levels, promotes normal blood pressure and plays a part in energy metabolism and protein synthesis.

MAGNESIUM CAN HELP KEEP INSULIN LEVELS LOW Magnesium influences the release and activity of insulin, the hormone that helps control blood glucose. A number of studies conducted in men and women show that those who consume the most magnesium in their diet are less likely to develop type 2 diabetes than those whose intake of the mineral is low.

If you have been told you have pre-diabetes, or insulin resistance, getting enough magnesium is especially important. Low levels of the mineral in your body may worsen insulin resistance. People with insulin resistance do not use insulin efficiently and require greater amounts of insulin to maintain blood sugar within normal levels. If you'll recall from Chapter 4, keeping your insulin levels low, thereby reducing insulin-signalling inside cells, is a key strategy to living longer. By helping you keep your blood-glucose levels under control, magnesium plays a vital role in promoting longevity.

MAGNESIUM CAN PROTECT YOUR HEART Magnesium may help reduce the risk of coronary heart disease and also protect against its consequences. Researchers have observed lower death rates from heart disease in populations who routinely drink "hard" water, which is higher in magnesium than soft water. (Water is "softened" through the removal of all minerals apart from naturally occurring sodium.) Studies have also associated higher blood levels of magnesium with a lower risk of coronary heart disease. There's evidence, too, that low body stores of magnesium increase the likelihood of abnormal heart rhythms (arrhythmia), a potentially fatal complication of heart attack.

HOW MUCH MAGNESIUM DO YOU NEED? The recommended daily intake for magnesium is 310 to 320 milligrams for women and 400 to 420 milligrams for men. That may not sound like much, but recent data shows that most Canadians don't get their daily requirement of this mighty mineral. (You'll find age-specific recommended dietary allowances, or RDAs, in "A Guide to Vitamins and Minerals" in the appendices.) Use the list below to identify magnesium-rich foods to work into your daily diet.

Magnesium content of selected foods

Food	Magnesium (milligrams)
Wheat bran, 2 tbsp (25 ml)	46
Wheat germ, 1/4 cup (50 ml)	91
Almonds, 1 oz (30 g) or 24 nuts	84
Brazil nuts, 1 oz (30 g) or 8 nuts	64
Peanuts, 1 oz (30 g) or 35 nuts	51
Sunflower seeds, 1 oz (30 g)	100
Black beans, cooked, 1 cup (250 ml)	121
Chickpeas, cooked, 1 cup (250 ml)	78
Lentils, cooked, 1 cup (250 ml)	71
Kidney beans, cooked, 1 cup (250 ml)	80
Navy beans, cooked, 1 cup (250 ml)	107
Soybeans, cooked, 1/2 cup (125 ml)	131
Tofu, raw, firm, 1/2 cup (125 ml)	118
Dates, 10	29
Figs, 10 dried	111
Green peas, 1/2 cup (125 ml)	31
Spinach, cooked, 1/2 cup (125 ml)	81
Swiss chard, cooked, 1/2 cup (125 ml)	76

Source: U.S. Department of Agriculture, Agricultural Research Service. 2009. USDA National Nutrient Database for Standard Reference, Release 22. Nutrient Data Laboratory Home Page, www.ars.usda.gov/nutrientdata.

DO YOU NEED A MAGNESIUM SUPPLEMENT? After scanning the list of magnesium-rich foods it's easy to see why so many Canadians don't get enough of this mineral. However, if you eat a variety of whole grains, legumes and dark green leafy vegetables you should be able to get enough of it to meet your daily requirements. If you're older, though, your body's ability to absorb magnesium from food is reduced, and certain medications such as antibiotics and diuretics can also affect the mineral's absorption. If you want to ensure you're getting enough, you can get a little help from a supplement.

Most multivitamin pills (which include minerals in the mix) supply 50 milligrams of magnesium. If you need to supplement your diet with calcium too, you can buy calcium/magnesium pills. Commonly called "Cal/ Mag" supplements, these products generally contain calcium citrate and magnesium citrate. I recommend buying a 2:1 formula, which means the product has twice as much calcium as magnesium (e.g., one tablet would provide 300 milligrams calcium and 150 milligrams of magnesium). If you don't need a calcium supplement, you can buy a stand-alone magnesium citrate supplement. They come in doses ranging from 100 milligrams to 250 milligrams. One word of caution: Don't take more than 350 milligrams of magnesium per day from a supplement—it can cause diarrhea. Magnesium in foods doesn't have this effect.

Omega-3 fatty acids (DHA and EPA)

Remember the exciting health benefits of eating salmon I told you about in Chapter 5? Oily fish are the natural source for DHA and EPA, two types of omega-3 fatty acids. A number of studies have documented longer life expectancies among people with higher intakes of these omega-3s, in particular for those who have been diagnosed with heart disease. What's more, large studies have shown that people with higher levels of DHA and EPA in their bloodstream are far less likely to develop heart disease, suffer a heart attack or die suddenly from cardiac arrest. To recap, there are many ways these fats protect the heart: they help lower triglycerides, prevent blood clots, reduce inflammation and protect against abnormal heart rhythms.

OMEGA-3S KEEP CELLS YOUNG Omega-3 fatty acids also work at the genetic level to help you live longer. Remember the University of California study I mentioned in Chapter 5, which studied the association between omega-3 levels and telomeric aging? The researchers followed people with stable coronary artery disease over a five-year period and found that those with the highest omega-3 levels in their blood had *less telomere shortening* than their peers with low omega-3 levels.[6] It's thought omega-3 fats put the brakes on telomere shrinkage—a key marker of aging—by combating oxidative stress. These fats may also increase the activity of telomerase, an enzyme that preserves telomere length and cell function.

HOW MUCH OMEGA-3 DO WE NEED? There aren't any official recommendations as to how much EPA and DHA we need. We don't yet know how much is enough to slow telomere shortening or to prevent Alzheimer's or macular degeneration. However, based on extensive evidence in the area of cardiovascular health, experts do advise getting at least 500 milligrams per day—the amount served up in 6 ounces (170 g) of salmon per week—to prevent heart disease. For people with heart disease or who have had a heart attack, the American Heart Association advises double that amount, 1000 milligrams daily, which 12 ounces (340 g) of salmon per week would provide.

I advise all my clients to aim for a daily intake of 1000 milligrams of DHA and EPA combined. Since omega-3 fats store in the body, you don't need to eat fish every day to reach these targets. Species of fish vary in their omega-3 fat content, with salmon at the top of the list (1800 milligrams DHA and EPA per 3 ounces/90 g) and lean white fish like tilapia at the bottom (115 milligrams per 3 ounces/90 g). Below you'll find a list of fish that are good sources of DHA and EPA.

Type of Fish	DHA plus EPA (milligrams per 3 ounces/90 g)
Herring, Atlantic, kippered	1827
Salmon, Atlantic, farmed, cooked	1825
Herring, Pacific, cooked	1806
Anchovy, European, canned in oil	1747
Herring, Atlantic, cooked	1712
Mackerel, Pacific, cooked	1571
Salmon, Atlantic, wild, cooked	1564

Type of Fish	DHA plus EPA (milligrams per 3 ounces/90 g)
Sablefish, smoked	1561
Sablefish, cooked	1519
Salmon, chinook, cooked	1476
Whitefish, cooked	1370
Tuna, bluefin, fresh, cooked*	1278
Oysters, Pacific, cooked	1170
Salmon, pink, cooked	1095
Salmon, coho, farmed, cooked	1087
Spanish mackerel, cooked	1059
Salmon, sockeye, cooked	1046
Mackerel, Atlantic, cooked	1023
Halibut, Greenland, cooked	1001

*This fish is high in mercury. Women who are pregnant or breastfeeding, women who could become pregnant and children aged 11 and younger should limit their intake to a very small portion once per month.

CONSIDER A FISH OIL SUPPLEMENT My advice: If you don't consistently eat two servings of omega-3 rich fish each week—or just don't like fish—take a fish oil supplement to make sure you get the omega-3s you need. If you go this route, read labels before you buy. Fish oil supplements vary in the amount of DHA and EPA they contain. Most capsules supply 300, 500 or 600 milligrams of DHA and EPA combined. If you eat only 6 ounces (170 g) of salmon each week, then you need to get 500 milligrams of DHA and EPA from a daily supplement. Many liquid fish oils contain as much as 1300 milligrams of DHA and EPA per teaspoon (5 ml). Fish liver oil and omega-3-6-9 supplements are typically low in omega-3 fatty acids. Most fish liver oil supplements are also high in vitamin A, which, when consumed over an extended period of time, can reduce bone density.

Multivitamin/mineral supplements

A principal theme of my Longevity Diet is to make the most of every calorie by choosing nutrient-rich foods. I will guide you on making food choices packed with vitamin C, folate, beta carotene and so on. You might be wondering why, then, I recommend you take a one-a-day vitamin and mineral supplement. For starters, it's pretty much impossible for women of reproductive age (who lose iron every month through menstruation) to meet their daily iron requirements—18 milligrams—from food alone. Consider that one of the very best sources of iron, beef, provides just 3 milligrams in a 3 ounce/ 90 gram serving. Plus, once you start my Longevity Diet, you won't be eating red meat every day (I'll tell you why in the next chapter). If you're a vegetarian, you'll also need the help of a supplement. That's because you require more iron each day than a meat eater—almost twice as much—since iron in plant foods is harder for your body to absorb.

A multi will also give you vitamin B12, a critical nutrient for making DNA and for clearing homocysteine out of your bloodstream. For B12 to be absorbed, it must first be separated from the proteins in food through the help of stomach acid (gastric acid). However, as many as three in ten older adults have atrophic gastritis—persistent inflammation in the stomach— which *reduces* the secretion of gastric acid. As a result, they absorb less B12 from their food. The B12 in vitamin pills, though, does not depend upon stomach acid for absorption. For this reason, I advise all of my clients over 50 to make sure they get their B12 from a supplement.

Some drugs can interfere with the absorption of B12 from food. Acid-blocking medications for ulcers, heartburn or GERD (gastroesopha-geal reflux disease), which slow the release of gastric acid, and metformin (Glucophage), a drug used to manage or prevent diabetes, can also reduce absorption of the vitamin. If you're on these medications, taking a multi-vitamin with B12 will help you meet your daily requirements. But there's another reason to take a multivitamin that's *directly* related to longevity.

MULTIVITAMIN USERS HAVE YOUNGER TELOMERES Researchers studying 586 women, aged 35 to 74, found that the women who took a multi every day had telomeres 5 percent longer than those who didn't take the supple-ment. This difference in telomere length corresponds to almost ten years of age-related telomere loss. In other words, multivitamin users had telomeres ten years *younger* than their peers who didn't supplement! Significantly longer telomeres were observed on the DNA of women who took multivitamins, one-a-day formulas and antioxidant combination supplements. There was no link, though, between telomere length and stress-tab or B-complex supplements.[7] (Stress-tabs supply a handful of B vitamins, and often vitamin C.)

When the researchers analyzed nutrients from foods the women ate, only vitamin C and vitamin E were associated with telomere length. Women who had the highest intakes of these two antioxidants had longer telomeres than their peers whose diets provided the least, even after multivitamin use was taken into account. And the higher their intake, the longer their telomeres. Among women who didn't use multivitamins, higher dietary intakes of beta carotene, folate, magnesium, and vitamins C and E were each associated with longer telomere length. My Longevity Diet contains plenty of these nutrients!

Sorting out which nutrients in multivitamins are responsible for this finding is an impossible task because different multivitamin have various formulations of vitamins and minerals. However, it's likely antioxidants play a role. Other studies have consistently associated higher intakes of vitamins C and E with longer telomeres.

HOW TO CHOOSE A MULTIVITAMIN Choose a standard one-a-day formula that offers 100 percent of the recommended daily intake for most nutrients. Use the following checklist as your guide.

A MULTIVITAMIN CHECKLIST

Vitamins

- Look for A, C, D, E, B1, B2, niacin, B6, folic acid and B12. Choose a formula that provides 100 percent of the RDA for B6 (1.3 to 1.7 mg), B12 (2.4 mcg) and folic acid (0.4 mg).
- Avoid products that supply more than 2500 IU of vitamin A from retinol (often called vitamin A palmitate or acetate). Excess vitamin A may increase the risk of osteoporosis and hip fracture. However, there's no evidence that beta carotene, also called pro-vitamin A on labels, is harmful to bones.
- If you take prescription anticoagulants (e.g., Coumadin), speak to your doctor before taking a formula with vitamin K.

Minerals

- Look for chromium, copper, iron, magnesium, selenium and zinc.
- Premenopausal women should choose a multivitamin supplement with 10 to 18 mg of iron; men of all ages and postmenopausal women should look for no more than 5 to 10 milligrams of iron.
- If you have high iron stores in your body (elevated ferritin in your blood), choose an iron-free multivitamin.

7
Food, drinks and nutrients to limit— or avoid

Ask any nutrition scientist the secret to longevity and you will hear that eating the healthiest diet possible is key. And that means eating a wide variety of foods packed with nutrients and antioxidants: whole grains, fruits, vegetables, legumes and nuts. I've featured many of these protective foods in the previous two chapters. We've heard over and over again that people whose diets are based on these types of foods live healthier *and* live longer.

But if you're hoping to add healthy years to your life, you need to do more than simply add nutritious foods to your diet. It's just as important to curb your intake of certain foods that can actually *speed* the aging process by damaging cells and tissues, which makes developing an age-related disease more likely. You probably already know which foods are on the hit list. But if you really do want to live longer, and to make your years as healthy and vital as possible, the list bears repeating. I promise to keep it short and sweet—I'll simply point you to what you need to limit in your diet and some easy ways to do so.

Red meat: Scale back to eat like a centenarian

I have bad news if you're a frequent eater of big, juicy steaks, hamburgers and ribs. Both historical accounts and scientific studies strongly suggest that heavy meat eaters don't live as long as their peers who eat meat less often. During

World Wars I and II, wartime food restrictions virtually eliminated meat consumption in Scandinavian countries and were followed by a decline in death rates. But once the meat restriction was lifted, mortality rates returned to pre-war levels. Data also show that life expectancy in Japan and certain Mediterranean countries is about two years longer than the typical lifespan for folks in Western countries where meat intake has been much higher for decades. And think back to the Blue Zone residents I described in Chapter 2. The Okinawan, Sardinian and Seventh-day Adventist diets are all character-ized by little or no red meat.

Okay, these observations are far from scientifically rigorous. They certainly don't prove cause and effect. However, well-controlled studies also point to meat's detrimental effect on life expectancy. One published review determined that in four of the six studies analyzed, people with a very low meat intake had a significantly lower risk of early death from any cause—from 25 percent lower to almost a twofold decrease—than folks who enjoyed a higher meat consumption.[1]

MEAT AND COLORECTAL CANCER RISK There is convincing evidence that a high intake of red meat increases the risk of colorectal cancer. Numerous studies have found a significantly greater risk of developing the cancer among those who eat a diet heavy in red meat versus those who eat little red meat.[2,3] There are several ways in which processed meats may contribute to colon cancer. Meats are a source of saturated fat, which has been linked to the cancer. The form of iron in meat—called heme iron—may also damage colon cells and trigger cancer growth. Cooking meats to high temperatures (e.g., grilling or frying) forms heterocyclic amines and polycyclic aromatic hydro-carbons, compounds linked to colon tumours in animals and precancerous colon polyps in humans.[4]

MEAT AND DIABETES RISK Studies also suggest that eating too much meat—more than twice per week—can up the risk of type 2 diabetes. A review of twelve large studies concluded that a high intake of red meat significantly increased the risk of diabetes by 21 percent. Eating processed meat raised the risk even more.[5] And researchers from Loma Linda University in California reported that among the 8401 men and women they followed for seventeen years, those who ate meat at least weekly—versus rarely or never—were 74 percent more likely to develop type 2 diabetes.[6] Researchers think that eating a lot of meat, a source of saturated fat, increases the risk of diabetes by promoting weight gain and, in turn, insulin resistance. It's also possible that iron in meat, called heme iron, causes oxidative stress that damages cells in the pancreas, the organ that produces insulin.

HOW MUCH MEAT? You don't have to completely give up red meat and adopt a vegetarian diet. After all, red meat is an important source of protein. But depending on how often you eat meat—and what your portion sizes are—you might have to cut back. Based on a review of 7000 studies on diet and cancer, experts advise that you limit your intake of red meat—beef, veal, pork, lamb, goat—to less than 18 ounces (500 g) per week. I recommend you eat even less if you can. When you follow my Longevity Diet, you will be eating fish, chicken, turkey, legumes, tofu and soy foods more often than red meat.

When you do eat red meat, choose lean cuts. For beef, that means sirloin, flank steak, eye of the round and tenderloin cuts, and lean and extra lean ground hamburger meat; for pork, tenderloin and centre cut chops. Keep in mind that any cut of meat that comes from an animal's stomach area—for example, rib-eye steak, rib chops, spareribs—will be high in saturated fat. Then, limit your portion size. Enjoy small amounts of red meat in stir-fries and pastas, and serve steak in thin slices rather than as a whole piece.

Processed meat: It's time to ditch the deli

If you're looking for a quick and easy lunch, it's hard to beat the convenience of sliced deli meats—a.k.a., luncheon meats or cold cuts—for building a sandwich. Yet, your ham and cheese on brown might not be as healthy as you think. Ever since the World Cancer Research Fund recommended in 2007 that people back off from processed meat, I've had clients wonder if they should trade in their pastrami for tuna fish.

The advice to steer clear of the deli counter was among other stark lifestyle recommendations put forward in a 517-page report released by the American Institute for Cancer Research and the World Cancer Research Fund. The international research team found that every 48 grams (1.5 oz) of processed meats consumed per day bumped up the risk of colorectal cancer by 21 percent. The evidence was convincing and strong enough that the report concluded people should eat little, if any, processed meat.

Some studies—but not all—have found high intakes of processed meats increase the risk of breast, lung, prostate, stomach and pancreatic cancers. And cancer isn't the only health risk: as I mentioned above, a review of twelve studies found a link between a steady diet of processed meat and developing type 2 diabetes.

What foods fall into the category of "processed meats"? The term is used inconsistently in studies but it commonly means red meats preserved by smoking, curing, salting or added chemicals. Ham, bacon, pastrami, salami and bologna are processed meats. So are sausages, hot dogs, bratwursts and frankfurters. Burgers sometimes fall into the "processed meat" category if they are preserved with chemicals. You're probably wondering about where smoked turkey or chicken fits in. A recent U.S. study found that men and women who ate the most processed meats—including poultry sausage—had an elevated risk of colon cancer compared to those who consumed little.[7] But few studies have defined processed meat as including turkey and chicken slices.

There are several ways in which processed meats may contribute to cancer. Red meat is a source of saturated fat, which has been linked to cancer. The form of iron in meat—heme iron—may also damage colon cells and trigger cancer growth. Just as it does for fresh red meat, cooking processed meats to high temperatures (e.g., grilling sausages or frying bacon) forms cancer-causing compounds that may lead to the development of colorectal cancer.

Processed meats including ham, corned beef, bologna, wieners and poultry products also list sodium nitrite as an ingredient. It's a preservative added to prevent botulism food poisoning and to give cured meats their characteristic red colour. (Soy-based veggie slices do not contain sodium nitrite.) During cooking, nitrite can react with compounds naturally present in meat to form N-nitroso compounds (nitrosamines and nitrosamides), several of which have been associated with certain cancers in humans and animals. It's also thought that N-nitroso compounds can be formed in the body from nitrites in food. However, the sodium erythorbate (a cousin of vitamin C) that food processing companies add to cold cuts inhibits the conversion of sodium nitrite to N-nitroso compounds and helps minimize the risk.

HOW MUCH PROCESSED MEAT? So, should you trade in your pastrami sandwich for one filled with tuna? That depends on how much pastrami—and other processed meats—you eat, and how often. If you eat it regularly or in large portions, I definitely suggest you cut back. Substitute healthy protein foods such as salmon, canned light tuna, fresh cooked chicken or turkey breast, and vegetarian alternatives such as soy-based deli slices in your sandwiches.

If you eat processed meat only *very occasionally*, don't fret. Keep in mind there are other important strategies that help guard against cancer. Eating plenty of fruits and vegetables and whole grains, limiting alcohol intake, maintaining a healthy weight and getting 30 minutes of daily activity are also linked with cancer prevention.

When you do eat processed meats, look for lower-fat choices to minimize saturated fat. Read nutrition labels to compare brands; choose processed meats that contain no more than 1 gram of saturated fat per 2 ounce (60 g) serving. "Light" cold cuts contain 25 percent less fat than the regular version. You can also look for nitrite-free deli meats at natural food and grocery stores. If these products aren't available, pair your sandwich with a vitamin C–rich food such as a bowl of strawberries, an orange or slices of raw red pepper. (Vitamin C helps block the conversion of nitrites to cancer-causing N-nitroso compounds.)

Added sugars: Rein in your sweet tooth

Cookies, cake, candy, chocolate, ice cream: the foods we crave when we're feeling blue, cranky or just plain bored. As a once-in-a-while treat, these sugar-laden goodies won't pose a threat to your health or longevity. But if sweets sneak into your diet on a daily or almost-daily basis, you'll need to learn how to tame your sweet tooth.

Of course, there are naturally occurring sugars in food, such as lactose in milk and yogurt and fructose in fruit and sweet vegetables. However, it's the sugar that manufacturers add to products—to enhance flavour, add bulk and texture or aid in browning during baking—that you need to watch out for.

It's estimated that Canadians consume, on average, 16 teaspoons (80 ml) of this added sugar each day. And it's not just the usual culprits like soft drinks, cookies and candy that deliver it. Sugar also lurks in salad dressings, frozen dinners, pasta sauces, soy milk, peanut butter, even bread. On food packages you'll see it listed in different forms: as brown sugar, corn syrup, dextrose, fructose, high fructose corn syrup, fruit juice concentrate, glucose-fructose, honey, invert sugar, liquid sugar, malt, maltose, molasses, rice syrup, table sugar and sucrose.

ADDED SUGAR RISKS YOUR HEART HEALTH There are several reasons why you should limit your intake of these added, or refined, sugars. Eating too much sugar can increase your risk for heart disease by lowering HDL (good) cholesterol and raising blood triglycerides. In a recent U.S. study, 6113 men and women were grouped by their intake of added sugar, which ranged from a low of 5 percent of daily calories to a high of 25 percent of calories or greater. As sugar consumption climbed, levels of HDL cholesterol fell. Compared to low sugar consumers (for whom sugar made up 5 percent of their daily calories or less), those whose diets contained the most were three times more likely to have low HDL cholesterol. Those who consumed the most sugar also had higher blood-trigylceride levels.[8]

A low HDL cholesterol level—less than 1.0 millimoles per litre (mmol/L) in men and less than 1.3 mmol/L in women—is associated with a greater risk of heart disease. (Estrogen increases a person's HDL cholesterol, which explains why women generally have higher levels than men do.)

It's not completely understood how excess sugar wreaks havoc on blood lipids. Studies suggest that fructose, a single sugar unit found in large quantities in nearly all added sugars, has something to do with it. Fructose makes the liver produce and release more triglycerides and impairs the body's ability to clear fat from the bloodstream.

ADDED SUGAR UPS OBESITY AND DIABETES RISK A steady intake of sugary foods can lead to overweight and obesity by adding a surplus of calories to your diet. Recent research has shown that over the past twenty years our increased use of sweeteners, especially high fructose corn syrup, correlates with rising obesity rates. While this correlation doesn't prove that high fructose corn syrup causes weight gain, some experts contend that our bodies process fructose in high fructose corn syrup differently than they do glucose in cane or beet sugar. Fructose doesn't trigger hormone responses that regulate appetite and satiety; without these natural curbs you could be "tricked" into overeating.

Sugar-laden foods, with their high glycemic index (GI), can also increase your risk for insulin resistance. Foods with a high GI are quickly digested and cause large spikes in blood sugar and an outpouring of insulin from the pancreas. Over time, the overworked pancreas can't keep up and insulin resistance develops—a condition in which the body cannot effectively remove sugar (glucose) from the bloodstream. The elevated sugar levels that result from insulin resistance in turn increase your risk for developing type 2 diabetes and metabolic syndrome, two potent predictors of heart disease.

HOW MUCH ADDED SUGAR? The World Health Organization recommends we limit added sugars to no more than 10 percent of daily calories.

But according to the American Heart Association, that's still too much. In August 2009, the association released a statement encouraging Americans, who swallow 22 teaspoons (110 ml) of sugar each day, to limit added sugars to an even greater extent than previously recommended. Adults were advised to cut added sugars to 5 percent of their daily calories—no more than roughly 5 teaspoons (25 ml, or 80 calories) per day for women and 9 teaspoons (40 ml, or 144 calories) for men. The Heart and Stroke Foundation of Canada doesn't give a specific guideline for added sugar intake; nor does Health Canada, advising only moderation.

To sleuth out hidden sugars, read nutrition labels. The Nutrition Facts box discloses the grams of sugars contained in one serving of the food (4 grams of sugar is equivalent to 1 teaspoon). Keep in mind, though, that this number doesn't tell you how much of the sugar is naturally occurring (fruit or milk sugars) and how much is added. To find the added sugars, you need to read the ingredient list too. You might be surprised to see how many different types of refined sugars are added to one product.

The following tips will help you curb your intake of added sugars.

- Avoid sugary drinks. Replace soft drinks, fruit punch, iced tea and VitaminWater with water, low-fat milk, vegetable juice or unsweetened tea. If you can't swear off sugary coffee drinks like Starbucks' Frappuccinos or Tim Hortons' Iced Capps, consider one your weekly dessert.
- Satisfy your sweet tooth naturally. Choose fruit, yogurt or homemade smoothies over candy, cakes, cookies and pastries.
- Choose breakfast cereals that have no more than 6 to 8 grams of sugar per serving. Exceptions include cereals with dried fruit.
- When buying packaged baked goods or cereal bars, choose products with no more than half the total carbohydrate content from sugars.
- Sweeten foods with spices instead of sugar. Add cinnamon to hot cereal, a dash of vanilla to lattes and grated fresh ginger to fruit and vegetables.
- Stay clear of the sugar bowl. Gradually cut back on the sugar that you add to coffee and tea or sprinkle over your cereal until you're taking it sugar-free. Believe it or not, your taste buds will adjust to a less sweet taste.
- Reduce sugar in recipes. As a rule, you can cut the sugar in most baked goods by one-third without affecting their taste or texture.

Refined starches: Purge your diet to manage your insulin

For decades we were told to eat more of these carbohydrate-rich starches— foods like bread, rice and pasta—as "healthy" substitutes for cholesterol-raising saturated fats. But we're learning that carbohydrates are not created equal. It seems the speed at which carbohydrate enters your bloodstream can influence your rate of aging and your risk for a number of age-related diseases.

Carbohydrates are traditionally classified as simple or complex depending on their chemical structure. Simple carbohydrates such as fructose (in fruit), lactose (in milk) and sucrose (table sugar) have one or two sugars linked together. Complex carbohydrates, or starches, are long chains of sugar (glucose) units linked together. While all carbohydrates ultimately end up as glucose in your bloodstream, they get there at different rates. It turns out that many complex carbohydrates, such as baked potatoes and white bread, cause even faster spikes in blood glucose than do simple sugars.

The glycemic index (GI) is a good indicator of the quality of carbohydrates you consume. The GI is a scale that ranks carbohydrate-rich foods by how fast they raise blood-sugar levels compared to a standard food, usually pure glucose, which is ranked 100. A food's GI value depends on the amount and type of fibre it contains and the extent of its processing. Foods with a high GI (70 or higher) are digested quickly and cause a rapid rise in blood glucose and, as a result, an outpouring of insulin, the hormone that removes sugar from the blood and stores it in cells.

GOOD CARBS, BAD CARBS It probably comes as no surprise that refined (white) carbohydrates, which are ground and milled and void of bran, have a high GI. Many carbohydrate-rich foods we eat on a regular basis are highly processed—for example, bread, rolls, pizza, white rice, instant oatmeal, cereal bars, many ready-to-eat cold breakfast cereals, cookies, honey, table sugar and sugary drinks.

Foods with a low GI (less than 55) release sugar more slowly into the bloodstream and don't produce a rush of insulin. Examples include grainy breads with seeds, 100% stone-ground bread, whole-meal rye bread and Pita Break's Finland Rye pitas; steel-cut oatmeal, Red River Hot cereal and 100% bran cereals; Ryvita and Finn Crisp crispbreads; barley, brown rice and wild rice; corn and sweet potatoes; pasta, both whole wheat and white; apples, citrus fruit, grapes and pears; nuts and all legumes; and milk, yogurt and soy beverages.

HOW TOO MUCH INSULIN CAN HARM Studies have clearly demonstrated that a steady intake of high GI carbohydrates can lead to chronically elevated blood levels of glucose and insulin and eventually to insulin resistance, a precursor for type 2 diabetes. A high-glycemic diet has also been linked to a greater risk of breast and colon cancers. It's thought that higher insulin levels in the body may promote the growth of precancerous and cancerous cells.

Eating a surplus of refined, highly processed carbohydrates can also damage your heart. In a study published in 2010, researchers compared the association between saturated fat and carbohydrates, respectively, with risk of heart attack among 53,644 healthy men and women living in Denmark. After twelve years of follow-up, 1943 people had suffered a heart attack. Substituting some carbohydrate in the diet with saturated fat did not alter the likelihood of heart attack—that is, consuming more saturated fat neither increased nor decreased the risk. However, replacing some saturated fat in the diet with high GI carbohydrate significantly raised the risk of heart attack, by 33 percent. On the flip side, substituting low GI carbohydrates for saturated fat lowered the risk of heart attack, although the decrease in risk wasn't statistically significant (that is, it could have been a chance finding).[9]

High-glycemic meals are thought to increase the risk of heart disease and heart attack by increasing blood triglycerides (fat), promoting inflammation and impairing blood vessel function. The adverse effects of a high-glycemic diet are especially harmful for people with insulin resistance.

Experts warn that our obesity epidemic and increasing consumption of highly processed carbohydrates have created a "perfect storm" for heart disease, a major cause of early death. For this reason, reducing your intake of refined carbohydrates and added sugars should be top priority. I've already given you strategies to help you slash sugar from your diet. Now it's time to replace "white" carbs with whole grains. Not only are many whole-grain foods low on the GI scale, they also have more fibre, vitamins, minerals and phytochemicals than their refined counterparts.

Next, use the following tips to add low-glycemic foods to your meals and snacks.

- Include at least one low GI food per meal. You'll find the GI value of the foods above and hundreds of others at www.glycemicindex.com. You can also refer to the table on page 58.

- Avoid eating high GI snacks like pretzels, tortilla chips and refined crackers. Opt for fresh fruit, yogurt, nuts, plain popcorn or low GI crackers and crispbreads such as those produced by Wasa, Ryvita and Finn Crisp.
- Choose fruits that are more acidic, such as oranges, grapefruit and cherries. They not only have a low GI but their acidity will lower the overall glycemic load of a meal.
- Use salad dressings made from vinegar or lemon juice—just as with citrus fruits and cherries, the acidity will further reduce the GI of your meal.
- Don't forget about portion size. When it comes to weight control, excess calories add up, regardless of their GI.

Sodium: Slash your intake to keep your arteries young

In North America, sodium has edged out trans fat to become public-health enemy number one. Hardly a day goes by without health associations and watchdog groups calling on the food industry to lower the sodium content of foods. And for good reason. Consuming sodium in excess of daily requirements—as most Canadians do—increases the risk of high blood pressure, stroke, osteoporosis and kidney stones. It may also increase obesity: researchers speculate that a high salt intake makes us thirstier, so that we consume more beverages, many of them calorie-laden.

Scan the nutrition labels on the foods in your kitchen cupboard and you'll quickly see that sodium is everywhere—and not just in tinned and packaged soups, frozen dinners, canned vegetables and cold cuts. Sodium is present in foods you wouldn't think to check, including hot chocolate mixes, instant oatmeal, frozen waffles, bread and, yes, breakfast cereals. It's even added to Heinz's toddler foods—one jar (213 g) of Toddler Chicken Cacciatore has 470 milligrams of sodium—half the daily sodium requirement for a 1-year-old.

HOW MUCH SODIUM IS OKAY? We *do* need a little sodium for good health. The mineral is needed to regulate fluid balance and blood pressure and keep our muscles and nerves working properly. But we need only a very tiny amount. For Canadians aged 9 to 50, all it takes is 1500 milligrams of sodium (two-thirds of a teaspoon of salt) to meet the body's requirements. People aged 50 to 70 need less, 1300 milligrams, and older individuals need just

1200 milligrams. (With age, the body becomes more sensitive to the blood-pressure-raising effects of sodium.) The daily upper limit for sodium—the most adults can safely take—is 2300 milligrams, but we should strive to consume less than that maximum.

If you sweat during exercise, you need a little more sodium than your recommended daily intake, but not much. You might have already guessed that we're unknowingly consuming far more sodium than we need. The latest survey estimates Canadians' daily sodium intakes are somewhere between 2300 and 2800 milligrams for women and between 2882 and 4066 milligrams for men.[10]

Manufacturers add salt (sodium chloride) to foods to enhance flavour, add texture, give colour and prevent spoilage. About 75 percent of the sodium we consume comes from processed and prepared foods, another 11 percent is salt we add during cooking and at the table, and the rest—12 percent—occurs naturally in low amounts in foods such as milk, meat, poultry and vegetables. Other compounds that add sodium to foods include monosodium glutamate (MSG), baking soda (sodium bicarbonate), baking powder and preservatives such as sodium benzoate, sodium nitrite and sodium propionate. (However, it's thought that sodium ingredients other than sodium chloride have a lesser impact on blood pressure since many contain less sodium.)

TIPS TO CUT SODIUM In our modern world of processed, packaged foods, reducing your sodium intake is a challenge. (You'll soon see that my Longevity Diet doesn't rely on packaged foods. They may have lots of sodium but they aren't usually brimming with vitamins, minerals or antioxidants.) Below are some tips to help you reduce sodium from your family's meals and snacks. Just as our taste buds get used to high levels of salt, they can adjust to eating less within a few weeks.

• *Read nutrition labels.* Sodium levels vary widely across different brands of like products. Sodium is listed in milligrams per one serving of food. You need to pay attention to the serving size, too: If your serving is bigger than the size in the Nutrition Facts box, your sodium intake will be correspond-ingly greater too. Use the serving size information to compare brands and choose one lower in sodium.

Sodium is also listed as a percentage of a "Daily Value" (% DV). The daily value is not based on individual daily sodium requirements;

rather, the DV for sodium you'll see on labels and packaging is based on 2400 milligrams, an outdated value that exceeds the needs of *all* Canadians plus the established daily *upper* limit of 2300 milligrams. (Health Canada is currently examining a number of issues related to helping Canadians reduce their sodium intakes, including labelling regulations.)

Nonetheless, you can use the Daily Value to quickly figure out whether there's a little or a lot of sodium in one serving of a food. A food that has a "% DV" of 5 percent or less is considered low in sodium. A food that has a "% DV" of 15 percent or greater is high in sodium.

- *Balance your sodium intake.* There will be times when for one reason or another your options don't include foods with a low % DV for sodium. On these occasions, use the % DV to balance your food choices over the course of the day. For instance, if you're going to have Lean Cuisine's Chicken Club Panini for lunch (36 percent of the DV for sodium), you'd be wise to pass on other high-sodium foods for snacks and dinner.

- *Dine out less often.* Thanks to salty ingredients and hefty portion sizes, restaurant meals are often overloaded with sodium. Consider these nutrition facts: Boston Pizza's Cajun Rice Bowl has 2050 milligrams of sodium; Kelsey's Chicken Quesadilla, 2480 milligrams; Swiss Chalet's Chicken Caesar Wrap, 1810 milligrams; Tim Horton's Chili, 1320 milligrams. Even the Old Spaghetti Factory's Veggie Lasagna clocks in at 1683 milligrams— more than a day's worth of sodium.

  If you eat meals frequently in food courts or chain restaurants, visit the company's website to review the nutrition facts of menu items. Doing so will help you choose a meal that's lower in sodium—and might prompt you to prepare more meals at home.

- *Order wisely.* When you do eat out, be aware of terms that signal the food is high in sodium: pickled, marinated, smoked, barbecued, teriyaki, soy sauce, broth, miso, gravy, bacon and, of course, salted. Order dressings, gravies and condiments on the side and use only a little. Request that your meal be prepared without added salt, MSG or ingredients containing sodium, such as soy sauce and broths.

- *Make it from scratch.* Make your own pasta sauces, chilis, soups and salad dressings. Simmer dried beans instead of buying them canned. Make these staples in big batches and freeze some for later use. It takes extra time but it's well spent if you're serious about cutting back on sodium.

- *Adjust recipes.* Reduce or omit the salt recipes call for whenever you can. In most casseroles, stews and main dishes you can leave out the salt entirely. In baked goods it's usually safe to halve the amount of salt specified without affecting quality or taste.

- *De-salt your breakfast.* Choose ready-to-eat breakfast cereals that have no more than 200 milligrams of sodium per serving. Brands like Nature's Path and Kashi are lower in sodium than most. A few, including Kashi Puffs and most of Post's Shredded Wheat products, are sodium-free. Instead of eating instant oatmeal (most brands have 180 milligrams' sodium per pouch), make a big batch of rolled oats in advance—leave out the salt in the directions—and reheat a (salf-free!) serving each morning.

- *Choose unsalted snacks.* Instead of pretzels, salty crackers or potato chips, snack on plain nuts, unsalted crackers or air-popped popcorn seasoned with a dash of chili powder.

- *Limit luncheon meats.* Ham, sausage, salami and smoked turkey are high in sodium. When preparing dinner, bake or grill some extra chicken, turkey breast or roast beef to have on hand for low-sodium sandwich fillings. If you must eat processed meats, look for brands that contain no more than 500 milligrams per serving (2 ounces/60 g).

- *Opt for low-sodium products.* Choose sodium-reduced or no-added-salt brands of vegetable juice, soups and canned vegetables. Rinse canned vegetables and beans to remove some of the added salt before using them.

- *Select lower-sodium convenience foods.* If you're buying convenience foods, choose premade and frozen dinners that contain no more than 200 milligrams of sodium per 100 calories. Select frozen burgers with less than 500 milligrams of sodium per patty. Look for store-bought soups with no more than 500 milligrams of sodium per serving. Choose commercial pasta sauces with no more than 400 milligrams of sodium—a generous cut-off—per half-cup (125 ml) serving.

- *Limit sodium-laden condiments.* Commercial dips, stir-fry sauces, salad dressings, Worcestershire sauce, barbecue sauce, ketchup and relish all contain sodium. Avoid the temptation to slather; use them sparingly.

- *Add herbs and spices.* Instead of salt, use cayenne pepper, rosemary, basil, thyme or wasabi to season foods. Or try a salt-free herb blend like Mrs. Dash. Acidic ingredients such as lemon or lime juice, vinegar or the zest from citrus fruit add flavour to meats, salads and vegetables. Remove the salt shaker from the table to break the habit of salting foods.

Alcoholic beverages: Weigh the risks against the benefits

If there ever was a double-edged sword, it's alcohol. No doubt you've heard that a moderate intake of alcoholic beverages—one to two drinks per day—can keep your heart healthy. Dozens of studies have revealed that light to moderate alcohol consumption is linked with a 30 percent to 50 percent lower risk of heart disease. That's pretty clear. Alcohol's protective effects are not just true for red wine—they've also been noted for white wine, beer and spirits. But contrary to common belief, there's no evidence whatsoever that it's the antioxidants in red wine that can ward off heart disease. Instead, it's the alcohol in these beverages that increases the level of HDL (good) cholesterol and reduces the ability of blood cells called platelets to clump together and form clots.

If you're thinking it might be wise to add a glass of wine—or a pint of beer—to your daily diet to protect your heart, think again. First of all, the Heart and Stroke Foundation of Canada does *not* recommend that you drink alcohol for the purpose of reducing your risk for heart attack and stroke. That's because the negative effects of alcohol can outweigh the positive. Drinking *more than* two drinks a day actually raises blood pressure and ups the long-term risk of developing hypertension. Alcoholic beverages can also increase your blood triglycerides (fats). In other words, too much alcohol can harm your heart.

ALCOHOL RAISES THE RISK OF CANCER Here's the problem: Even that moderate intake that can guard against heart disease increases the risk of several cancers. In an ongoing study in the United Kingdom called the Million Women Study, researchers followed more than 1.2 million middle-aged women for an average of seven years. Compared to teetotallers, women who consumed, on average, one drink per day had a higher overall cancer risk, especially for cancers of the breast, liver, rectum, mouth, throat and esophagus. What's more, each additional drink increased the risk further.

The researchers estimated that alcohol could be to blame for 13 percent of the cancers in the women in the study. (Most of the cancers were breast cancers.) The study also found that women who drank only wine had the same risk of developing cancer as those who drank beer, spirits or a combination of alcoholic beverages. Based on these findings, the researchers concluded that from the standpoint of risk for cancer, there is no level of alcohol consumption that can be considered safe.[11]

There are plenty of ways in which alcohol can increase cancer risk. It damages DNA in cells, harms the liver and reduces the amount of folate in the bloodstream (remember, folate is needed to repair faulty DNA). Alcohol can also make breast cells more permeable to carcinogens and increase estrogen levels in the body. (Estrogen can trigger the growth of cancerous breast cells.)

THE RED WINE–LONGEVITY CONNECTION There's one more reason you might want to reconsider including alcohol—red wine in particular—in your longevity diet, especially if you don't drink right now. It has to do with resveratrol, a potent antioxidant found in red grape skins and seeds. It's the compound that's often attributed to the so-called "French Paradox"—the fact that the French have relatively low rates of heart disease despite their high saturated fat intake. (The fact is, the French paradox may have nothing at all do with alcohol. It's possible the French experience less heart disease than North Americans because they exercise more, weigh less and eat smaller portions.)

We know that the resveratrol in red wine activates longevity genes that slow aging: Feed the compound to middle-aged mice and they become healthier and live 25 percent longer than mice not fed it. Resveratrol mimics the effects of calorie restriction at the genetic level. (You'll learn how calorie restriction blunts aging in the next chapter.) Resveratrol turns on those sirtuin genes that shut down cellular aging and increase disease resistance. But don't get too excited. So far there's nothing proven in humans, and the clinical trials necessary to create a drug for human consumption take a lot of time and even more money. And at this point, the amount of resveratrol that's required to activate longevity genes in animals would be equivalent to about twenty bottles of red wine per day for humans. At that level, liver disease would get you long before resveratrol could exert its anti-aging magic.

ALCOHOL INTAKE RECOMMENDATIONS The question of whether and how much you can safely drink should be based on your current health, medical history, family history, age and gender, among other factors. If you are healthy, limit yourself to one drink per day if you are a woman and two drinks if you are a man. Keep in mind that for elderly people, even two drinks may be too much. One drink is considered 12 ounces (340 ml) of regular beer, 5 ounces (145 ml) of wine or 1-1/2 ounces (45 ml) of 80-proof (40 percent) distilled spirits.

One last point to think about: Alcoholic beverages provide empty calories. And on your path to a longer and healthier life, empty calories are ones you cannot afford.

PART 3

LESLIE BECK'S LONGEVITY DIET

8

The calorie–longevity connection

If someone told you that you could add ten healthy years to your life simply by eating five hundred fewer calories each day—starting now—would you do it?

Would you downsize your food portions and pass up second helpings? Save dessert for a once-in-a-while treat? Break the after-dinner snack habit? Would you adopt a special diet to fend off the usual diseases of old age and extend your lifespan? I'm willing to bet you'd agree to sacrifice a few hundred calories each day for a longer, healthier life.

This special diet, known as calorie restriction, is the one tried-and-true method of extending *maximum* lifespan and improving disease resistance. It's worked in every species it's been tested on: yeast, worms, flies, mice, rats, dogs and rhesus monkeys. Animals on a restricted-calorie diet have lived 20 percent to 50 percent longer than normal. And not only did they live much longer, they stayed youthful, energetic and healthy.

What is "calorie restriction"?

Calorie restriction—CR for short—isn't what it sounds like. It's *not* a drastic diet based on deprivation or vegetarian fare, and it's *not* about starvation—far from it. In these animal studies, CR was about lowering—by 25 percent to 45 percent—the number of calories needed to maintain an animal's body weight while providing all the protein, vitamins, minerals and other nutrients essential for life. So CR is calorie restriction *without* malnutrition. And that's a fundamental point. Eating an unbalanced, low-calorie diet that skimps on important nutrients doesn't bestow anti-aging benefits. Instead, it only brings on all the nutrient deficiencies and health problems one might expect from a poor diet.

When it comes to humans, a 45 percent calorie restriction is far too severe. But a 25 percent reduction is entirely feasible. How many calories does that mean you'd have to slash from your diet? Well, supposing you consume roughly 2500 calories each day, cutting 25 percent of them means you'd drop your daily intake to 2000 calories. If you usually eat, say, 2000 calories per day, you'd have to cut back to 1500. Certainly not a drastic reduction, as will become clear as you read on. What's more, short-term studies in humans suggest that cutting calories by 25 percent may, indeed, lengthen life.

FROM MICE TO MONKEYS

The evidence linking calorie restriction to longevity dates back to 1935 when a scientist at Cornell University, Dr. Clive McCay, unexpectedly discovered that rats on a low-calorie diet lived 30 percent longer than their lab mates fed a normal diet. McCay's influential work spurred researchers over the next seventy-five years to test—and confirm—the calorie-restriction theory in all sorts of species. Caloric restriction has been evaluated repeatedly under well-controlled conditions by many laboratories using different animal species. It is the only intervention that has consistently been shown to slow the aging process. And it doesn't just increase life expectancy, the *average* age you can expect to live to. Amazingly, animals on calorie-restricted diets live well past their *maximum* lifespan—the age at which the oldest known species member has died—about *20 percent to 50 percent longer* than animals fed their usual chow!

It's not only yeast, insects and rodents that thrive on a calorie-restricted diet. A twenty-year study from the University of Wisconsin revealed that among rhesus monkeys—a species genetically closer to humans—those who consumed fewer calories lived longer and experienced significantly less cancer, diabetes and heart disease than their fellows on a regular diet. Starting in 1989, researchers put seventy-six adult rhesus monkeys, aged 7 to 14 years, on a diet with either 100 percent or 70 percent of their usual calorie intake. Waiting for the results of this experiment took patience because rhesus monkeys live an average of 27 years and a maximum of 40.

By 2009, 37 percent of the monkeys who'd been permitted to eat freely had died from conditions related to old age, compared with only 13 percent of the dieting monkeys. The incidence of cancer and heart disease in animals on the restricted diet was half that of the animals eating their usual diet. Remarkably, two health conditions that are very common in monkeys fed all they want—diabetes and impaired blood-sugar control—were not observed in any of the calorie-restricted monkeys. The spartan diet appeared to benefit the monkeys' brains: it preserved volume in some areas, in particular those regions responsible for motor control, memory and problem solving.[1] We'll have to wait another ten years to find out if calorie restriction makes it possible for monkeys to live past their maximum lifespan of 40 years.

WHAT ABOUT HUMANS?

The results from the Wisconsin study are very exciting. Essentially, they say that the anti-aging effects of calorie restriction are translatable to some long-lived primates. But what about humans? Can CR extend lifespan and dramatically delay the onset of age-related diseases in people?

Unfortunately, it's not feasible to conduct a study in humans to answer these questions. Such a study would take 125 years to complete! And unlike lab animals living in carefully controlled environments, people are free-living and prone to temptation. For a study to produce reliable results, people would have to adhere to a calorie-restricted diet almost their entire life. In my clinical experience, it's tough enough to get people to stick to a healthy eating plan for more than six months! Let's face it: We all know how our motivation and focus can waver under stress. Although there isn't a life-long trial underway in humans, we do have other clues that suggest CR can help us lead a longer, healthier life.

THE OKINAWANS The Okinawan centenarians are living what you might call a natural experiment. Because of poverty, long-term calorie restriction was a way of life for these islanders. It's estimated that Okinawans eat roughly 10 percent to 20 percent fewer calories each day than mainland Japanese, who in turn consume roughly 20 percent fewer calories daily than North Americans. However, the Okinawans' diet had enough nourishing food in it that they suffered no dietary deficiencies and fended off infectious diseases, which would have compromised their health and longevity. The combination of fewer calories and plenty of nutrients is thought to have helped these people reach very old ages in extremely good health.

LIVING IN A BIOSPHERE In September 1991, the door was sealed on a crew of eight humans for two years in a laboratory in the Arizona desert known as Biosphere 2. This artificial environment was a huge enclosed space—the size of two and a half football fields—made up of many different types of terrain, including rain forest, desert, ocean and agricultural land. The purpose of the experiment was to see if the scientists could create a self-sustaining ecosystem. The crew's medical doctor was Dr. Roy Walford, a pioneer in calorie-restriction research from the University of Los Angeles, California.

During their stay inside Biosphere 2, the crew learned early on that they could not produce as much food as they thought. As a result, their diet was limited to roughly 1800 calories per day. Despite their low calorie intake, the biospherians ate a nutrient-dense diet of vegetables, fruits, nuts, grains and legumes, with small amounts of dairy, eggs and meat.

As you might expect, the eight researchers experienced a dramatic weight loss during the first year. Men lost, on average, 18 percent of their weight, and women shed 10 percent. They also observed big improvements in a number of health measurements. The food shortage resulted in marked reductions in their blood pressure, fasting blood-glucose levels, fasting insulin levels, thyroid hormone levels (an indication that their metabolisms had slowed) and white blood cell counts. These were the very same effects that had been observed in calorie-restricted rodents in the animal studies mentioned earlier! Although it was not a controlled study, Biosphere 2 did provide evidence that calorie restriction could slow aging in humans.[2]

DATA FROM "CRONIES" Dr. Walford's research—as well as his published books on caloric restriction and longevity—inspired many people to voluntarily cut calories from their diet in the hopes of living longer, healthier. Many of these calorie restriction practitioners, often referred to as CRONies (the name coming from "Caloric Restriction Optimal Nutrition"), have joined an international online organization called the Calorie Restriction Society (CRS). The organization boasts more than 16,000 members, most of them in North America and Western Europe. While some followers eat very sparsely and meticulously track their calories day in and day out, others are far less stringent and will occasionally eat dessert or even a big juicy steak. Most CR adherents say they are doing it for quality of life rather than for length of life. Most believe, on the basis of the animal study findings, that calorie restriction will let them live a full life without illness or aches and pains and with more energy.

According to researchers from the Washington University School of Medicine, CRONies might be well on their way to accomplishing their mission. The research team compared eighteen members of the CRS who had independently eaten a calorie-restricted diet for at least six years and eighteen healthy, non-obese study participants of similar age who followed a typical North American diet. The CR folks consumed between 1000 and 2000 calories per day, whereas the control group consumed between 2000 and 3500 calories daily.

The calorie-restricted subjects scored immensely better on all major risk factors for heart disease, including total cholesterol, LDL (bad) cholesterol, HDL (good) cholesterol and blood triglycerides. In fact, the CRS members had cholesterol and triglyceride levels in the bottom 10 percent for people in their age groups. They also had remarkably low blood pressure and extremely low levels of C-reactive protein, a marker of chronic inflammation in the body.

And that's not all. The CR group had substantially less—40 percent less—plaque located in their carotid arteries than did the individuals on a typical Western diet.[3] Carotid arteries are the major blood vessels that supply your brain with blood. The thicker the plaque is in the carotid artery, the less space there is for blood to travel through, putting you at risk for heart disease. In fact, the thickness of the carotid artery is an independent predictor of heart disease, heart attack and stroke. The astoundingly low level of cardio-vascular risk factors observed in the eighteen CR practitioners provides strong evidence that cutting calories can dramatically delay—and even prevent altogether—the onset of heart disease.

Calorie restriction has been shown to consistently reduce the level of circulating sex hormones in lab animals, an effect that may slow aging and halt the development of hormone-related cancers such as prostate cancer. (The male sex hormone testosterone is thought to feed prostate cancer cells.) To find out if restricting calories had the same effect in humans, the Washington University researchers compared levels of sex hormones among members of three groups of men, all the same age: twenty-four who had been practising CR for seven years; 24 who were endurance runners; and 24 who were sedentary and ate a "normal" (an unrestricted, Western) diet.

Just like long-lived CR mice and rats in earlier animal studies, men following a CR diet had significantly lower levels of testosterone and higher levels of sex hormone-binding globulin (SHBG)—a protein that binds to sex hormones in the blood—than the exercise and sedentary groups.[4] (When the level of SHBG is higher, there is less free testosterone in the blood that could come into contact with tissues.) Reducing sex hormone levels may be one way calorie restriction fends off cancer.

Putting CR to the test in humans: The CALERIE study

You have to agree that these short-term human studies have turned up pretty promising results. Many of the same biological effects researchers saw in animals on CR have now been observed in people on this type of diet. In fact, the data were so promising that the U.S. National Institutes of Medicine has funded a two-year study to see if a prolonged calorie-restricted diet slows the signs of aging in men and women. The study intends to find out if fewer calories can allow people to grow old in better health with less disease, fewer drugs and shorter hospital stays. The findings may also shed light on whether calorie restriction can extend lifespan.

Known as CALERIE—which stands for Comprehensive Assessment of Long-Term Effects of Reducing Intake of Energy—the study began enrolling people in 2007. It's being carried out at three research centres: Pennington Biomedical Research Center (Baton Rouge, Louisiana), Human Nutrition Research Center on Aging at Tufts University (Boston, Massachusetts) and the Washington University School of Medicine (St. Louis, Missouri). The final recruits signed on in February 2010, which means we won't know the final results until sometime in 2012, the end of the two-year period for these final recruits.

Two hundred men and women, with body weight ranging from "healthy" to "slightly overweight," are taking part in the study. One-third of them have been assigned to the control group and will eat their usual diet and not add any physical exercise. The remaining two-thirds are following a 25 percent calorie-restricted, nutrient-rich diet. After determining how many calories each subject in the CR group needed to maintain his or her weight at enroll-ment, the researchers prescribed individualized calorie targets based on a 25 percent reduction.

For the first month, all meals and snacks were custom-prepared for each participant and packaged in coolers to be picked up and taken home. After that, participants followed the diet on their own with plenty of coaching from the study dietitians. Those in the CR group were taught how to assess portion sizes, count calories and pick nutrient-packed foods. These highly motivated and organized people are required to keep a detailed journal of their food and calorie intake.

As I write this, the study is still underway. But so far, it appears the participants are doing a good job of sticking to their diet. Participants in the CR group had lost 10 percent to 17 percent of their body weight by the one-year mark. After twelve months, their body mass index (BMI) values ranged from 18.5 to 25, down from a starting range of 22 to 28. (There's more on BMI in the next chapter, including how to calculate your own. In brief, A BMI of 18.5 to 24.9 is defined as normal weight and is linked to a lower risk of health problems.)

TWO TYPES OF AGING CALERIE is investigating whether energy (that is, calorie) restriction affects the aging process and its associated illnesses such as heart disease, diabetes, Alzheimer's and cancer. The aging process, often called *primary aging* by researchers, refers to the damage that normally builds up in our cells as we grow older. *Secondary aging* refers to diseases that prevent people from reaching their expected lifespan. In other words, they're the illnesses that take years from your life.

The CALERIE study will determine if cutting calories by 25 percent can prevent age-related illness by looking at *biomarkers* such as inflammation, insulin secretion and blood-sugar levels. (A biomarker is a term often used to refer to a protein measured in blood whose concentration reflects the risk or presence of some disease.) They will also assess the participants' core body temperature and metabolic rate, which are indicators of caloric restriction. Animals and humans on calorie-restricted diets have slower metabolisms and lower body temperatures than their peers with normal calorie intakes. While these two consequences of calorie restriction might not sound like a good thing—who wants a sluggish metabolism, for example?—they might slow the aging process. Scientists speculate that at lower temperatures, the body may be more efficient at repairing damaged DNA. As well, if cells generate energy more slowly, they also produce fewer harmful free radicals.

The first results of CALERIE are hopeful: Six months into the study, the CR subjects had reduced levels of damaged DNA, a marker of aging.

THE PHASE 1 CALERIE STUDY We'll have to wait until 2012 to find out if calorie restriction fends off aging in humans. But a smaller study, called PHASE 1 CALERIE, generated some impressive preliminary results. Phase 1 CALERIE included three pilot studies, all of which ended in 2006. The studies assigned forty-eight healthy but overweight men and women, aged 24 to 42 years, to either a 25 percent CR diet or a control diet, and for either six months or one year.

Both six and twelve months of calorie restriction resulted in significant decreases in body weight, body fat, liver fat deposits, core body temperature, energy expenditure, T3 (a thyroid hormone), damage to DNA, fasting blood glucose, fasting insulin and improvement in insulin sensitivity.[5–10] These exciting findings strongly suggest that calorie restriction affects a number of biomarkers of both primary and secondary aging. However, the participants of Phase 1 were overweight when they enrolled. Even after they lost weight, their BMIs were in the upper normal to moderately overweight range at the end of the study, so it is possible that some results were due to weight loss rather than the effect of calorie restriction. The current Phase 2 CALERIE study will give us more definitive answers, since the researchers enrolled men and women of healthy weight.

What matters more: Calorie restriction or weight loss?

It's an easy conclusion to draw: Cutting calories results in weight loss, which in turn, reduces your odds of developing an age-related disease that can shorten your life. In other words, it's the consequence of losing weight— body fat—that triggers all the health benefits, not the effect of depriving your body of calories. Certainly there is truth to this. It's well established that if you're overweight or obese, losing excess weight, especially pounds around your middle, reduces your risk of type 2 diabetes, heart disease and many cancers—breast, ovarian, uterine, cervical, prostate and pancreatic. Achieving a healthy BMI can also lower the odds you'll suffer a stroke or macular degeneration.

There's no question that being overweight can shorten your life. Data from the ongoing Framingham Heart Study, which began enrolling residents of Framingham, Massachusetts, in 1948, revealed that being overweight at age 40 (BMI of 25 to 29.9) shortens life by three years; being obese at age 40 (BMI of 30 or greater) reduces life expectancy by seven years.[11] Research has also shown that men and women classified as super obese (with a BMI greater than 45) can expect to subtract thirteen and seven years, respectively, from their life expectancy.[12]

In my private practice in Toronto, not a day goes by that I don't help clients lose weight on their way to an important health goal such as lowering their blood cholesterol, blood pressure or blood sugar. Getting leaner can also greatly improve insulin sensitivity and reduce inflammation in the body. There's no doubt that losing weight improves health and improves many biomarkers of secondary aging. So does exercise. Working out on a regular basis is clearly linked with better health and a longer average lifespan. Among its many health benefits, exercise helps prevent weight gain, boosts HDL (good) cholesterol and improves insulin sensitivity.

CALORIES MATTER! So why not lose weight by eating a little less or exercising more—or both—to live longer, rather than by cutting a chunk of calories out of your daily diet? You can certainly do this. If you are obese, the risk of dying from heart disease, diabetes and cancer diminishes after a sustained weight loss. Losing weight and regular exercise both have health benefits and can extend your average lifespan. In other words, shedding pounds can help you live a few years longer than the expected average of 80.7 years. In the lab, rats that maintain a low body weight by exercising live longer on average. But here's the key point: They do not have a longer *maximum lifespan*. Even though they are leaner and more insulin-sensitive than sedentary rats, they don't live past the oldest of their species. But guess what? Sedentary rats *who are food-restricted* have both a longer average and a longer maximum lifespan.

The animal research clearly shows that when it comes to influencing primary aging and extending maximum lifespan, it's calorie restriction that matters. Weight loss is just a side effect of calorie restriction. What's more, the greater the calorie restriction—up to 45 percent—and the earlier animals start after puberty, the better. (Restricting calories more than 45 percent is counterproductive to longevity. Animals begin to lose bone mass, their immune system declines and they become infertile.)

The question remains, what's at work here? How is calorie restriction able to achieve such a remarkable anti-aging effect?

How CR regulates your lifespan

The exact mechanism by which calorie restriction slows aging and increases maximum lifespan isn't known yet. However, scientists believe a number of factors play a role. The four most important ways calorie restriction is thought to work involve:

1. Influencing hormones
2. Prevention of inflammation
3. Increasing resistance to stress and
4. Protection against free radical damage.

CR PROVOKES HORMONE ADAPTATIONS It's been known for many years that calorie restriction alters levels of key hormones and that some of these changes are associated with longevity. In studies on rodents, CR lowers blood levels of IGF-1 (insulin-like growth factor 1) by 40 percent. This is thought to be a key anti-aging and anti-cancer effect, because when IGF-1 binds to receptors on cells, it sets into motion signalling that stimulates cell growth and proliferation and inhibits programmed cell death. Programmed cell death plays a crucial role in maintaining our health by eliminating old cells, unnecessary cells and unhealthy cells.

Calorie restriction triggers other adaptations in the body, all of which are thought to slow aging and extend life. It reduces the levels of hormones that regulate metabolism, as well as the levels of hormones that promote cell growth, such as insulin and testosterone, and it increases insulin sensitivity and the levels of hormones that suppress inflammation.

CR GUARDS AGAINST INFLAMMATION Chronic inflammation damages tissues, causes organ dysfunction and induces gene mutations that may promote cancer development. It's implicated in the development of many, many age-related diseases and in the aging process itself. (If you recall from Chapter 4, chronic inflammation can be caused by cigarette smoking, lack of sleep, sun exposure, a poor diet, high blood pressure, elevated blood sugar and abdominal obesity.)

Data in animals and humans—namely, very low levels of C-reactive protein and inflammatory chemicals in the bloodstream—bear witness to calorie restriction's powerful anti-inflammatory effect. Calorie restriction has many biological effects that shut off inflammation in the body. It reduces abdominal fat and, as a result, the secretion of inflammatory chemicals from fat tucked deep in the abdomen. Calorie restriction also combats inflammation by lowering blood glucose. Improved blood-glucose levels mean reduced levels of harmful compounds called *advanced glycation products*, proteins bound to glucose that can accumulate, disrupt cell function and promote inflammation. CR is also thought to influence hormone levels and activity of the nervous system in such a way as to lower inflammation.

CR SUPPRESSES OXIDATIVE STRESS One of the most accepted explanations of aging is free radical damage that accumulates over time. A high level of free radicals in the body causes a state of oxidative stress, overwhelming the body's built-in antioxidant defences. As a result, free radicals roam the body and damage proteins, lipids and DNA within cells, accelerating the aging process. As we grow older, our bodies produce more and more free radicals and their damage accumulates. Injury from free radicals and weakened antioxidant defences are well documented for many diseases—cancer, heart disease, arthritis and dementia, to name only a few.

CR's ability to combat oxidative stress is evident in all animal models tested. CR has suppressed free radical damage, increased production of antioxidant enzymes, enhanced repair of free radical damage and deactivated many inflammatory genes (chronic inflammation also creates harmful free radicals). Calorie-restricted animals have lower levels of free radical damage to proteins, lipids and DNA. There's no reason to think that calorie restriction wouldn't have this protective effect in people, too. Indeed, a recent small study found that a 20 percent CR diet significantly reduced oxidative damage to human DNA over one year.[13]

CR IS A STRESS THAT ENHANCES SURVIVAL Many experts believe that the effects of calorie restriction are an evolutionary response to food scarcity. In times of famine, the body's resources switch from supporting breeding to focusing on tissue maintenance. This adaptive response slows down aging and increases the animal's (or human's) resistance to disease so that it can survive until such time as it can reproduce. The theory is called *hormesis*, from the Greek word *hormaein*, which literally means "to excite." The hormesis theory proposes that calorie restriction puts a low-grade stress on the animal and triggers a defence that protects it from aging. This defensive state allows the animal to survive adversity, resulting in better health and a longer life. Hormesis, therefore, is a beneficial stressor that increases an individual's resistance to a more intense stress.

This theory does explain why calorie-restricted animals are more resistant to a wide range of stressors such as surgery, acute inflammation and exposure to heat. What's more, calorie restriction has been shown to enhance DNA repair systems, promote the removal of damaged proteins and lipids and increase the production of antioxidant enzymes. All of these CR-mediated effects may be a defence response to a prolonged food reduction.

LONGEVITY GENES IN ACTION It's widely believed that many of CR's anti-aging mechanisms are activated at the genetic level. The key may be a set of seven genes called sirtuins that help cells withstand stress by regulating the pace of aging. When stimulated, sirtuins can extend the lifespan of yeast cells and worms, and it turns out that it's calorie restriction that stimulates them. SIRT1, the most studied sirtuin in mammals, turns off a number of age-promoting activities in human cells when calories are limited. (SIR stands for Silencing Information Regulator; it "silences" certain chemical signals inside cells.) Perhaps one day in the future scientists will discover a drug that stimulates SIRT1, setting off its anti-aging activities. In the meantime, cutting calories is the best strategy we have for turning back the biological clock.

The idea that calorie restriction can slow aging and ward off the illnesses that accompany middle and old age is incredibly exciting. The overwhelming animal data and the promising, although preliminary, findings in human studies ought to convince many of us to follow a lower-calorie, nutrient-rich diet. If reading this chapter has motivated you to revamp your diet in the quest for longer, healthier life, it's time to get started! The next chapter will give you the tools you need to cut calories safely, while still enjoying nutritious meals that are delicious and satisfying.

9
Leslie's Longevity Diet in five easy steps

It's finally time to translate everything you've learned so far into a plan that will help you live a longer, healthier life. On the pages that follow, I outline a step-by-step guide to transforming your diet into one that's rich in nutrients, antioxidants and phytochemicals and lower in calories. And there's no rush—take your time implementing each step so that it becomes a lifestyle habit. Make small changes, one at a time. Even if you decide to stop at step 1 or 2, that's perfectly fine. Not only will you be feeling more alert and energetic, you'll also be feeding your body foods that will help it fight disease. You might even lose a few unwanted pounds along the way.

But if you want to be vital and healthy into your nineties—and perhaps beyond—your diet needs to be nutritious *and* lower in calories. On my Longevity Diet you'll reduce your current calorie intake by 25 percent. This level of calorie restriction is realistic. You won't feel hungry or deprived. Your body might take a few days to a week to adjust to eating less, but that's it. The rewards—better health and more energy—are well worth it. Just imagine feeling like you're 40 when you're 50. Or 50 when you're 65. Imagine having the blood work to prove your body's a good ten years younger than your chronological age!

EXPECT TO LOSE WEIGHT AND BODY FAT
There is a side effect that comes with following my Longevity Diet: you'll lose weight. Weight loss is not the purpose of this diet, but it is a natural consequence of eating fewer calories. If you follow this diet for life—which is my intention—you can expect to shed 10 percent to 15 percent of your current body weight, perhaps a little more. Those extra pounds and body fat will be gone forever. You'll fit into a smaller-sized wardrobe, perhaps even

the one that's hanging in the back of your closet. Losing weight will be a plus for many people, but stay focused on your primary motivation for adopting this way of eating—to live longer and in better health. It's about being able to remain physically active when you're older without aches and pains. It's about staying mentally alert in old age and having plenty of energy to play with your grandchildren. It's about eluding high blood pressure, heart disease, diabetes and so many other illnesses that can take years from your life, and life from your years.

CUTTING CALORIES—EVEN MODESTLY— ISN'T RIGHT FOR EVERYONE

That said, not everyone should follow this diet. Some people need to eat a higher number of calories each day. Pregnant women and nursing moms shouldn't restrict their calories. Nor should kids or teenagers who need extra energy and nutrients for growth. If you already have a low body mass index, say 20 or less (in Chapter 10, you'll learn how to calculate your BMI; see page 194), cutting your usual calorie intake by 25 percent could result in a calorie intake that's too low. If you eat too few calories you'll consume fewer nutrients, the very opposite of what my Longevity Diet is intended to accomplish. Dropping from a BMI of 20 to 18 isn't healthy. Being underweight (having a BMI of 18 or less) increases the chance of developing osteoporosis, a weakened immune system, poor wound healing, heart problems and, in women, cessation of menstruation. In fact, being underweight may actually contribute to inflammation in the body and up the risk of heart disease.

People who are extremely physically active—such as athletes and manual labour workers—might find a 25 percent calorie cut makes them feel too hungry or lacking energy for heavy exercise. Even if you're not an athlete it is possible this diet will make you feel hungry if you work out on a daily basis. If this happens but you also want to reap the anti-aging benefits of calorie restriction, you will have to take your exercise down a notch.

GET YOUR DOCTOR INVOLVED

It's always a good idea to let your doctor know you're changing your diet, especially if you have a pre-existing health problem. But there's another reason why you should talk to your doctor. In the previous chapters you've learned the many ways calorie restriction positively influences biomarkers of aging. Before you make changes to your diet and start the Longevity Diet, schedule a medical checkup to get your baseline measurements. Ask your doctor to measure your lipid profile (your blood cholesterol and triglyceride numbers), fasting blood sugar, fasting insulin, C-reactive protein and thyroid hormones. Have your blood pressure and body weight checked too. If possible, get your body fat measured by a fitness professional at your local gym.

After following the plan for three to six months, have these health measures retested. It's very exciting to see the improvements in these tests, and a powerful motivator to stick with the program. In the appendices you'll find a Health Measurement Tracker that you can use to record your health data and to see how they change over time.

Getting started on the Longevity Diet

The basic idea of my Longevity Diet is to substitute foods that have more nutrition per calorie for foods that have fewer nutrients per calories while gradually reducing the number of calories you consume. In other words, you want better nutrition for fewer calories. But before you jump right in to the meal plan, there are a few things you need to do. First, to ensure your success, it's important that you phase in your new eating plan, step by step. This way you'll learn which foods are the very best sources of various nutrients, as well as the calorie content of different foods. You must have this knowledge to reap the benefits of the diet and to keep on track for the long term.

Step 1: Clean up your diet

Where to start? The first and most obvious place is with your current diet. Assessing what you're doing now and making a few tweaks will help you ease some healthier, more nutritious foods into your diet. Then, by the time you're ready to segue into the Longevity Diet Meal Plan, eating these foods will feel natural. The eight tips below will help you tidy up your diet. Reviewing Chapter 7, "Food, Drinks and Nutrients to Limit—or Avoid," will help you put these tips into practice. (If you already follow these principles, move on to Step 2.)

EIGHT TIPS TO TUNE UP YOUR DIET
- *Swap white for whole-grain.* White bread, white crackers, white rice and white pasta don't deliver much for their calories besides carbohydrate. What's more, most of these and other refined starchy foods have a high glycemic index, so that your blood sugar and insulin levels spike soon

after you eat them. Whole grains—which still have the nutrient-rich germ and bran portions of the grain kernel (stripped out of refined grains)—deliver carbohydrate along with fibre, vitamins, minerals, antioxidants and phytochemicals. And many whole-grain foods are low on the GI scale. What's more, folks who choose whole grains over their refined counterparts have a lower risk of becoming obese and developing heart disease, type 2 diabetes and certain cancers. And, they're less likely to die of an inflammation-related disease!

Whole-grain foods

Barley (hulled)	Quinoa
Brown rice	Rye berries
Buckwheat groats (kasha)	Rye flakes; rye meal
Bulgur	Spelt berries
Flaxseed	Wheat berries
Kamut berries	100% whole-wheat bread
Millet	100% whole-wheat pasta
Oats	Wild rice

Read ingredient lists when buying bread, crackers and ready-to-eat breakfast cereals. Ideally, choose a product that is made from 100 percent whole grains (i.e., it does not contain any refined grains). For products not made entirely of whole grains, make sure a whole grain is listed as the first ingredient. (Ingredients are listed in order of the amount of the ingredient in the product so the first item is the most abundant.)

Choose whole grains that have a low glycemic index. You'll find tips for adding these slow-burn carbohydrate-rich foods to your diet in Chapter 7.

- *Rid your diet of sugary drinks* such as soft drinks, sweetened iced tea, fruit drinks and energy drinks—they're empty calorie foods that spike your insulin level. Limit sweets such as candy, cookies and cake to a once-a-week treat. Refer to Chapter 7 for more ways to reduce your intake of refined sugar.

- *Cut back on saturated fat,* the type that raises LDL (bad cholesterol) in your bloodstream. Choose lean cuts of meat (sirloin, tenderloin, inside round), skinless poultry breast and low-fat dairy products (skim or 1% milk, yogurt with 1% milk fat or less). Trim visible fat from meat and poultry before cooking. Start eating red meat less often, and when you do, eat it in smaller portions.

- *Choose unsaturated fats in small portions* to improve health and moderate calories. Healthy cooking oils include canola, grapeseed, peanut, sunflower and safflower. Reserve extra virgin olive oil—the highest quality olive oil produced—for salads, where you can taste its wonderful flavour. But remember, oil is calorie-dense, delivering 120 calories per tablespoon. So drizzle, don't pour.

- *Add oily fish to your diet* to boost your intake of omega-3 fatty acids. Aim to eat fatty fish such as salmon, rainbow trout, Arctic char, sardines and herring at least twice per week. See the section on "Salmon and other omega-3-rich fish" in Chapter 5 for tips on how to add fish to your diet.

- *Start eating more vegetables, of any kind,* to add disease-fighting phytochemicals and antioxidants to your diet. Your target: at least 4 servings each day. (One serving is equivalent to 1/2 cup/125 ml of cooked or raw vegetables, 1 cup/250 ml of salad greens or 1/2 cup/125 ml of 100% vegetable juice.) To accomplish this task include vegetables at lunch (e.g., spinach leaves in your sandwich, vegetable soup, green salad), snack on raw veggies and always serve two different vegetables at dinner. Increasing your portion size is another way to bump up your vegetable intake and to feel full at the end of a meal.

- *Include 2 to 3 fruit servings in your diet* each day. (One serving is equivalent to 1 medium-sized fruit, 1 cup/250 ml berries, 2 tablespoons/ 25 ml of dried cranberries or 1/2 cup/125 ml of 100% fruit juice.) Many people don't think about fruit until they realize it's missing from their diet. It's easy to get into the habit of grabbing a muffin or cereal bar instead of an apple or a banana. If this sounds familiar, it's now time to make a permanent place for fruit in your diet. Start by including some at breakfast every day and by snacking on a piece of fruit between meals.

- *Substitute nutritious snacks* for less healthy ones. Potato chips, candy, chocolate bars, white bagels, coffee shop muffins and white crackers are a far cry from the nutrient-rich snacks that you'll be enjoying on my Longevity Diet Meal Plan. If you routinely snack on these types of foods, start replacing them gradually with fruit, raw vegetables and hummus, low-fat yogurt, a small handful of nuts or homemade smoothies made with low-fat milk or soy milk and berries.

Step 2: Make nutrient-rich food choices

Now it's time to learn which foods give you the most bang for your buck when it comes to vitamins and minerals. There's no point reducing your calorie intake if you don't make wise food choices. As you eat fewer calories, it's very important that you meet your daily requirements for all nutrients. And as you learned in Chapter 6, many vitamins play a vital role in shielding your cells from harm that accelerates aging.

In this section I've highlighted seven nutrients that are important for healthy longevity. They're nutrients that many people don't get nearly enough of in their day-to-day diet. Earlier in the book, I told you how these nutrients work to slow aging and fight disease. Here, you'll find tables that list the top 20 food sources for each nutrient, ranked highest to lowest for the serving sizes typically eaten. Use these tables as handy reference tables when planning your meals and snacks. (Refer to Chapter 6 to learn the precise nutrient content of selected foods.)

Beta carotene: Top 20

Carrot juice	Cabbage, Chinese
Pumpkin	Frozen mixed vegetables
Sweet potato	Cantaloupe
Carrots	Red peppers
Spinach, cooked	Vegetable juice
Collard greens	Green peas
Kale	Vegetable soup
Turnip greens	Spinach, raw
Beet greens	Broccoli, cooked
Winter squash, all types	Mango

Vitamin C: Top 20

Orange juice, from frozen concentrate	Kiwifruit
Red peppers	Oranges
Papaya	Vegetable cocktail
Orange juice, fresh-squeezed	Cantaloupe
Green peppers	Mangos
Grapefruit juice	Cabbage, all types
Broccoli	Cauliflower
Strawberries	Tomato juice
Brussels sprouts	Raspberries
Pineapple	Grapefruit

Vitamin E: Top 20

Sunflower seeds	Turnip greens
Almonds	Pine nuts
Spinach, frozen, cooked	Beet greens
Sunflower oil	Crab
Safflower oil	Canola oil
Turnip greens, cooked	Red peppers
Hazelnuts	Mangos
Spinach, cooked	Broccoli, cooked
Mixed nuts, dry roasted	Papayas
Carrot juice	Peanuts

Vitamin K: Top 20

Kale, cooked	Spinach, raw
Collard greens, frozen, cooked	Endive, raw
Spinach, cooked	Lettuce, green leaf
Collard greens, fresh, cooked	Broccoli, raw
Beet greens, cooked	Okra, frozen, cooked
Turnip greens, cooked	Green peas
Mustard greens, cooked	Lettuce, romaine
Broccoli, cooked	Celery, cooked
Brussels sprouts, cooked	Cabbage, raw
Cabbage, cooked	Rhubarb, cooked

Calcium: Top 20

Milk	Cottage cheese
Yogurt	White kidney beans
Hard cheese	Salmon, canned, with bones
Soy beverages*	Okra, frozen, cooked
Rhubarb, cooked	Lettuce, green leaf
Spinach, frozen, cooked	Broccoli, raw
Collard greens, cooked	Okra, frozen, cooked
Edamame	Soybeans
Turnip greens, cooked	Tofu, firm, prepared with calcium sulfate
Spinach, fresh, cooked	Cabbage, Chinese, cooked

*Rice beverages and almond beverages are also excellent sources of calcium but, unlike milk and soy beverages, they are low in protein.

Magnesium: Top 20

Halibut	Navy beans
Spinach, cooked	Refried beans
Pumpkin seeds	Okra, frozen, cooked
Soybeans	Oat bran muffins, homemade
White kidney beans	Pinto beans
Black beans	Brown rice
Edamame	Red kidney beans
Brazil nuts	Chickpeas
Lima beans	Cashews
Beet greens, cooked	Almonds

OTHER IMPORTANT NUTRIENTS

FIBRE In addition to selecting foods for their vitamins and minerals, you need to focus on making fibre-rich choices each day. Found mainly in fruits, vegetables, whole grains and legumes, fibre is best known for its ability to prevent or relieve constipation. But eating a high-fibre diet can also lower your risk of type 2 diabetes and heart disease. And it may even guard against colon and breast cancers.

Men and women aged 19 to 50 need 38 and 25 grams of fibre per day, respectively. After age 50, daily fibre requirements decrease to 30 grams for men and 21 grams for women. Below is a list of fibre-rich foods.

Fibre: Best food sources

Fruits	Vegetables	Grains	Legumes & Nuts
Apple, with skin	Broccoli	100% bran cereals	Black beans
Blackberries	Brussels sprouts	100% whole-grain breads	Kidney beans
Blueberries	Collard greens	Brown rice	Navy beans

Fruits	Vegetables	Grains	Legumes & Nuts
Mango	Green peas	Bulgur	Pinto beans
Oranges	Lima beans	Oat bran, cooked	
Pears	Snow peas	Oatmeal	Almonds
Raspberries	Sweet potato	Quinoa	Peanuts
Strawberries		Red River Cereal	Pecans
		Whole-wheat pasta	Walnuts
		Wild rice	

PROTEIN It's important to meet—but not exceed—your daily protein requirements. An adequate protein intake keeps your immune system healthy and your bones strong. It's also critical to preserving your muscle mass as you age. Eating more protein than your body needs adds unnecessary calories to your diet; unlike with carbohydrate and fat, the body does not store the protein it can't use. Here are the protein-rich foods that you will be including in your meals and snacks when you begin the Longevity Diet.

Protein: Best food sources

Chicken breast	Soybeans	Soy beverages, unflavoured
Turkey breast	Tofu, firm or extra firm	Milk
Lean beef	Edamame	Yogurt
Lean pork	Lentils	Kefir
Fish—all types*	Black beans	Hard cheese, skim or part skim
Shellfish	Kidney beans	Cottage cheese, 1% or non-fat
Egg whites	Navy beans	Chickpeas
	Pinto beans	

*Avoid fresh and frozen tuna, shark, swordfish, marlin, orange roughy, escolar and canned albacore (white) tuna because these fish are high in mercury.

Step 3: Determine your personal calorie prescription

Your daily calorie requirements are based on your gender (men need more calories than women because they have more muscle mass), your age (calorie needs drop as we age), your current weight (heavier bodies use more calories) and your activity level. In order to determine which calorie level is right for you on my Longevity Diet, you first need to know how many calories your body requires to maintain your current weight. If your weight has been stable, this is the same thing as the number of calories you consume each day.

To learn how many calories you are eating, you can track your daily food intake on an online diet journal such as FitDay.com or Sparkspeople.com. But there's another way to figure out how many calories your body needs. You can use an online tool to calculate your daily calorie requirements. Simply Google "calorie requirement calculator" and you'll get pages of results. These calculators ask you to input your age, height, weight, gender and activity level. They use a mathematical formula to estimate the number of calories required to maintain your body weight.

HOW MANY CALORIES DO YOU NEED RIGHT NOW?

To save you time, I've made the process even simpler. The chart below shows calorie requirements for men and women at various ages and activity levels (sedentary to active). The numbers of calories are based on Estimated Energy Requirements from the U.S.–based Institute of Medicine.[1] They have been calculated by gender, age and activity level for "reference sized" adults. (The "reference size" is based on average height and weight to give a BMI of 21.5 for women and 22.5 for men.)

Your estimated daily calorie requirements

	Age	Sedentary[a]	Moderately Active[b]	Active[c]
Females	19–30	2000	2000–2200	2400
	31–50	1800	2000	2200
	51+	1600	1800	2000–2200

	Age	Sedentary[a]	Moderately Active[b]	Active[c]
Males	19–30	2400	2600–2800	3000
	31–50	2200	2400–2600	2800–3000
	51+	2000	2200–2400	2400–2800

a. *Sedentary* means a lifestyle that includes only light physical activity associated with day-to-day life.

b. *Moderately active* means a lifestyle that includes moderate activity (e.g., brisk walking, cycling, aerobics classes) about two or three times per week.

c. *Active* means a lifestyle that includes at least 30 minutes of moderate activity most days of the week or 20 minutes of vigorous activity (e.g., running, spinning, working out at the gym) at least three days per week.

REDUCE YOUR CALORIES BY 25 PERCENT

Now that you know how many calories your body needs right now, it's time to determine the calorie level you will follow on the Longevity Diet. Quite simply, it will be 25 percent fewer calories than the amount required to maintain your current weight. Plug the number of calories you determined above—your current daily calorie requirement—in the following equation:

1. Multiply your daily calorie requirement by 0.25

_____ × 0.25 = _____

This is your "calorie deficit." It's the number of calories you will subtract from your current calorie requirement.

For example, a 45-year-old woman who is sedentary requires approximately 1800 calories per day. To consume 25 percent fewer calories, she will need to subtract 450 calories from 1800. (1800 x 0.25 = 450)

A 50-year-old man who is active needs roughly 2900 calories per day. To consume 25 percent fewer calories, he will need to subtract 725 calories from 2900. (2900 x 0.25 = 725)

2. Subtract your calorie deficit from your daily calorie requirement to determine your personal Longevity Diet calorie prescription.

_____ – _____ = Your Longevity Diet calorie prescription

For example, the sedentary women described above will be consuming 1350 calories each day on her Longevity Diet Meal Plan (1800 − 450 = 1350). The active man will scale back his calorie intake to 2175 calories to slow his body's aging process (2900 − 725 = 2175).

Below, I've crunched the numbers for you. (Where necessary, I have rounded to the nearest 100 calories.) Use this table to find your Longevity Diet calorie prescription.

Your Longevity Diet calorie prescription

	Age	Sedentary[a]	Moderately Active[b]	Active[c]
Females	19–30	1500	1600	1800
	31–50	1400	1500	1700
	51+	1200	1400	1600
Males	19–30	1800	2000	2300
	31–50	1700	1900	2200
	51+	1500	1700	2000

a. *Sedentary* means a lifestyle that includes only light physical activity associated with day-to-day life.
b. *Moderately active* means a lifestyle that includes moderate activity (e.g., brisk walking, cycling, aerobics classes) about two or three times per week.
c. *Active* means a lifestyle that includes at least 30 minutes of moderate activity most days of the week or 20 minutes of vigorous activity (e.g., running, spinning, working out at the gym) at least three days per week.

Step 4: Choose your Longevity Diet Meal Plan

Below you'll find two Meal Plans—one for women and one for men. They are designed to provide 1500 calories for women and 1900 calories for men. If the calorie prescription you worked out above doesn't match, not to worry! It's easy to adjust the plans to meet your personal calorie target—you'll learn how to do this on page 179. The meal plans also include what supplements to take to ensure you are meeting your daily requirements for all nutrients, especially those that can be challenging—or impossible—to get from diet alone. And as you learned earlier, some may extend lifespan by preserving the length of your telomeres!

The Longevity Diet Meal Plan for women (1500 calories)

	Food Group Choices
Breakfast (350 calories)	2 Starchy Food Choices 1 Fruit Choice 1 Milk/Milk Alternative Choice
Lunch (450 calories)	3 Protein Choices 2 Starchy Food Choices 2 Vegetable Choices 2 Fat Choices
Dinner (450 calories)	3 Protein Choices 2 Starchy Food Choices 2 Vegetable Choices 2 Fat Choices
Snacks (250 calories)	1 Fruit Choice, 1 Milk/Milk Alternative Choice, 1 Vegetable Choice, 1 Fat Choice
Water*	9 cups (2.2 L)

*All beverages, with the exception of alcoholic beverages, contribute to your daily water requirements. Besides plain water, count the milk, soy beverages, 100% juice, coffee, tea and herbal tea you drink as part of your water intake.

The Longevity Diet doesn't prohibit alcoholic drinks, but it doesn't encourage them either. Women can have up to one drink per day, or seven per week. One drink is defined as 341 ml (12 oz) of 5% (alcohol by volume) beer, 142 ml (5 oz) of 12% wine or 43 ml (1-1/2 oz) of 80 proof (40%) distilled spirits. Keep in mind that alcohol provides empty calories and is counterproductive to the principles of calorie restriction. Every glass of wine, bottle of light beer or 1-1/2 ounces of spirits has about 100 calories; regular beer has even more.

Daily Supplements

Women aged 19–49
Multivitamin and mineral supplement
Vitamin D, 1000 IU
Calcium (300–500 mg) once daily
Fish oil (omega-3) providing 500–600 mg of DHA plus EPA (combined)

Women aged 50+
Multivitamin and mineral supplement
Vitamin D, 2000 IU
Calcium (300–500 mg) once or twice daily
Fish oil (omega-3) providing 500–600 mg of DHA plus EPA (combined)

The Longevity Diet Meal Plan for men (1900 calories)

	Food Group Choices
Breakfast (400 calories)	2 Starchy Food Choices 1 Fruit Choice 1 Milk/Milk Alternative Choice 1 Fat Choice
Lunch (550 calories)	4 Protein Choices 2 Starchy Food Choices 2 Vegetable Choices 2 Fat Choices
Dinner (600 calories)	5 Protein Choices 2 Starchy Food Choices 2 Vegetable Choices 2 Fat Choices
Snacks (350 calories)	2 Fruit Choices, 1 Milk/Milk Alternative Choice, 1 Vegetable Choice, 1 Fat Choice
Water*	13 cups (3 L)

*All beverages, with the exception of alcoholic beverages, contribute to your daily water requirements. Besides plain water, count the milk, soy beverages, 100% juice, coffee, tea and herbal tea you drink as part of your water intake.

The Longevity Diet doesn't prohibit alcoholic drinks, but it certainly doesn't encourage them either. Men can have up to one to two drinks per day, or nine per week. One drink is defined as 341 ml (12 oz) of 5% (alcohol by volume) beer, 142 ml (5 oz) of 12% wine or 43 ml (1-1/2 oz) of 80 proof (40%) distilled spirits. Keep in mind that alcohol provides empty calories and is counterproductive to the principles of calorie restriction. Every glass of wine, bottle of light beer or 1-1/2 ounces of spirits has about 100 calories; regular beer has even more.

Daily Supplements

Men aged 19–49
Multivitamin and mineral supplement
Vitamin D, 1000 IU
Calcium (300–500 mg) once daily
Fish oil (omega-3) providing 500–600 mg of DHA plus EPA (combined)

Men aged 50+
Multivitamin and mineral supplement
Vitamin D, 2000 IU
Calcium (300–500 mg) once or twice daily
Fish oil (omega-3) providing 500–600 mg of DHA plus EPA (combined)

THE LONGEVITY DIET FOOD GROUPS AND SERVING SIZES

The Longevity Diet Meal Plans indicate how many servings from each food group you need to eat each day and how you should combine them at meals to maximize your feeling of energy. The serving size for 1 choice is listed beside each food. Serving sizes are measured *after* cooking, not before.

Protein food choices

	1 Choice =
Meat, Poultry, Fish & Seafood	
Lean beef (Tenderloin, sirloin, inside round, eye of the round, extra-lean ground)	1 ounce (30 g)
Lean pork (Tenderloin, centre-cut chops, lean ham, peameal bacon)	1 ounce (30 g)
Veal (Sirloin, loin chop, ground)	1 ounce (30 g)
Chicken (Skinless breast meat, extra-lean ground)	1 ounce (30 g)
Turkey (Skinless white or dark meat, extra-lean ground)	1 ounce (30 g)
Fish, all types	1 ounce (30 g)
Mussels	3 medium
Sardines, Atlantic, canned, 1-1/2 inches (7.5 cm) long	2 pieces
Scallops, sea or bay	7 small or 3 large
Shrimp, large	5 pieces (30 g)
Oysters, raw or broiled	7 medium

Eggs & Cheese

Egg, large, whole	1
Egg whites	2
Egg whites, liquid	1/4 cup (50 ml)
Cheese, hard, lower-fat (less than 20% milkfat)	1 ounce (30 g)
Cheese string, part skim	1
Cottage cheese, 1% or fat-free	1/4 cup (50 ml)

Vegetarian Protein Choices

Beans/lentils, cooked, e.g., black beans, garbanzo beans, kidney beans, navy beans, soy beans, lentils	1/3 cup (75 ml)
Soy burger, 75 g patty	1/2
Soy ground round	1/4 cup (50 ml)
Soy hot dog, 52 g	1/2
Soy nuts, roasted	2 tbsp (25 ml)
Tempeh, cooked	1/3 cup (75 ml)
Tofu, extra firm, chopped	1/4 cup (50 ml)
Textured soy/vegetable protein (TSP/TVP), dry	3 tbsp (45 ml)

Milk & milk alternative choices

	1 Choice =

Dairy

Milk, 1% or skim	1 cup (250 ml)
Milk, powdered, skim	1/3 cup (75 ml)
Milk, evaporated, skim	1/2 cup (125 ml)
Yogurt, plain, 1% or skim	1 cup (250 ml)
Yogurt, flavoured or fruit bottom, 1% or skim	3/4 cup (175 ml or 175 g)

Non-dairy

Soy beverage, plain, calcium-enriched	1 cup (250 ml)

Starchy food choices

	1 Choice =
Breads (a whole grain must be the first ingredient)	
Bread	1 slice (30 g)
Bagel, small	1/2 (30 g)
Bagel, regular size	1/4 (30 grams)
Bun (e.g., Kaiser roll, hamburger roll)	1/2
English muffin	1/2
Pita pocket, 6-inch	1/2 (30 grams)
Tortilla, soft, 6-inch	1
Tortilla, soft, 10-inch	1/2
Cereals (a whole grain must be the first ingredient)	
Cold cereal, dry flake (e.g., Bran Flakes, Cheerios, Shreddies, Spoon Size Shredded Wheat)	3/4 cup (175 ml)
Cold cereal, denser flake (e.g., Kashi Go Lean, Nature's Path Flax Plus, Nature's Path Optimum)	1/2 cup (125 ml)
Cold cereal, 100% bran	1/2 cup (125 ml)
Cold cereal, Kellogg's Bran Buds	1/3 cup (75 ml)
Cold cereal, granola	1/4 cup (50 ml)
Cold cereal, shredded wheat	1 biscuit
Oats, uncooked, dry	1/4 cup (50 ml)
Oatmeal, cooked	1/2 cup (125 ml)
Oatmeal, instant, unflavoured	1/2 packet
Crackers	
Soda crackers, whole-wheat	7
Finn Crisp crispbread	3 slices
Rice cakes, brown	2
Rice crackers, small	10
Ryvita crispbread	3 slices
Wasa crispbread	1-1/2 slices
Grains & Potatoes	
Barley or bulgur, cooked	1/3 cup (75 ml)
Couscous, cooked	1/3 cup (75 ml)
Corn	1/2 cup or 1/2 cob
Pasta, whole-wheat, cooked	1/2 cup (125 ml)
Rice, brown or wild, cooked	1/3 cup (75 ml)
Potato, new or yellow flesh	1/2 medium or 1/2 cup (125 ml)

	1 Choice =
Potato, sweet	1/2 medium or 1/2 cup (125 ml)
Quinoa, cooked	1/3 cup (75 ml)

Other Starchy Food

Granola bar, low-fat, small (~ 90 calories)	1
Muffin, very small, low-fat, whole-grain	1/2
Popcorn, air-popped or low-fat microwave	3 cups (375 ml)
Soup, broth-based with potato, rice or pasta	1 cup (250 ml)

Fruit choices

	1 Choice =

Fresh & Dried Fruit

Berries, fresh (blackberries, blueberries, raspberries)	1 cup (250 ml)
Berries, fresh (cranberries, strawberries)	1-1/2 cups (375 ml)
Grapes	1 cup (250 ml) or 40 grapes
Fruit, fresh (apple, pear, kiwifruit, orange, peach, nectarine)	1 medium-sized
Fruit, fresh (banana, grapefruit)	1 small
Fruit, fresh (mango, papaya)	1/2 medium-sized
Fruit, fresh, small (apricots, plums, prunes)	4
Fruit, fresh, small (figs)	2
Fruit, canned, packed in water or juice	1 cup (250 ml)
Fruit, dried (apricots)	7 halves
Fruit, dried (dates, figs)	3
Fruit, dried (raisins, cranberries)	2 tbsp (25 ml)
Melon (cantaloupe, honeydew)	1/2 small or 1 cup (250 ml) cubes
Melon (watermelon, diced)	1-1/2 cups (375 ml)
Pineapple, fresh or canned in water or juice	3/4 cup (175 ml)

Unsweetened, 100% Fruit Juices

Apple, grapefruit, orange, pineapple	1/2 cup (125 ml)
Grape, prune, cranberry	1/3 cup (75 ml)

Vegetable choices

1 Choice = 1/2 cup (125 ml) cooked or raw, or 1 cup salad greens, or 1/2 cup of vegetable juice

Your goal: Choose at least 4 vegetable servings per day and 3 of them must be different colours to increase your intake of antioxidants and phytochemicals.

Green	Yellow/Orange	Red
Artichokes	Butternut squash	Beets
Arugula	Carrots	Red peppers
Asparagus	Yellow peppers	Radishes
Beet greens	Pumpkin	Radicchio
Broccoli	Rutabagas	Red onions
Broccoflower	Yellow summer squash	Tomatoes
Brussels sprouts	Yellow tomatoes	Tomato juice
Chinese cabbage	Winter squash	
Collard greens		
Green beans		
Green cabbage		
Green leaf lettuce	**White**	**Blue/Purple**
Celery	Cauliflower	Purple cabbage
Cucumbers	Jicama	Purple carrots
Endive	Kohlrabi	Eggplant
Green pepper	Mushrooms	Purple endive
Kale	Onions	Purple peppers
Okra	Parsnips	
Peas	Turnips	
Rapini		
Romaine lettuce		
Snow peas		
Spinach		
Swiss chard		
Watercress		
Zucchini		

Fat & oil choices

	1 Choice =
Spreads	
Butter, margarine (non-hydrogenated)	1 tsp (5 ml)
Margarine, light	2 tsp (10 ml)
Cream cheese, fat reduced	2 tbsp (25 ml)
Goat's cheese, soft, 20% MF or less	1 tbsp (15 ml)

	1 Choice =
Dressings & Oils	
Mayonnaise	1 tsp (5 ml)
Mayonnaise, fat-reduced	2 tsp (10 ml)
Peanut sauce, calorie-reduced	2 tbsp (25 ml)
Salad dressing, vinaigrette	2 tsp (10 ml)
Salad dressing, fat-reduced	4 tsp (20 ml)
Vegetable oil (e.g., olive, canola, flaxseed, walnut)	1 tsp (5 ml)
Other Fats	
Avocado	1/8 of one whole
Dips (hummus, tzatziki)	2 tbsp (25 ml)
Nuts (almonds, dry roasted)	6 whole
Nuts (walnuts)	4 halves
Nuts (peanuts, dry roasted)	1 tbsp (15 ml)
Nuts (pecans, dry roasted)	5 halves
Nut butter	1-1/2 tsp (7 ml)
Olives, medium	6
Parmesan cheese, grated	2 tbsp (25 ml)
Pesto sauce, bottled	1-1/2 tsp (7 ml)
Seeds	1 tbsp (15 ml)
Sour cream, fat-reduced, 7%	2 tbsp (25 ml)

Step 5: Personalize your Longevity Diet Meal Plan

ADJUSTING THE CALORIE LEVEL If your daily calorie target doesn't match the calorie level of the Longevity Diet Meal Plans, you'll need to adjust them to hit your goal. The list below shows you 100-calorie portions of nutrient-rich foods. Use the list to add—or drop—calories from your diet. When adding or subtracting calories from the Meal Plans, keep the following principles in mind:

- If you need to subtract calories, do not remove a Vegetable Choice. *You must consume at least 4 vegetable servings each day.* With the exception of green peas, winter squash, tomato sauce and tomato/vegetable juice, vegetables are considered "free" because they are so low in calories. That means they are unlimited—you may exceed 4 servings per day.

- If you need to subtract calories, do not remove a Milk & Milk Alternative Choice. Doing so would reduce your daily protein and calcium intake.
- If you need to increase calories, you may add 1 Milk & Milk Alternative Choice. In this case, remove 1 calcium supplement (300–500 mg) from your daily plan.
- If you increase your calorie intake from packaged foods such as breakfast cereal, whole-grain crackers or a commercial soup, you will need to read the nutrition label to determine calories per serving. Pay attention to the serving size. Depending on the food, you will likely need to eat less or more of the stated serving size to reach 100 calories.

100-Calorie food portions*

Protein Foods

Lean meat, chicken	2 oz (60 g)
Fish, salmon	2 oz (60 g)
Fish, tuna	3 oz (90 g)
Fish, halibut, sole	2-1/2 oz (75 g)
Seafood, shrimp/scallops	3 oz (90 g)
Egg, whole	1 large
Egg whites	6
Cheese, part skim (20% MF or less)	1-1/2 oz (45 g)
Cottage cheese, 1%	2/3 cup (150 ml)
Chickpeas, cooked	1/3 cup (75 ml)
Kidney beans, cooked	1/2 cup (125 ml)
Lentils, cooked	1/2 cup (125 ml)
Tofu, firm	1/2 cup (125 ml)

Milk & Milk Alternatives

Milk, skim or 1%	1 cup (250 ml)
Yogurt, plain, low-fat	3/4 cup (175 ml)
Yogurt, low-fat, fruit-flavoured	1/2 cup (125 ml)
Soy milk, unflavoured	1 cup (250 ml)

Starchy Foods

Cereal, e.g., Bran Flakes, Cheerios	1 cup (250 ml)
Cereal, 100% bran	1/2 cup (125 ml)
Oatmeal, cooked	3/4 cup (175 ml)
Pasta, cooked	1/2 cup (125 ml)
Popcorn, air-popped	3 cups (750 ml)
Rice, barley or bulgur, cooked	1/2 cup (125 ml)
Pasta, cooked	1/2 cup (125 ml)

Corn, kernels, cooked	2/3 cup (150 ml)
Sweet potato, mashed	1/2 cup (125 ml)
Whole-grain bread	1 slice
Tortilla, whole-wheat, 6-inch	1

Fruits

Apple	1 medium
Applesauce	1 cup (250 ml)
Apricots	3 whole or 6 halves
Banana	1 medium
Blueberries	1 cup (250 ml)
Dates	5
Fruit juice, unsweetened	3/4 to 1 cup (175–250 ml)
Pear	1 medium
Prunes, dried	5
Raisins	1/4 cup (50 ml)
Strawberries	1 cup (250 ml)
Orange	1 large

Fats & Oils

Almonds, unsalted	14 whole
Avocado	1/4
Cashew nuts, unsalted	11 whole
Peanuts, unsalted	17 whole (2 tbsp/25 ml)
Peanut/almond butter	1 tbsp (15 ml)
Pecans	10 halves
Salad dressing, vinaigrette, homemade	4 tsp (20 ml)
Sunflower seeds	2 tbsp (25 ml)
Vegetable oil	2 tsp (10 ml)
Walnuts	8 halves

*Calorie values range from 90 to 115.

MOVING FOOD CHOICES BETWEEN MEALS The Longevity Diet Meal Plans have been designed to help you feel fuller at meals and to keep your blood-sugar levels stable longer after eating. Eating the right combinations of food groups at meals and as snacks at regular intervals during the day will reduce the likelihood you'll feel hungry and low in energy. You'll notice that each meal has a source of protein and of carbohydrate (Starchy Food Choices and/or Fruit Choices) to help accomplish this.

That said, the Meal Plans are not cast in stone. You can make the following changes, if you wish:

- You may move 1 Starchy Food Choice from one meal to another. If you'd like to move 1 Starchy Food Choice from a meal to your snack, that's fine. For instance, you might want to have three whole-grain Ryvita crackers with almond butter for a mid-afternoon snack. That's fine. If you do move 1 Starchy Food Choice from a meal to a snack, be sure to eat the alternate snack (e.g., fruit, yogurt, milk, soy milk, veggies and hummus) at another time during the day.
- You may move 1 Protein Choice from one meal to any other meal.
- You may move your Fat & Oil Choices from one meal to another, or from one meal to a snack. For example, if you'd like to have peanut butter on your whole-grain toast at breakfast, feel free to move a Fat & Oil Choice from lunch or dinner to breakfast.
- Remember, you may add more "unlimited" vegetables to any meal you like. Each meal plan includes a minimum 4 daily vegetable servings. (Green peas, winter squash, turnip, tomato sauce and tomato/vegetable juice are not unlimited because they have more calories than other vegetables.)

Because your meal plan is designed to prevent you from feeling hungry between meals, or overly hungry before meals, keep the following rules in mind when you make changes to your Meal Plan:

- Do not skip meals. Always eat three meals plus one or two midday snacks, depending on your schedule.
- Breakfast must always include at least one protein-rich food serving, either a Milk & Milk Alternative Choice or a Protein Food Choice.
- The midday and evening meals must always include servings from the Protein Food group.
- It's okay to move a few food group servings from lunch to supper in anticipation of a big meal, but it is not all right to skip lunch entirely to "bank" calories. You'll end up feeling ravenous by the time you get your supper, making it far more likely you'll overeat.

A Seven-Day Menu Plan for the Longevity Diet: 1500 Calories

To help you see what meals and snacks could look like on your meal plan, I've created a one-week menu plan using everyday nutritious foods and many of the tasty recipes you'll find in "Part 4: The Longevity Diet Recipes." Use this as a guide to help you build your own menu plans.

To bump up the calorie level, increase portion sizes at meals and snacks. For men following the 1900-calorie Longevity Diet, make the following adjustments to the menu plan below:

- **Add 3 Starchy Food Choices each day**. To do so, choose foods from the list of Food Choices on pages 176 to 177, or increase your portion sizes at meals. Increase the portion size of Starchy Foods at meals. For example, on Day 1 add 1 cup (250 ml) cooked oatmeal to breakfast (2 Starchy Food Choices) and 1/3 cup (75 ml) brown rice to dinner (1 Starchy Food Choice). And …
- **Add 4 Protein Food Choices each day**. Simply increase your portion size of fish, poultry or lean meat by 2 ounces (60 g) at lunch and 2 ounces (60 g) at dinner.

Or, if you prefer, you can simply add 400 calories' worth of food using the "100-Calorie Food Portions" list on pages 180 to 181.

Monday

Breakfast
1 cup (250 ml) cooked large-flake or steel-cut oatmeal
1/2 cup (125 ml) blueberries
1 tbsp (15 ml) ground flaxseed, sprinkled over cereal
3/4 cup (175 ml) plain yogurt (1% MF or less) *or* 1 cup (250 ml) skim milk
   or plain soy milk
1/2 cup (125 ml) 100% orange juice
Coffee, tea or herbal tea (if needed, with added milk instead of cream)

Morning snack
1 medium apple, sliced, with 1 tbsp (15 ml) almond or peanut butter

Lunch
Chicken and Arugula Sandwich with Lemon Chive Mayonnaise (p. 279)
1/2 cup (125 ml) baby carrots
2 cups (500 ml) water

Afternoon snack
1 energy bar such as Luna Bar, Lärabar, Elevate Me! Bar, or Proteins Plus Express
   Bar (150 to 200 calories and no more than 3 g saturated fat)
1 cup (250 ml) water

Dinner
Salmon with White Wine, Lemon and Garlic (p. 288)
2/3 cup (150 ml) steamed brown rice
1 cup (250 ml) broccoli and cauliflower, steamed
2 cups (500 ml) water

Nutrient breakdown: 1494 cal, 92 g pro, 42 g total fat (9 g saturated fat), 189 g carb, 23 g fibre, 146 mg chol, 1160 mg sodium.

Tuesday

Breakfast
2 slices of 100% whole-grain toast (70 to 90 calories per slice) with 2 tsp (10 ml) almond or peanut butter
1 cup (250 ml) of mixed fruit salad
3/4 cup (175 ml) vanilla yogurt (1% MF or less) or 1 cup (250 ml) skim milk or soy milk
Coffee, tea or herbal tea (if needed, with added milk instead of cream)

Morning snack
1 medium-sized (12 oz or Starbucks' "tall") non-fat or soy latte

Lunch
1-1/2 cups (375 ml) Lemon Chickpea Soup (p. 259)
1 small whole-grain roll *or* 3 slices of Ryvita crispbread
1 medium apple
2 cups (500 ml) water

Afternoon snack
1 small red pepper sliced plus 1/4 cup (50 ml) hummus (chickpea dip)

Dinner
Ginger Tomato Chicken Pasta (p. 280)
Small green side salad with 4 tsp (20 ml) of a vinaigrette dressing
2 cups (500 ml) water

Nutrient breakdown: 1483 cal, 85 g pro, 45 g total fat (6 g saturated fat), 196 g carb, 31 g fibre, 78 mg chol, 1884 mg sodium.

Wednesday

Breakfast
Pumpkin Orange Banana Smoothie (p. 235)

1 breakfast-sized pita such as Pita Break's Finland Rye pita (it has a low glycemic index!)

Add 2 tsp (10 ml) apple butter or low-sugar fruit spread if desired

Coffee, tea or herbal tea (if needed, with added milk instead of cream)

Morning snack
4 dried apricots plus 10 plain almonds

Lunch
Open-faced tuna salad sandwich on 1 slice of 100% whole-grain bread. To make the salad, mix half of a 6 oz (170 g) tin of tuna with 2 tbsp (25 ml) plain non-fat yogurt, 1 tsp (5 ml) Djion mustard and a bit of chopped celery.

1/2 cup (125 ml) raw veggie sticks with 2 tbsp (25 ml) hummus

1 medium apple

2 cups (500 ml) water

Afternoon snack
1 medium pear plus 1 oz (30 g) part-skim cheese such as 1 Mini Babybel Light (20% MF or less)

Dinner
4 oz (120 g) grilled or roasted pork tenderloin (brush with hoisin sauce before cooking)

Roasted Broccoli (p. 267)

Sautéed Cherry Tomatoes with Garlic and Fresh Basil (p. 269)

5 small new potatoes, steamed or boiled

2 cups (500 ml) water

Nutrient breakdown: 1505 cal, 97 g pro, 40 g total fat (8 g saturated fat), 203 g carb, 30 g fibre, 147 mg chol, 1376 mg sodium.

Thursday

Breakfast
1 cup (250 ml) whole-grain ready-to-eat breakfast cereal* (e.g., Post Shredded
   Wheat Spoon Size Wheat'n Bran, Nature's Path Organic Flax Plus Flakes or
   President's Choice Blue Menu Bran Flakes)
1 cup (250 ml) skim or 1% milk or unflavoured soy milk
1/2 small banana, sliced, and 1/2 cup (125 ml) strawberries, sliced
Coffee, tea or herbal tea (if needed, with added milk instead of cream)

* Choose a whole-grain cereal with at least 5 grams of fibre, no more than 8 grams of sugar and no
more than 240 milligrams of sodium per serving.

Morning snack
3/4 cup (175 ml) low-fat yogurt (1% MF or less) plus 2 tbsp (25 ml) dried cranberries and 2 tbsp (25 ml) unsalted sunflower seeds

Lunch
White Bean, Garlic and Arugula Wrap (p. 303)
1 cup (250 ml) vegetable soup—if store-bought, choose a brand that contains no
   more than 500 mg of sodium per 250 ml serving
2 cups (500 ml) water

Afternoon snack
1/2–1 cup (125–250 ml) baby carrots plus 1/4 cup (50 ml) Black Bean Hummus
   (p. 237)

Dinner
Thai Roasted Trout with Fresh Lime (p. 291)
Spicy Sautéed Kale (p. 271)
2/3 cup (150 ml) steamed brown basmati rice
2 cups (500 ml) water

Nutrient breakdown: 1494 cal, 80 g pro, 41 g total fat (8 g saturated fat), 219 g carb, 36 g fibre,
83 mg chol, 1820 mg sodium.

Friday

Breakfast
1 whole-grain toaster waffle topped with 1 cup (250 ml) mixed berries and
   3/4 cup (175 ml) vanilla yogurt (1% MF or less)
1/2 cup (125 ml) 100% orange juice
Coffee, tea or herbal tea (if needed, added milk instead of cream)

Morning snack
1 medium apple with 10 walnut halves

Lunch
1 cup (250 ml) Black Bean and Avocado Salad with Toasted Cumin Dressing
   (p. 247)
1 small whole-grain roll or 3 slices of Ryvita crispbread
1 medium orange
2 cups (500 ml) water

Afternoon snack
1 energy bar such as Luna Bar, Lärabar, Elevate Me! bar or Proteins Plus Express
   Bar (150–200 calories and no more than 3 g saturated fat)

Dinner
Baked Pita Pizza with Chicken, Spinach and Fresh Basil (p. 277)
2 cups (500 ml) tossed green salad with 4 tsp (20 ml) of vinaigrette dressing
2 cups (500 ml) water

Nutrient breakdown: 1457 cal, 75 g pro, 42 g total fat (8 g saturated fat), 208 g carb, 36 g fibre,
64 mg chol, 1775 mg sodium.

Saturday

Breakfast
1 Raspberry Ginger Muffin (p. 311)
3/4 cup (175 ml) plain or vanilla yogurt (1% MF or less)
1 cup (250 ml) blueberries or 3/4 cup (175 ml) 100% orange juice
Coffee, tea or herbal tea (if needed, with added milk instead of cream)

Lunch
Sesame Salmon Wrap (p. 289)
1/2–1 cup (125–250 ml) raw veggies: carrots, celery, cucumber
2 cups (500 ml) water

Afternoon snack
Kale "Chips" with Sea Salt (p. 238)

Dinner
4 oz (120 g) of lean steak, grilled (e.g., tenderloin, sirloin)
Zesty Sweet Potato Wedges (p. 272)
Simple Sautéed Spinach (p. 270)
2 cups (500 ml) water

Dessert
Chocolate Fruit Fondue (p. 313)

Nutrient breakdown: 1496 cal, 95 g pro, 52 g total fat (23 g saturated fat*), 177 g carb, 26 g fibre, 143 mg chol, 1911 mg sodium.

The higher saturated fat content of Saturday's menu comes mainly from the dark chocolate. But not to worry—the type of saturated fat in chocolate does not raise blood cholesterol. Good news for chocolate lovers!

Sunday

Breakfast

Red Pepper and Asparagus Omelet (p. 222)

2 small slices of 100% whole-grain toast with 2 tsp (10 ml) nut butter or
non-hydrogenated margarine

1 cup (250 ml) mixed berries

Coffee, tea or herbal tea (if needed, with added milk instead of cream)

Lunch

Red Lentil Soup (p. 260)—batch cook for quick meals next week

1 small whole-grain roll or 3 slices of Ryvita crispbread

2 cups (500 ml) water

Afternoon snack

3/4 cup (175 ml) plain yogurt (1% MF or less) plus 1/2 cup (125 ml) crushed
pineapple (canned in its own juice)

Dinner

4 oz (120 g) grilled turkey or soy burger; place in 1 whole-wheat pita pocket or thin
whole-grain hamburger roll (160–190 calories per bun)

Crunchy Broccoli Salad with Apple Dijon Dressing (p. 245)

2 cups (500 ml) water

Nutrient breakdown: 1536 cal, 84 g pro, 53 g total fat (9 g saturated fat), 195 g carb, 28 g fibre,
283 mg chol, 1843 mg sodium.

10

Leslie's Longevity Diet: Eight strategies for success

The Longevity Diet is a means of improving your health and living a longer life. Adopting a lower-calorie, nutrient-rich diet is a way to change your metabolism and body chemistry to ultimately slow the aging process. You'll feel better, too, just days after starting the plan. You'll have considerably more energy. Any nagging aches and pains associated with carrying excess weight will diminish as your body gets leaner.

And, of course, your health will be enhanced. Your cholesterol, blood-sugar and insulin levels will decline, even if these numbers are not elevated right now. If you have high blood pressure, the Longevity Diet can help you lower it. Once you experience the many benefits of the diet, you won't want to lose them. Which brings me to a critical point: This total nutrition plan will benefit you only as long as you follow it. You need to make eating less—and eating smartly—a permanent part of your life. It's as simple as that.

Too often I witness clients in my private practice who have successfully reached their health and weight goals through diet change slide back into old habits. Inevitably life interferes—be it through long work hours, family stress or a string of food-focused social events—and slowly, but ever so surely, eating habits deteriorate and achievements are undone. We're human. We sometimes turn to food for reward or consolation. We give in to temptation from time to time. That's to be expected. But the key is not to let small slips accumulate and unravel your progress.

HOW TO STAY ON TRACK
FOR THE LONG HAUL

Read on for a number of strategies that will help you make the Longevity Diet an integral part of your life today, next month and for years down the road. Some of these strategies, such as keeping a food journal and measuring food portions, you will apply in the early stages of following the diet to help you adhere to it successfully. But you may also need to revisit these strategies down the road if you find that your eating habits are starting to slip. Every so often, it's wise to refocus your attention on your food choices and portion sizes. For long-term success, you'll also need to learn how to adapt your meal plan to regular life. Skills such as interpreting food labels and navigating restaurant menus will help you fit a wide variety of foods and meals into your meal plan. Below are eight strategies to help you master a lower-calorie, nutrient-rich diet for the rest of your life.

Success strategy #1: Track your progress

Self-monitoring is a powerful tool that's critical to your success on the Longevity Diet Meal Plan. Recording and tracking your food intake, body weight and health measurements will give you immediate feedback. It'll let you know how well you're doing or if you need to make a few changes to stick more closely to the plan. In the appendices I have provided you with two tools you can use to keep on target: a Daily Food and Nutrient Tracker and a Health Measurement Tracker.

A. THE DAILY FOOD AND
NUTRIENT TRACKER

One of the most important things you can do as you make changes to your diet is to keep a food journal. Your food journal will keep you aware of how you're doing and committed to your goals. It will highlight, in black and white, the nutrients and foods you're consuming and in what portion sizes. It will also help you recognize which nutritious foods you might not be eating enough of. Writing down what you eat will make you think twice about reaching for seconds at dinner or sneaking a few bites from your child's plate. It will also help you avoid "mindless eating" (those nibbles you don't pay attention to and easily forget), uncover emotional eating patterns and identify overeating triggers.

You'll find a Daily Food and Nutrient Tracker in the appendices, page 319. I suggest you photocopy these pages so that you have plenty of extras to use as you follow the Longevity Diet. You can carry the Tracker with you during the day. Or, if you prefer, create your own food journal in a notebook or even in a bound diary. Write down the time of day you ate, the foods you ate and your portion sizes. On the Food and Nutrient Tracker you'll also be able to tally your total intake of food group choices for the day and assess how closely you're following the meal plan. As well, you can check off your intake of nutrient-rich foods to ensure you've met your daily targets.

I recommend you keep a food journal for at least one month. Continue to log your meals and snacks beyond that if you find it motivates you to keep with the plan. Don't wait until the end of the day to complete the entries because you're likely to forget a few foods. Instead, record your food intake after each meal. If you prefer, you can use your Food and Nutrient Tracker as a planning tool. Rather than recording what foods you eat as you eat them, fill out your journal one day in advance. It'll help you prepare for the day ahead by organizing what you will eat and ensuring the right foods are on hand.

B. THE HEALTH MEASUREMENT TRACKER

You've committed to change your diet for a purpose: to improve your health and longevity. You've already read how calorie restriction can enhance a number of biomarkers linked with longevity in both animals and humans, such as blood pressure, cholesterol levels, insulin sensitivity and inflammation. In Chapter 8, I recommended you consult with your family doctor before starting the Longevity Diet. If you doctor is supportive of your goals then ask if you could have a few tests done to determine your current health status. Have them completed before you start the plan so that there's a baseline you can measure your progress against along the way.

Recording your health measurements provides another check point you can use to see how you're doing and where you're going. Your results are tangible. They'll tell you that the diet is doing what it's supposed to do. Improving your health is a powerful motivator. Many of my clients who come to see me to lose weight tell me that watching their cholesterol level plummet or blood pressure drop is an even more powerful motivator than seeing the number on the scale go down. By tracking your health measurements, you'll be able to see the extent to which your new diet enhances your health, knowledge that'll inspire you to stick with all the healthy changes you've made.

In the appendices of this book, you'll find the Health Measurement Tracker. Use it to record your starting weight, body mass index (BMI), body measurements, percentage of body fat (if possible), blood pressure and the results of various blood tests. Check and record these measures again at three months, six months and one year. Use the following guide to record your body measurements as accurately as possible.

YOUR BODY MASS INDEX (BMI)

Your weight is considered to be healthy if your BMI is between 18.5 and 24.9 (research suggests the healthiest weight corresponds to a BMI between 18.5 and 22). Overweight is defined by a BMI of 25 to 29.9 and obesity is defined as a BMI over 30. Here's how to calculate your BMI (you'll need a pencil and a calculator):

1. Determine your weight in kilograms (kg).   Weight (kg)
   (Divide your weight in pounds by 2.2.)   _____

2. Determine your height in centimetres (cm).   Height (cm)
   (Multiply your height in inches by 2.54.)   _____

3. Determine your height in metres.   Height (metres)
   (Divide your height in centimetres by 100.)   _____

4. Square your height in metres   Height (metres^2)
   (Multiply your height in metres by height in metres.)   _____

5. Now, calculate your BMI.   BMI
   (Divide your weight [in kg] by height [in metres^2].)   _____

For example, let's say your weight is 150 pounds (150 ÷ 2.2 = 68.1 kilograms) and your height is 5 feet and 5 inches (65 inches x 2.54 = 165 centimetres or 1.65 metres). That means your height in metres squared is 2.72 (1.65 x 1.65 = 2.72). Now, to determine your BMI, all you need to do is divide your weight (68.1 kilograms) by this number (e.g., 68.1 ÷ 2.72 = 25.03). Your BMI is 25. If you don't feel like doing the math yourself, there are online calculators that will do this for you. Google "BMI calculator" and you'll find a number to choose from.

YOUR BODY MEASUREMENTS

You will need a measuring tape for this exercise. If you find it tricky to take your own measurements, ask a family member—or a personal trainer if you have one—to do this for you.

Your Waist: Without holding the measuring tape too tightly or too loosely, measure your waist circumference. Your waist is the narrowest part of your trunk, about one inch above your belly button.

Your Hips: Stand with your heels together and measure your hips around the fullest part of your buttocks.

Your Chest/bust: Take your measurement around the fullest part of your chest.

Success strategy #2:
Master portion control

Many of my clients tell me they know their portion sizes are too big. They snack on crackers out of the box, eat too much pasta at dinner, polish off a steak meant to serve two people and often admit to going back for seconds. They recognize that a lack of portion control is a big reason why their cholesterol or blood pressure is too high and why they're overweight. But they aren't sure what an appropriate portion size is supposed to be. Even nutritious foods can add a surplus of calories to your diet if you eat them in large portions. Clients are often surprised to learn that their habit of snacking on multiple pieces of fruit or drinking two large glasses of milk at dinner is contributing to their weight problem. Many people eat the right foods but in portions that are just too big.

Reducing your portion size is paramount to being successful on the Longevity Diet. In order to stick to your 25 percent calorie reduction, you will need to get used to eating smaller-sized portions. Learning portion control isn't as difficult as you think. All you have to do is learn how to recognize an appropriate serving size for different foods. There are three ways you can assess the portion size of the foods you eat, and I recommend you try all three to find what works best for you. Once you get into the habit of monitoring your portions, it becomes second nature. (But you absolutely should refresh your memory every so often, since portion sizes have a way of creeping up.)

A. MEASURE YOUR FOOD

The best way to figure out how much you're eating is to measure it. *For the first two weeks of your meal plan I strongly advise that you measure your foods in a measuring cup or with measuring spoons.* Weigh your meat, poultry and fish on a digital kitchen food scale. You'll find a few different models at kitchen stores or department stores. Use measuring cups to serve your food once it's cooked. You'll need to learn what, say, 1 cup of cooked pasta, 1 cup of breakfast cereal and 3 ounces of cooked chicken looks like on your plate, or what 4 teaspoons of salad dressing looks like drizzled over your salad. After two weeks, you'll have become an expert at knowing what an appropriate portion size is just by looking and you won't need to measure as often.

You will also need to read nutrition labels on food packages to become familiar with serving sizes of your favourite brands of cereal, crackers, soup and salad dressings. The numbers on the Nutrition Facts box—the calories, grams of fat, protein, sugar, fibre and so on—apply to *one* serving of the food. Pay particular attention to the serving size and calorie information. Think about how the number of calories for one serving of the food fits into your daily calorie target. If you eat two servings, then double the numbers. You might be surprised to learn that one serving is much less than what you're used to eating.

B. EYEBALL YOUR PORTIONS

If measuring your food makes you crazy, you can eyeball your foods to make sure you're eating the correct serving size. While it's easy to translate serving size information into something visual that's easy to remember, this method won't be as precise as measuring your foods, which means your calorie intake might be a little off. That said, this is a good technique to use when you're eating in restaurants and can't actually weigh or measure your foods. Use the following list to compare serving sizes of particular foods with familiar objects.

A serving of ...	Looks like the size of ...
3 ounces (90 g) meat, fish, chicken	1 deck of playing cards
3 ounces (90 g) thin baked/grilled fish	a chequebook
1-1/2 ounces (45 g) cheese	3 dominos
1/2 cup (125 ml) cooked pasta or rice	1/2 of a baseball or 1 ice cream scoop
1 small muffin	one large egg
1/2 bagel	one hockey puck
1 pancake	a compact disc

A serving of ...	Looks like the size of ...
1/2 cup (125 ml) cooked vegetables	1/2 baseball or a small fist
1 cup (250 ml) salad greens	1 baseball
1 medium-sized fruit	1 baseball
1 small baked potato	a computer mouse
1 teaspoon (5 ml) butter, margarine	the tip of your thumb or 1 dice
2 tablespoons (25 ml) peanut butter	1 ping pong ball

C. USE THE PLATE MODEL

This method of portion control forces you to look at your plate and think about the proportion of food on it and the portion sizes you eat. Take a look at your dinner plate—is half of it covered by a slab of meat? Is it overflowing with spaghetti and meat sauce? Here's how the plate model works to help you eat appropriate portion sizes:

- Divide your dinner plate into four sections, or quarters.
- Fill one quarter with your protein food choice such as meat, chicken, fish or tofu.
- Fill another quarter with your starchy food choice, such as cooked brown rice, whole-wheat pasta, sweet potato or quinoa.
- The remaining half of your plate is to be filled with vegetables and salad greens.

Some people find it easier to visualize their plate as a clock and then fill the 12–6 P.M. slot with veggies, the 6–9 P.M. slot with starchy foods and the 9–12 A.M. slot with protein.

Courtesy of iDesign® Inc

Success strategy #3: Plan meals and snacks in advance

We've all been through it. We start out with great expectations, the best intentions, a wonderful plan—but they come to nothing because we haven't got the pieces in place that'll let us follow through. Not being organized is a sure-fire way to sabotage your success. To make the Longevity Diet work you need to plan so that you have the right foods on hand.

I know how busy our lives can be. My head spins when I hear about my clients' hectic weekday schedules. With both spouses working and rushing home to pick up kids or deliver them to after-school activities, it can be a real challenge to put a nutritious meal on the table. And if you leave it to chance, let's face it—it's not likely to happen. Too often, take-out or delivery saves the day.

The good news is that just a little organization upfront will pay off. Read on for some suggestions that my clients have found really work.

PLAN WEEKLY MENUS AHEAD Most people don't plan menus—that is, they don't write them down in advance. Menu planning means thinking about what foods you and your family will eat together—for a meal, for a day, for a week. I encourage you to sit down for fifteen minutes on the weekend (before you go grocery shopping) to map out your family's meals for the week. You'll need to think about your family's scheduled activities—who will be home for meals and who won't—so that you can decide if you need to cook ahead on the weekend or plan for leftovers. And once this is done, it's easy to prepare your grocery list.

You don't have to be feeding a family to benefit from mapping out the week's meals. I have plenty of clients who cook for one and find menu planning extremely useful. With the plan in place they don't need to figure out dinner at the last minute when they get home from work—they have the foods ready to go. Devising a menu plan also helps my single clients eat restaurant or take-out foods less often and save money.

In Chapter 9 I outlined the basic structure of your Longevity Diet Meal Plan, and provided a sample menu plan for a week. Use those pages as a guide when you sit down to make your own plan, and don't forget to add some of the delicious meals and snacks you'll find in "Part 4: The Longevity Recipes."

Planning ahead may sound like a lot of extra work, but believe me, once it becomes routine you'll find it'll save you heaps of time during your busy week. You'll have healthy foods on hand and fewer stops at the grocery store during the week. Planning enough for leftovers also cuts down on preparation time. And best of all, it'll set you up for a week of eating wholesome, nutritious meals.

SCHEDULE TIME FOR GROCERY SHOPPING (ONCE A WEEK) Once you've completed your weekly menu plan, you more or less have your grocery list. Your menu plan tells you what foods you need to buy. You may need to restock fresh vegetables and fruit mid-week but otherwise will have all the essentials to last through the week.

A weekly trip to the grocery store is important even if you don't create a menu plan. You still need to have healthy foods in the house. When you shop, stick to the perimeter of the store—the outer aisles are where you'll find the nutritious, unprocessed foods. Stay clear of the snack food or frozen entree aisles. And never shop on an empty stomach—you'll come home with more food items than you planned, some of them not that good for you.

If you find you really don't have time to visit a grocery store (or you just don't like to grocery shop), take advantage of a home delivery service. Today many supermarkets and specialty food shops deliver for a small fee. Some stores offer online ordering and will even deliver in the evening.

Success strategy #4: Read nutrition labels

Reading nutrition labels and grocery shopping go hand in hand. Many of the core foods of the Longevity Diet don't have nutrition labels. Fruit, vegetables, fish, lean poultry and nuts aren't required to disclose nutrition information. That's fine because these foods are very nutritious and many are naturally low in calories. However, you do need to become savvy at reading the nutrition labels on packaged foods.

The healthiest diet doesn't rely on many processed, packaged foods, many of which are made from refined starch and high in sugar or sodium or both. That said, you will have some packaged foods in your diet, such as breakfast cereals, whole-grain crackers, nut butters, even the occasional frozen meal. Use the tips below to help you understand what the nutrient numbers on food labels mean to you.

DECIPHERING NUTRITION LABELS

1. Serving size information. This is the first number to look at and that's why it's listed first. All nutrient amounts that follow are based on 1 serving of the food. The Nutrition Facts give the serving size in familiar household units—cups, tablespoons or a portion of the food (e.g., 1/4 pizza, 1 slice of bread)—follow it with the metric equivalent.

Many people don't pay attention to serving size information and end up eating more calories than they realize. In many cases, the serving size is not the whole package or the entire bottle. Products to watch out for include fruit juice, snack personal-size pizzas, pita bread, flatbreads and bagels. For example, the nutrition information for many whole-grain bagels is given for 1/2 bagel; if you eat the whole bagel you'll need to double the numbers. Read the serving size and figure out how much you typically consume.

When you compare two brands of a similar food, make sure you're comparing nutrient numbers for identical serving sizes. For instance, most brands of salad dressing list numbers for 1 tablespoon (15 ml), but some specify 2 tablespoons (25 ml) as a serving.

2. Calories. It's essential to pay attention to the calories per serving. Knowing the calories per serving—and how many servings you're actually eating—will help you succeed on my Longevity Diet. How you prepare a food also affects the number of calories you consume. Packaged rice and pasta dishes (too high in sodium to be nutritious) and muffin and cake mixes require you to add oil, milk and eggs. To know how much you are consuming, always check calories and nutrient amounts under the "as prepared" heading.

Memorize your personal calorie prescription for the Longevity Diet (you probably already have). Then, when you read labels in the grocery store, consider how a serving of the food in question fits into your daily target.

3. Fat, saturated and trans fat. The combined amount of saturated, polyunsaturated and monounsaturated and trans fats is listed next. If you're trying to find a lower-fat choice among, say, cookies or crackers, you can compare brands on grams of total fat per serving.

But a food product with a lot of fat grams isn't necessarily unhealthy. For instance, vinaigrette salad dressings, packages of nuts and nut butters contain heart-healthy monounsaturated fats. What's more important than the total fat for these products is the grams of combined saturated and trans fats—listed below total fats in the Nutrition Facts. These two fats are linked to a higher risk of heart disease because they raise LDL (bad) cholesterol.

Current guidelines recommend consuming no more than 10 percent of daily calories from these so-called bad fats. For a 2000-calorie diet, that means no more than 22 grams of saturated plus trans fat per day. (The math: 2000 calories x 10% = 200 calories. One gram of fat equals nine calories, so 200/9 = 22 grams.)

4. Cholesterol. Current guidelines recommend limiting your daily intake to 300 milligrams per day. If you have heart disease, limit your intake to 200 milligrams per day.

5. Sodium. Adults aged 19 to 50 need 1500 milligrams per day for health while older adults require 1200–1300 milligrams. The daily upper limit for sodium is 2300 milligrams. Since the majority of your meals aren't based on packaged foods, don't panic over a big sodium number for one food. A serving of tomato juice with 700 milligrams of sodium is okay as long as you eat lower-sodium foods for the rest of the day. On the other hand, you might want to pass on a frozen dinner that delivers 1000 milligrams of sodium. (If occasionally you need to rely on a frozen meal, choose one that contains no more than 200 milligrams of sodium per 100 calories.)

6. Carbohydrate, fibre, sugars. Next on the label come grams of total carbohydrate, all of the starch, fibre and sugar that's in 1 serving of the food. If you have diabetes and your diet requires you to "count carbohydrates" this is useful information. Otherwise, the numbers that follow—fibre and sugars—are more important.

Women aged 19 to 50 should strive for 25 grams of fibre per day; men in this age range, 38 grams. Women aged 51 and up need 21 grams, while their male counterparts need 30 grams. Look for foods with at least 2 grams of fibre per serving; breakfast cereals should deliver at least 5 grams per serving.

The sugar numbers include both naturally occurring sugars (e.g., fruit or milk sugars) *and* refined sugars added during food processing (e.g., sucrose, glucose-fructose, honey, corn syrup). You need to read the ingredient list if you want to limit added sugars in your diet. Look for names such as sucrose, dextrose, glucose, fructose, honey, molasses, malt, corn syrup, rice syrup, cane juice, invert sugar and fruit juice concentrate. You might be surprised to see how many types of sugar appear on the ingredient list of just one product!

7. Protein. If you eat a mixed diet that contains meat, poultry, fish, eggs, legumes and dairy you're more than likely meeting your daily protein requirements. Since protein helps keep you feeling full longer after eating, choose snack foods that provide a little protein, such as yogurt, nuts, soy beverages, energy bars and food bars made from nuts and fruit.

8. *Percentage daily value.* Fat, saturated plus trans fat, cholesterol, carbo-hydrate, fibre, sodium, vitamins A and C, calcium and iron are also expressed as a percentage of a Daily Value (% DV). Daily Values are based on recommendations for a healthy diet and represent the contribution (from 0 percent to 100 percent) that 1 serving of the food makes towards the particular nutrient's recommended intake.

You can use the % Daily Value to see whether nutrients you are trying to consume more of—fibre, vitamins A and C, calcium and iron—have a high percentage in a food product. For example, if you want to boost your fibre intake, compare similar serving sizes of two brands of a breakfast cereal, then choose the one with the highest % Daily Value for fibre per serving. If you want to buy a yogurt that provides the most calcium, choose the brand with the highest % Daily Value for calcium.

If 1 serving of food has a 15% Daily Value or more for fibre, vitamins A and C, calcium or iron, it's considered a good source of these nutrients; a 25% Daily Value or greater means it's an excellent source.

It's not always wise to strive for a higher % Daily Value. In the case of saturated plus trans fat and sodium, choose food products with a lower percentage. Foods with a 5% Daily Value or less for fat, cholesterol or sodium are considered low in these nutrients. Foods with a 10% Daily Value or less for saturated plus trans fat is also low in these bad fats.

READ INGREDIENT LISTS All packaged foods must list their ingredients in order, from greatest to least amount used. The first few ingredients usually make up the bulk of the food. Often, the fewer the ingredients the better, especially if there are a lot of unhealthy extras like chemical additives or refined sugars. If you're limiting added sugars, watch out for sucrose, dextrose, glucose, fructose, honey, molasses, malt, corn syrup, cane juice and fruit juice concentrate. And with grain products, such as cereals and crackers, scanning the ingredient list is often the only way you can tell if they are made from 100% whole grains.

Success strategy #5: Listen to your hunger cues

Many people equate feeling full with being satiated or satisfied. Many clients tell me that they push away from the dinner table when they are full and a little uncomfortable. That full feeling in their stomach to them signals the end of the meal. The problem is that by this point they have already *over*eaten and consumed more calories than they needed.

It's the same thing for many of my clients who snack after dinner. They tell me they snack because they feel hungry. But when they really think about it, it's not really hunger they feel at all. They simply no longer feel *full*. Sometimes we lose touch with what it truly feels like to be hungry, or satisfied, or full. Identifying and distinguishing between these different feelings is key to managing how much we eat at mealtime.

RATE YOUR HUNGER LEVEL FOR TWO WEEKS

For the first two weeks on the Longevity Diet Meal Plan, use the following hunger scale to assess how hungry or full you feel at three points during mealtime—(1) before you start eating, (2) halfway through your meal and (3) when you're done. *Your goal is to stop eating when you reach level 5.*

The hunger scale

1	You feel starving. You can't concentrate because you feel so empty. You need food *now!*
2	You feel hungry and know that your stomach needs food, but you could wait a few minutes before eating.
3	You feel slightly hungry. You could eat something, but you couldn't eat a large meal.
4	Your hunger has almost disappeared. You could eat another bite.
5	**You are no longer hungry. You feel satisfied, not full.**
6	You feel slightly full.
7	You feel overly full and uncomfortable. Your waistband is noticeably tighter.
8	You feel stuffed, bloated, even nauseous. Some people call this the "Thanksgiving Day" full.

I guarantee it: Your body will get used to eating less food. For some people this adjustment happens quickly, within a matter of days. For others, who have become used to overeating, it may take a week or two—at the most. But trust me, over time your appetite will become smaller and you will be satisfied with a smaller amount of food. In fact, you will find that the amount of food that used to satisfy your appetite at a meal will make you feel stuffed.

Success strategy #6:
Remove overeating triggers

Most of us have overeaten at least once or twice because our eyes were bigger than our stomachs. Part of the problem is letting ourselves get too hungry before a meal (see the next Success Strategy, #7). But how food is presented can also prompt us to overeat. Just picture an inviting banquet spread, or a groaning buffet table: the more types of food in front of us—and the bigger the portions served—the more likely it is we'll overeat. But besides these obvious examples that tempt us to excess, it turns out there are many environmental triggers below our radar screens that catch us unaware and make us overeat.

Take package size for instance. Research shows that if you give people a larger package, they'll pour more, whether it's pasta, vegetable oil, candy or pet food. In fact, if you eat from a larger versus a smaller package, you'll eat 25 percent more! And those extra calories are enough to derail you from your meal plan. Practise the tips below to curb overeating.

BINGE-BUSTING STRATEGIES

- *Use smaller plates.* A few of my clients say this trick really works. Instead of filling a large eleven-inch dinner plate with food, serve less food on a smaller, nine-inch "luncheon" plate. The plate looks full and you'll end up eating less food!
- *Use smaller glassware.* People perceive tall, skinny glasses as holding more liquid than short, stubby glasses. In fact, people drink almost 20 percent more from short, wide glasses than they do from tall, narrow glasses. We look at the height of an object but usually under-account for the width. So when you do drink higher-calorie beverages such as fruit juice or an alcoholic cocktail use tall, skinny glasses. You'll drink less, but think you drank more.
- *Plate your snacks.* Never snack out of the bag or box. When your hand keeps dipping back in for more, you don't get a sense of how much you're actually eating. It just doesn't register. And you will have no idea how many

calories you've consumed. Whether your snack is whole-grain crackers and low-fat cheese, popcorn or apple slices, measure out 1 serving and put it on a plate. And don't forget to consider the calories per serving.

- *Keep tempting treats hidden.* Nearby food makes us nosh. One study found that if office workers had Hershey Kisses on their desk, they ate about 9 per day if the kisses were in a clear bowl, and just 6.5 if they were in an opaque bowl. But if that bowl of chocolates was placed six feet away, the number they ate dropped down to 4 per day. So, if you bring treats into the house for your kids, the secret is to keep them where you can't see them—either at a distance that is inconvenient to reach or hidden away at the back of a cupboard. If possible, don't bring them in the house at all.
- *Keep variety to a minimum.* Variety prompts overeating. That's because we tend to get bored with familiar tastes so stop eating sooner. A study from the University of Illinois found that people who were presented with M&Ms in ten colours ate 30 percent more than when they were given just seven colours. Studies have found the same holds true for pasta shapes and sandwich fillings. The take-home message: When it comes to healthy foods like fruit, keep a variety of them in your kitchen or in a bowl at your desk at work. But if you're treating yourself to a sweet or another higher-calorie food, select just one type to prevent overeating.
- *Snack before you go out.* When you're going out to a restaurant or to a cocktail party, eat a snack before you head out so you don't arrive famished. Taking the edge off your hunger will help prevent overeating. A piece of fruit, a serving of yogurt, a non-fat latte or a bowl of vegetable soup—all are good snack choices.
- *Slow down your pace.* After every bite, put down your knife and fork and chew your food thoroughly. Remember that it takes 20 minutes for your brain to get the signal that your stomach has had enough food. Stop eating when you feel satisfied, before you feel stuffed.

Success strategy #7: Stave off hunger

You might need to employ a few tricks to keep hunger at bay during the first few weeks of following your meal plan until your appetite adjusts to your new calorie intake. Your meal plan has been designed to prevent you from becoming overly hungry between and before meals. Each meal includes a good source of protein to slow digestion and keep you feeling full longer. As well, most of the starchy foods I recommend are also slowly digested, since they're higher in fibre and lower on the glycemic-index scale.

Keep in mind that you *should* feel hungry—just not overly hungry—right before a meal. Feeling a bit hungry is a welcome sign that you're not overeating and that your body is using your food efficiently. People who routinely skip meals or who have a sluggish metabolism often go through the day not feeling hungry at all. Use the following strategies to reduce the likelihood you'll feel too hungry.

HUNGER PREVENTION STRATEGIES

* *Don't skip meals.* And don't skimp at mealtime either. Be sure to eat all the food choices assigned on your meal plan.
* *Eat every three hours.* Eating at regular intervals will keep your energy level stable and hunger at bay. The Longevity Diet Meal Plan gives you two snacks a day. Depending on your schedule, you might have one snack mid-morning and the other in the afternoon. Or, if the lag between lunch and dinner is quite long, you might prefer to put both snacks in the afternoon—one at, say, 3 P.M. and the second at 5:30. And if you're just not a snacker, be sure to add your assigned snack food group choices to breakfast and lunch to hold you over until the next meal.
* *Boost fibre at meals.* Fibre-rich foods like bran cereals, whole grains, legumes, fruit and vegetables can help you stay full on fewer calories. Because fibre slows the passage of food through your digestive tract, the gut sends out satiety signals for a longer period, promoting the feeling of fullness. Fibre-rich foods also take more time to chew, which also contributes to satiety. See Chapter 9, pages 167 to 168, for a list of foods with higher fibre.
* *Fill up on vegetables at meals.* Not only are vegetables low in calories and loaded with anti-aging antioxidants, they also provide fibre to fill you up. Your goal: eat *at least* 2 vegetable servings at lunch and at dinner, and preferably more.
* *Serve vegetable soup as a first course.* Research shows that starting your meal with a broth-based soup (not a cream soup!) can help you to eat 100 fewer calories at the meal that follows. Soup's liquid volume fills up your stomach and activates the stomach's "stretch receptors," sending satiety messages to your brain. Even though the calories are low, the volume of soup makes your stomach do the same amount of work!

- *Drink enough water.* Many of my clients say that drinking water helps them fill up so that they eat less food at a meal. However, studies have not found that drinking water before or with a meal does actually reduce food intake. Even so, it's important to drink the recommended amount of water outlined on the Meal Plan. Besides the fact that your body needs a certain amount of water each day for health, if you feel thirsty you might confuse that sensation with hunger. Sometimes people reach for food when what their body really needs is water.

Success strategy #8: Dine out defensively

Your new meal plan must fit into your life. You need to be able to entertain friends for dinner, dine in restaurants and attend family gatherings that, yes, often celebrate food. And you can, too. You'll likely end up consuming more calories on these occasions than you would if you ate a home-prepared meal, but that's perfectly fine as long as you get back on your meal plan the next meal or the next day. It's the big picture, your overall intake over the days and weeks, that matters.

I always advise my clients to check out a restaurant's menus on its website before they go there to eat. That way they can see what healthy options are available and plan their meal in advance. If you do this too you'll find that knowing what types of foods the restaurant serves helps you ask for a food to be specially prepared. For example, if a dish features breaded, crispy chicken, you'll most certainly be able to request grilled or roasted chicken instead.

Many large chain restaurants provide nutrition information on their websites. I encourage you to look at this and choose your order ahead of time. You just might be shocked at how many calories lurk in seemingly healthy appetizers and entrees. It's not uncommon for an entree to have as many as 1000 calories! (Sodium numbers are even more appalling.) Thanks to hefty-sized portions, it's not hard to eat a day's worth of calories in one meal.

Always practise portion control, no matter how healthy or low-calorie your meal seems. If your meal is too large, don't eat it all—take half home. Ask the waiter to bring a doggie bag when he brings your meal. As soon as it arrives at the table, portion off the extra and put it away. If you leave it sitting on your plate you'll be more likely to eat it! Instead of a large entree, order two appetizers, or an appetizer and a salad, as your meal. Or consider sharing an entree with a friend.

Be assertive when you're dining out. Remember that you're the one paying for your meal. If you don't know what's in a dish or don't know the serving size, ask. Below are plenty more tips to help you save calories when eating out.

DEFENSIVE DINING TIPS

- Cut down on starchy side dishes. Skip the bread basket that comes before the meal. Or better yet, ask that your server doesn't bring it to the table. Order extra vegetables instead of the white potatoes or white rice that comes with the meal. Order a half portion of pasta.
- When ordering meat, fish or chicken, ask that the food either be grilled without butter or prepared lightly with only a little olive oil.
- Choose tomato-based pasta dishes rather than creamy ones. Tomato sauces are much lower in calories than cream-based alfredo sauces, and they contain virtually no saturated fat. (Alfredo and rose sauces are made with whipping cream, which delivers a sizeable amount of saturated fat.) A serving of tomato sauce (1/2 cup/125 ml) counts as a vegetable serving too.
- When ordering soup, stick with broth-based ones instead of cream-based soups or chowders. To increase your intake of magnesium- and fibre-rich legumes, choose minestrone, lentil and bean soups most often.
- Order sandwiches made with whole-grain breads instead of high-fat croissants or white breads.
- Ask for salsa with a baked potato instead of butter, sour cream, cheese or bacon. Salsa is fat-free and very low in calories.
- Order sandwiches without butter or "special sauce." Ask for mustard, which adds flavour but virtually no calories.
- Watch out for healthy-sounding salads. Salad entrees that come laden with cheese, bacon and plenty of dressing can have more fat and calories than an all-dressed burger.
- Order salad dressings, sauces and sour cream "on the side." That way you can control how much you use.
- Request low-fat items even if they are not on the menu—fat-reduced salad dressings, salsa for a baked potato or fresh fruit for dessert.
- If you're craving dessert, opt for something healthy like fresh berries or fruit.
- If you really want the rich dessert, share it with a friend.

You're truly ready to get started on my Longevity Diet! You now have plenty of tips to incorporate my 25 longevity foods into your diet and you've figured out your personal calorie prescription. And, in this chapter, you've learned about eight very important strategies that will help you make this way of eating a *permanent* part of your lifestyle. The many recipes that follow will show you that my Longevity Diet is not only nutritious, it's also delicious. Enjoy and let your journey to a longer, healthy life begin.

PART 4

THE LONGEVITY DIET RECIPES

Contents

Breakfasts
eggs

whole grains

Beverages

Snacks

Salads
vegetables

whole grains and legumes

seafood

Soups

Side dishes
vegetables

whole grains and legumes

Entrees

poultry

fish and seafood

legumes and soy

Salad dressings, condiments and marinades

Muffins

Desserts

Healthy Recipes Featuring Top Longevity Foods

almonds

avocados

beets

berries

black beans and other dried beans

broccoli

cabbage

dark chocolate

flaxseed

green tea

kale

lentils

oats

oranges

pomegranate

red bell peppers

red grapes

salmon and other omega-3-rich foods

soybeans

spinach

sweet potatoes

tomatoes

walnuts

Breakfasts

Eggs

Red Pepper and Asparagus Omelet

Sautéed red bell pepper, red onion and asparagus team up to deliver plenty of flavour and colour in this low-calorie omelet. One serving has only 150 calories and is an excellent source of vitamins C, E and K. Make it for breakfast, or enjoy it as a quick weeknight dinner when you're short on time.

2	eggs	2
2	egg whites	2
1/8 tsp	sea salt	0.5 ml
	freshly ground black pepper, to taste	
2 tsp	canola oil	10 ml
1/4 cup	finely chopped red onion	50 ml
1/2 cup	thinly sliced red pepper strips (about 1/2 pepper)	125 ml
1/2 cup	asparagus stems and spears, cut into 1-inch pieces	125 ml
2	cloves garlic, finely chopped	2

In a large mixing bowl, whisk together eggs, egg whites, salt and pepper until slightly frothy, about 30 seconds. Set aside.

Heat oil in a skillet over medium heat. Add onions; sauté for 8 to 10 minutes till they are soft and transparent. Add red pepper and asparagus; sauté for another 4 to 5 minutes. Add garlic; sauté for another minute. Remove contents from pan and set them aside.

Reheat the skillet over medium heat. Add the egg mixture and cook, without stirring, for 4 to 5 minutes, or until the eggs are set and slightly firm. Run a spatula around the edges of the omelet and under it to loosen it from the pan.

Add the red pepper mixture to half of the omelet's surface, then gently fold the other half of the omelet over it. Continue to cook for 3 to 4 minutes, or until the eggs are slightly golden brown on the outside and firm on the inside.

Remove from heat and serve immediately.

Serves 2.

Per serving (1/2 omelet): 150 cal, 10 g pro, 9 g total fat (2 g saturated fat), 7 g carb, 2 g fibre, 164 mg chol, 255 mg sodium

Excellent source of: vitamin C, vitamin E, vitamin K
Good source of: folate, beta carotene
Low in saturated fat

Soft Scrambled Eggs with Fresh Chives

Substituting egg whites for whole eggs, or using a combination of the two, as in this recipe, is an easy way to cut calories, cholesterol and saturated fat. Unlike egg yolks, egg whites are free of fat and cholesterol and still deliver a hefty dose of high-quality protein, riboflavin and selenium.

2	eggs	2
2	egg whites	2
1 tbsp	low-fat (1% MF or less) milk or soy milk	15 ml
1 tbsp	chopped fresh chives	15 ml
1/8 tsp	sea salt	0.5 ml
	freshly ground black pepper, to taste	
1 tsp	canola oil	5 ml

In a large mixing bowl, whisk together eggs, egg whites, milk, chives, salt and pepper until slightly frothy, about 30 seconds.

Heat the oil in a skillet over medium heat. Add the egg mixture but do not stir until it begins to set on the bottom, about 1 minute, then gently draw a spatula through the eggs to form large curds. Continue cooking until the eggs are cooked through, but still moist, about 5 to 7 minutes.

Serve immediately.

Serves 2.

Per serving: 103 cal, 9 g pro, 7 g total fat (2 g saturated fat), 1 g carb, 0 g fibre, 164 mg chol, 255 mg sodium

Low in saturated fat

Whole Grains

Almond Orange Granola Parfait

The granola in this recipe uses a fraction of the oil and sugar you'll find in store-bought brands. Mixing a small portion of the crunchy blend with low-fat yogurt and fresh berries is a delicious way to keep the calories down at breakfast. Though it's often thought of as a breakfast food, granola doubles as a healthy midday snack.

Tip: Double the granola recipe and keep it in an airtight container for a quick grab-and-go breakfast during the week.

Granola

1/2 cup	rolled oats	125 ml
1/4 cup	sliced almonds	50 ml
1 tbsp	flaxseeds	15 ml
1/4 tsp	almond extract	1 ml
1 tbsp	canola oil	15 ml
1/2 tbsp	maple syrup	7 ml
1 tbsp	freshly squeezed orange juice	15 ml

Parfait

3 cups	low-fat (1% MF or less) plain yogurt	750 ml
2 cups	sliced strawberries	500 ml

Preheat oven to 350°F (180°C).

In a large mixing bowl, toss together oats, almonds and flaxseeds. Add almond extract, oil, maple syrup and orange juice. Stir until the dry ingredients are evenly coated with the orange juice mixture and they begin to clump together.

Spread oat mixture evenly across a large baking sheet. Place the sheet in the oven on the middle rack and bake the mixture for 10 to 12 minutes, or until it begins to brown. Remove from oven; let granola cool on the sheet.

To make parfait, scoop 3/4 cup (175 ml) yogurt into four bowls, top each bowl with 1/2 cup (125 ml) sliced strawberries. Sprinkle with 1/4 cup (50 ml) granola mixture.

Serve immediately.

Serves 4.

Per 1/4 cup (50 ml) granola with 3/4 cup (175 ml) yogurt and 1/2 cup (125 ml) strawberries: 249 cal, 13 g pro, 9 g total fat (1 g saturated fat), 31 g carb, 4 g fibre, 3 mg chol, 134 mg sodium

Excellent source of: vitamin C, calcium, magnesium, potassium
Good source of: vitamin E, folate
Low in sodium
Low in saturated fat
Low in cholesterol
High source of fibre

Cinnamon Stovetop Oatmeal with Fresh Berries

Oats are an excellent source of soluble fibre, which helps prolong feelings of fullness and keep LDL (bad) blood-cholesterol levels in check. This recipe uses quick oats so it's ready in less than 10 minutes, making it a perfect breakfast even for a busy mid-week morning. If you don't have fresh blueberries on hand, other antioxidant-rich berries work just as well, such as blackberries or raspberries.

1-1/2 cups	water	375 ml
1 tbsp	dark brown sugar	15 ml
1/4 tsp	cinnamon	1 ml
1/8 tsp	vanilla extract	0.5 ml
1/8 tsp	salt	0.5 ml
3/4 cup	quick oats	175 ml
1/2 cup	fresh blueberries	125 ml
1/2 cup	sliced strawberries	125 ml

In a saucepan stir together water, brown sugar, cinnamon, vanilla and salt. Bring to a boil over high heat.

When water comes to a rolling boil, add oats and immediately reduce heat to low, while stirring to prevent any clumps. Continue stirring for 1 to 2 minutes, until most of the liquid is absorbed and oats begin to thicken.

Remove from heat. Sprinkle with fresh blueberries.

Serve immediately.

Makes 2 cups (500 ml).

Serves 2.

Per 1 cup (250 ml): 197 cal, 6 g pro, 3 g total fat (1 g saturated fat), 39 g carb, 5 g fibre, 0 mg chol, 166 mg sodium

Good source of: vitamin C, iron
Low in fat
Low in saturated fat
Low in cholesterol
High source of fibre

Field Berry Almond Pancakes

These hearty, stick-to-your-ribs pancakes are packed with oats, almonds and berries. As a result, they are an excellent source of fibre, which will help you feel full all morning long. Their small size means they're ideal for freezing and popping in the toaster for a quick workday breakfast before you dash out the door.

Tip: Fresh or frozen berries work equally well in this recipe.

3/4 cup	whole-wheat flour	175 ml
1/4 cup	all-purpose flour	50 ml
1/3 cup	quick oats	75 ml
1/4 cup	sliced almonds	50 ml
1 tsp	baking powder	5 ml
1/4 tsp	baking soda	1 ml
1/4 tsp	nutmeg	1 ml
1/8 tsp	salt	0.5 ml
4	egg whites	4
3/4 cup	low-fat (1% MF or less) plain yogurt	175 ml
1/4 cup	low-fat (1% MF or less) milk or soy milk	50 ml
1/2 tsp	almond extract	2 ml
1-1/2 tsp	canola oil	7 ml
1/2 cup	blueberries	125 ml
1/2 cup	raspberries	125 ml

In a large mixing bowl combine flours, oats, almonds, baking powder, baking soda, nutmeg and salt. Set aside.

In a large mixing bowl, whisk together egg whites till white and fluffy, about 30 seconds. Add yogurt, milk and almond extract; whisk to combine. Add dry ingredients to bowl, whisk together until ingredients are just combined.

Heat oil in a large skillet over medium-high heat. When pan is hot, reduce heat to medium and pour 1/4 cup (50 ml) batter into pan to make each pancake. Sprinkle each pancake with 2 tbsp (25 ml) berries. When bubbles start to appear at edges of pancakes, about 4 to 5 minutes, flip and continue cooking for another 4 to 5 minutes or until pancakes are brown.

Remove from heat and serve immediately.

Makes 8 pancakes.

Serves 4.

Per 2 pancakes: 255 cal, 13 g pro, 7 g total fat (1 g saturated fat), 38 g carb, 6 g fibre, 2 mg chol, 401 mg sodium

Excellent source of: magnesium
Good source of: vitamin E, calcium, folate, iron, potassium
Low in saturated fat
Low in cholesterol
Very high source of fibre

Rye Breakfast Bars with Flaxseed and Cranberries

Rye flakes (also known as rolled rye) give these high-fibre breakfast bars a lovely nutty flavour, but other grains such as spelt flakes or rolled oats work just as well. I suggest making these ahead of time and storing them in the fridge (they will keep for 5 days) for an easy grab-and-go breakfast during the busy week.

2 cups	rye flakes, such as Bob's Red Mill Creamy Rye Flakes	500 ml
1/2 cup	brown sugar	125 ml
1/3 cup	dried cranberries	75 ml
3 tbsp	ground flaxseed	50 ml
2 tsp	cinnamon	10 ml
1 tsp	ground ginger	5 ml
1 tsp	baking powder	5 ml
1-1/2 cups	low-fat (1% MF or less) milk or soy milk	375 ml
1/2 cup	unsweetened applesauce	125 ml
2 tbsp	canola oil	25 ml
2	egg whites	2
1 tsp	vanilla extract	5 ml

Preheat oven to 375°F (190°C).

Lightly grease a 13 x 9 inch (3.5 L) glass baking dish. Set aside.

In a large mixing bowl combine rye flakes, brown sugar, cranberries, flaxseed, cinnamon, ginger and baking powder.

In another mixing bowl, whisk together milk, applesauce, oil, egg whites and vanilla.

Pour wet ingredients over dry ingredients and mix well to combine.

Pour batter into the greased baking dish. Bake for 30 minutes, or until cooked through, turning once.

When cool, cut into 10 pieces. Serve cold.

Serves 10.

Per bar: 194 cal, 6 g pro, 5 g total fat (1 g saturated fat), 34 g carb, 5 g fibre, 2 mg chol, 64 mg sodium

Low in sodium
Low in saturated fat
Low in cholesterol
High source of fibre

Beverages

Açaí Pomegranate Smoothie

Açaí (pronounced ah-sah-ee) berries and pomegranates are both excellent sources of disease-fighting antioxidants. Here, they team up to make a delicious and vibrant-coloured smoothie. Look for an açaí-pomegranate juice blend in the refrigerator near the produce section of most grocery stores and health food stores.

1 cup	açaí-pomegranate blend, such as Bolthouse Farms	250 ml
1	banana, sliced	1
1 cup	low-fat (1% MF or less) vanilla yogurt	250 ml

In a blender, combine juice, banana and yogurt. Purée until smooth.

Serve cold.

Serves 2.

Per 1 cup (250 ml) serving: 200 cal, 8 g pro, 2 g total fat (1 g saturated fat), 40 g carb, 2 g fibre, 7 mg chol, 101 mg sodium

Good source of: calcium, magnesium, potassium
Low in sodium
Low in fat
Low in saturated fat
Low in cholesterol

Blueberry Raspberry Smoothie

Berries are recognized as superfoods, and for good reason. Studies suggest eating plenty of antioxidant-rich berries can help ward off cancer, heart disease and other age-related conditions. Fresh or frozen berries work equally well in this recipe.

Tip: Swap the blueberries for blackberries or the raspberries for strawberries for a delicious variation.

1/2 cup	blueberries	125 ml
1/2 cup	raspberries	125 ml
1/2 cup	low-fat (1% MF or less) plain yogurt or soy yogurt	125 ml
1/2 cup	low-fat (1% MF or less) milk or soy milk	125 ml
1/2 cup	100% pure unsweetened orange juice	125 ml
1/2 tsp	grated fresh ginger root	2 ml

Combine all ingredients in a blender and purée until smooth.

Serve cold.

Serves 2.

Per 1 cup (250 ml) serving: 122 cal, 6 g pro, 1 g total fat (0 g saturated fat), 23 g carb, 3 g fibre, 4 mg chol, 72 mg sodium

Excellent source of: vitamin C
Good source of: vitamin D, calcium, folate, potassium
Low in sodium
Low in fat
Low in saturated fat
Low in cholesterol

Lemon Iced Green Tea

This refreshing iced tea has very little sugar, making it a much healthier alternative to store-bought versions. For variety, use different types of green tea, including tea leaves blended with dried fruit or flowers.

6	green tea bags	6
6 cups	boiling water	1.5 L
1/4 cup	lemon juice	50 ml
2 tbsp	honey	25 ml
	fresh mint leaves, optional	

Pour boiling water over tea bags in a large pitcher. Steep for 5 to 10 minutes, depending on desired strength.

Remove tea bags; stir in lemon juice and honey.

Let tea cool completely, then pour into 6 tall ice-filled glasses. Garnish with fresh mint leaves and serve immediately.

Makes 6 cups (1.5 L).

Serves 6.

Per 1 cup (250 ml): 30 cal, 0 g pro, 0 g total fat (0 g saturated fat), 8 g carb, 0 g fibre, 0 mg chol, 3 mg sodium

Pumpkin Orange Banana Smoothie

Canada's Food Guide recommends eating at least one bright orange vegetable, such as pumpkin, each day. Smooth and creamy, this unconventional smoothie is as delicious as it is nutritious. Its deep orange colour is a clear sign this smoothie is brimming with antioxidants—it's packed with beta carotene and vitamin C.

Tip: Pure pumpkin purée is sold in a can in grocery stores. Unlike pumpkin pie filling, pure pumpkin purée does not have added sugar, fat or spices. Pure pumpkin purée has about one-third of the calories of pumpkin pie filling.

1 cup	low-fat (1% MF or less) milk or soy milk	250 ml
1/2 cup	pure pumpkin purée	125 ml
1/2 cup	100% pure unsweetened orange juice	125 ml
1	banana, sliced	1
4	ice cubes, optional	4

Combine all ingredients in a blender and purée until smooth. If you are making this to enjoy later in the day, chill until serving.

Serves 2.

Per 1 cup (250 ml) serving: 153 cal, 6 g pro, 2 g total fat (1 g saturated fat), 31 g carb, 3 g fibre, 6 mg chol, 58 mg sodium

Excellent source of: vitamin C, vitamin D, potassium, beta carotene
Good source of: calcium, magnesium, folate
Low in sodium
Low in fat
Low in saturated fat
Low in cholesterol

Strawberry Kiwi Smoothie

My taste-testers loved this delicious vitamin C–rich smoothie! You can't go wrong with the combination of strawberries, kiwifruit and mango juice. One serving of this smoothie contains more than twice the recommended daily intake of vitamin C, an antioxidant that helps prevent telomeres from shrinking, a marker of biological aging.

Tip: Choose a brand of mango juice with no added sugar, such as Ceres Fruit Juices mango juice.

1 cup	sliced strawberries	250 ml
1 cup	100% pure mango juice	250 ml
1/2 cup	low-fat (1% MF or less) plain yogurt or soy yogurt	125 ml
2	kiwifruit, peeled	2
4	ice cubes, optional	4

Combine all ingredients in a blender and purée until smooth. If you are making this to enjoy later in the day, chill until serving.

Serves 2.

Per 1-1/4 cup (300 ml) serving: 166 cal, 5 g pro, 1 g total fat (0 g saturated fat), 38 g carb, 4 g fibre, 1 mg chol, 53 mg sodium

Excellent source of: vitamin C, vitamin K
Good source of: vitamin E, potassium
Low in sodium
Low in fat
Low in saturated fat
Low in cholesterol
High source of fibre

Snacks

Black Bean Hummus

Hummus has a long history in the Middle East where it is traditionally made with chickpeas. This version uses black beans instead; gram for gram, black beans have 15 percent more fibre and 25 percent fewer calories than chickpeas. And they beat out other beans when it comes to antioxidants. This hummus is a delicious dip for vegetables and also makes a tasty spread on whole-grain crackers.

1	can (19 oz/540 ml) black beans, drained and rinsed	1
1/4 cup	tahini	50 ml
3 tbsp	freshly squeezed lemon juice	50 ml
2 tbsp	olive oil	25 ml
1	clove garlic, crushed	1
1/8 tsp	red pepper flakes	0.5 ml
1 tbsp	finely chopped parsley, optional	15 ml

In a mixing bowl combine black beans, tahini, lemon juice, olive oil, garlic and red pepper flakes. Using the back of a fork, mash ingredients until smooth.

Alternatively, place ingredients in a food processor and pulse until smooth.

Place in a serving bowl and garnish with fresh parsley. Serve cold.

Serves 8.

Per 1/4 cup (50 ml) serving: 128 cal, 5 g pro, 8 g total fat (1 g saturated fat), 12 g carb, 4 g fibre, 0 mg chol, 219 mg sodium

Good source of: magnesium, folate
Low in saturated fat
Low in cholesterol
High source of fibre

Kale "Chips" with Sea Salt

These yummy "chips" are a far healthier alternative to potato chips and provide an easy way to boost your intake of leafy green vegetables. Kale is an excellent source of beta carotene and one serving of these chips provides more than a day's worth of vitamins C and K. Kale's sturdy leaves are ideally suited to making these crispy chips. I suggest making extra—they won't last long!

4 cups	kale, washed, trimmed and torn into bite-sized pieces	1 L
1 tbsp	olive oil	15 ml
1/2 tsp	sea salt	2 ml
	freshly ground black pepper, to taste	

Preheat oven to 350°F (180°C).

In a large mixing bowl toss together kale, olive oil, salt and pepper. Use clean hands to gently rub oil into kale.

Spread kale on a large baking sheet. Bake for 15 minutes, or until kale is crispy.

Cool and serve.

Serves 4.

Per 1 cup (250 ml) serving: 63 cal, 2 g pro, 4 g total fat (1 g saturated fat), 7 g carb, 2 g fibre, 0 mg chol, 321 mg sodium

Excellent source of: vitamin C, vitamin K, beta carotene
Good source of: vitamin E
Low in saturated fat
Low in cholesterol

Sweet Potato Cranberry Drop Biscuits

Somewhere between cookies and scones, these soft and chewy biscuits are a real winner, with only 110 calories and less than a gram of saturated fat per serving. They're also an excellent source of beta carotene. If you don't have spelt flakes, use rolled oats instead—they work well and taste just as great.

Tip: To prepare sweet potato for mashing, begin by covering peeled and diced sweet potato with water in a small saucepan. Bring to boil; cover and reduce heat to low. Simmer for 10 minutes or until sweet potato is soft when pierced with a fork. Remove pan from heat; drain liquid and mash the potato with the back of a fork. Be sure to cool sweet potato completely before adding it to biscuit dough. One medium-sized sweet potato will yield roughly 2 cups (500 ml) of mashed potato.

1 cup	whole-wheat flour	250 ml
1 cup	all-purpose flour	250 ml
1 cup	spelt flakes	250 ml
1/2 cup	dried sweetened cranberries	125 ml
1 tsp	baking powder	5 ml
1/2 tsp	baking soda	2 ml
1/2 tsp	ground cloves	2 ml
1/2 tsp	ground nutmeg	2 ml
1/4 tsp	salt	1 ml
2	egg whites	2
3/4 cup	brown sugar	175 ml
1/4 cup	non-hydrogenated soft margarine	50 ml
1 cup	mashed sweet potato	250 ml
1/4 cup	low-fat (1% MF or less) milk or soy milk	50 ml
1 tsp	vanilla extract	5 ml

Preheat oven to 350°F (180°C).

In a large mixing bowl, combine flour, spelt flakes, cranberries, baking powder, baking soda, cloves, nutmeg and salt.

In another large mixing bowl, whisk together egg whites, brown sugar and margarine until creamy and smooth. Add sweet potato, milk and vanilla. Whisk again until all ingredients are blended.

Pour dry ingredients into mixing bowl with wet ingredients; fold together until just combined.

To make biscuits, drop dough onto baking sheet in dollops of about 2 tbsp (25 ml), three inches apart, and gently flatten dough with moist fingers. Bake for 14 to 16 minutes, turning once, till the biscuits are golden brown on the bottom.

Makes 24 biscuits.

Per biscuit: 110 cal, 2 g pro, 2 g total fat (1 g saturated fat), 21 g carb, 2 g fibre, 0 mg chol, 101 mg sodium

Excellent source of: beta carotene
Low in sodium
Low in fat
Low in saturated fat
Low in cholesterol

Salads

Vegetables

Arugula, Red Grape and Toasted Walnut Salad

Walnut oil may be more expensive than olive and canola oil, but it's well worth the extra cost thanks to its exceptional ALA content (an omega-3 fat) and rich nutty flavour. Walnut oil can vary widely in flavour; for the best-tasting oil, look for a product that's unrefined.

Tip: Walnut oil is susceptible to damage from heat and light and has a limited shelf life. Keep it in a cool, dark place or in the refrigerator for up to 6 months.

Salad

1/2 cup	coarsely chopped walnut halves	125 ml
4 cups	tightly packed arugula (about 5 oz/142 g)	1 L
2 cups	red grapes, halved	500 ml

Dressing

4 tbsp	walnut oil	60 ml
2 tbsp	freshly squeezed lemon juice	25 ml
2 tsp	honey	10 ml
1 tsp	whole-grain mustard	5ml

Preheat oven to 350°F (180°C).

Arrange walnuts on a baking sheet and place in the oven for 5 to 7 minutes, or until fragrant; remove from heat and cool.

In a large mixing bowl toss together arugula, grapes and toasted walnuts; set aside.

In a small mixing bowl whisk together walnut oil, lemon juice, honey and mustard.

Drizzle dressing over salad; serve immediately.

Serves 6.

Per 1 cup (250 ml) salad and 1 tbsp (15 ml) dressing: 182 cal, 2 g pro, 15 g total fat (1 g saturated fat), 13 g carb, 1 g fibre, 0 mg chol, 15 mg sodium

Excellent source of: vitamin K
Low in sodium
Low in saturated fat
Low in cholesterol

Broccoli with Sesame Thai Dressing

This combination of rice wine vinegar, sesame oil, ginger and sesame seeds tastes delicious on broccoli. Steam the broccoli until it's still slightly crunchy—if it's overcooked it will get soggy sitting in the dressing. This salad can be eaten warm or cold.

1 tsp	canola oil	5 ml
3	cloves garlic, chopped	3
3 cups	broccoli, cut into bite-sized pieces	750 ml
1 tbsp	seasoned rice wine vinegar	15 ml
1 tbsp	dark sesame oil	15 ml
1 tsp	ginger root, chopped	5 ml
1 tbsp	sesame seeds	15 ml

In a skillet, heat oil over medium heat. Add garlic and broccoli, and sauté until garlic is fragrant and broccoli is still tender, about 4 to 5 minutes.

Empty contents of skillet into a large bowl, and allow to cool.

Meanwhile, in a small bowl, whisk together rice wine vinegar, sesame oil and ginger root. Drizzle over broccoli and garlic, sprinkle with sesame seeds.

Serves 6.

Per serving: 127 cal, 10 g pro, 5 g total fat (1 g saturated fat), 18 g carb, 8 g fibre, 0 mg chol, 86 mg sodium

Excellent source of: vitamin A, vitamin C, vitamin K, folate, iron, magnesium
Good source of: potassium
Very high in fibre

Cabbage and Carrot Coleslaw

Studies show that eating plenty of cruciferous vegetables, including cabbage, can help protect against breast, lung, prostate, bladder and pancreatic cancers, as well as boost heart health and ward off stroke. Best of all, cabbage is available year-round and is one of the least expensive vegetables.

1/4 cup	rice vinegar	50 ml
2 tbsp	olive oil	25 ml
1 tbsp	sugar	15 ml
2 cups	shredded purple cabbage	500 ml
2 cups	shredded green cabbage	500 ml
2 cups	shredded carrot (about 2 medium)	500 ml
1/4 tsp	sea salt	1 ml
	freshly ground black pepper, to taste	

In a large mixing bowl, combine rice vinegar, olive oil and sugar. Whisk together until sugar is dissolved.

Add purple cabbage, green cabbage and carrot. Toss until cabbage and carrot are evenly coated with dressing. Season with salt and pepper.

Cover and refrigerate for at least 2 hours before serving.

Serves 6.

Per 1 cup (250 ml) serving: 76 cal, 1 g pro, 5 g total fat (1 g saturated fat), 9 g carb, 2 g fibre, 0 mg chol, 134 mg sodium

Excellent source of: vitamin K, beta carotene
Good source of: vitamin C
Low in sodium
Low in saturated fat
Low in cholesterol

Crunchy Broccoli Salad with Apple Dijon Dressing

This tangy salad is low in calories and it's packed with nutrients, including vitamin C, vitamin K and folate. Leave the skin on the apple for a boost of colour and soluble fibre.

Tip: This salad tastes best when made a day in advance.

4 cups	broccoli florets, cut into bite-sized pieces	1 L
1 cup	sliced Red Delicious apple (about 1 medium)	250 ml
1 cup	red grapes, halved	250 ml
1/4 cup	apple cider vinegar	50 ml
2 tbsp	100% pure apple juice	25 ml
2 tbsp	olive oil	25 ml
1 tsp	grainy Dijon mustard	5 ml
1/4 tsp	salt	1 ml
	freshly ground black pepper, to taste	

In a large mixing bowl, combine broccoli florets, apple and grapes.

In a small mixing bowl, whisk together apple cider vinegar, apple juice, olive oil, mustard, salt and pepper.

Pour dressing over broccoli mixture and stir to combine. Cover and refrigerate for at least 2 hours before serving.

Serves 4.

Per 1-1/2 cup (375 ml) serving: 145 cal, 3 g pro, 7 g total fat (1 g saturated fat), 20 g carb, 3 g fibre, 0 mg chol, 194 mg sodium

Excellent source of: vitamin C, vitamin K, folate
Good source of: vitamin E, potassium
Low in saturated fat
Low in cholesterol

Fig and Roasted Walnut Salad

Dried figs, red onion and roasted walnut pieces not only give this salad a rich helping of alpha-linolenic acid (an omega-3 fat), but also plenty of flavour and texture.

1/4 cup	walnut pieces	50 ml
12	dried figs, cut into eighths	12
8 cups	spinach (about 1 lb/454 g)	2 L
1/2 cup	red onion, sliced	125 ml
1/4 cup	crumbled feta cheese	50 ml

Preheat oven to 350°F (180°C).

Place walnut pieces on a baking sheet and place in oven for 5 to 7 minutes, or until nuts are golden brown and fragrant. Remove from heat and cool.

In a large salad bowl, toss figs, spinach, onion, roasted walnuts and feta cheese.

Drizzle with Honey Balsamic Dressing (p. 305) or another reduced fat dressing.

Serves 6.

Per 1 serving salad (1-1/2 cups/375 ml) without dressing: 131 cal, 5 g pro, 8 g total fat (1 g saturated fat), 14 g carb, 3 g fibre, 6 mg chol, 102 mg sodium

Per 1 serving salad with 1 tbsp (15 ml) Honey Balsamic Dressing: 205 cal, 5 g pro, 14 g total fat (2 g saturated fat), 18 g carb, 3 g fibre, 6 mg chol, 119 mg sodium

With dressing:
Excellent source of: vitamin A, vitamin K, magnesium
Good source of: potassium
Low in sodium
Low in saturated fat
Low in cholesterol

Whole Grains and Legumes

Black Bean and Avocado Salad
with Toasted Cumin Dressing

Black beans and avocados team up to bring plenty of longevity nutrients to this salad, including fibre, folate, potassium and heart-healthy monounsaturated fat. Purchase avocados a few days before making this salad to give them time to ripen. You may also quicken the ripening process by putting them in a paper bag with a banana or apple.

Salad

2	cans (19 oz/540 ml) black beans, drained and rinsed	2
1 cup	finely chopped red pepper	250 ml
1/2 cup	finely chopped cilantro	125 ml
1/4 cup	chopped green onion	50 ml
2	avocados, diced	2

Dressing

1 tbsp	cumin seeds	15 ml
1/3 cup	freshly squeezed lime juice	75 ml
2 tbsp	olive oil	25 ml
2	cloves garlic, crushed	2
1/2 tsp	red pepper flakes	2 ml
	freshly ground black pepper, to taste	

In a large mixing bowl combine black beans, red pepper, cilantro, green onions and avocados; gently toss to combine. Set aside.

Heat a skillet over high heat; add cumin seeds and toast until fragrant, about 2 minutes. Remove from heat and cool.

In a small mixing bowl, whisk together toasted cumin seeds, lime juice, olive oil, garlic, red pepper flakes and pepper.

Pour dressing over black bean mixture; toss to coat.

Serves 8.

Per 3/4 cup (175 ml) serving: 203 cal, 8 g pro, 9 g total fat (1 g saturated fat), 24 g carb, 11 g fibre, 0 mg chol, 438 mg sodium

Excellent source of: vitamin C, vitamin E, vitamin K, folate, potassium
Good source of: magnesium, iron
Low in saturated fat
Low in cholesterol
Very high source of fibre

Lentil Salad with Citrus Yogurt Dressing

Lentils may be small in size but they pack a powerful punch when it comes to nutrition. A member of the legume family, lentils are loaded with folate, iron, potassium, thiamin and fibre. Here they're combined with antioxidant-rich orange segments, orange bell pepper and cilantro for a colourful and disease-fighting salad.

Salad

3 cups	water	750 ml
1-1/2 cups	green lentils, rinsed	375 ml
1/4 cup	freshly squeezed lemon juice	50 ml
2 cups	diced orange segments	500 ml
1-1/2 cups	finely chopped orange bell pepper	375 ml
1-1/2 cups	diced cucumber	375 ml
1 cup	finely chopped cilantro	250 ml
3 tbsp	freshly squeezed lemon juice	50 ml
1/2 tsp	salt	2 ml
1/4 tsp	cayenne pepper	1 ml

Dressing

1/2 cup	low-fat (1% MF or less) plain yogurt	125 ml
1/4 cup	freshly squeezed orange juice	50 ml
1 tbsp	honey	15 ml

Heat water and lemon juice in a saucepan over high heat; bring to a boil. Add lentils; stir and bring back to a boil. Cover with a lid, reduce heat to low; simmer until lentils are cooked, but still tender, about 20 to 22 minutes. Drain any excess liquid. Set aside to cool.

In a large mixing bowl, combine cooked lentils with orange segments, bell peppers, cucumber, cilantro, lemon juice, salt and cayenne pepper. Toss to combine.

In a small mixing bowl, whisk together yogurt, orange juice and honey.

Drizzle honey mixture over lentil salad. Toss to combine.

Serve cold.

Serves 6.

Per 1-1/2 cup (375 ml) serving: 224 cal, 12 g pro, 1 g total fat (0 g saturated fat), 44 g carb, 9 g fibre, 0 mg chol, 221 mg sodium

Excellent source of: vitamin C, potassium
Good source of: vitamin K, iron, beta carotene
Low in fat
Low in saturated fat
Low in cholesterol
Very high source of fibre

Salmon Quinoa Salad with Spicy Ginger Dressing

This simple salad is big on taste and packed with nutrients. One serving contains more than a day's worth of vitamins A, B12, C and K and a whopping 9 grams of fibre. I recommend dressing the salad just prior to serving to prevent it from going soggy.

Tip: Look for quinoa, an ancient grain, in natural food stores and large supermarkets. It's usually sold next to the rice.

Salad

1 cup	water	250 ml
1/2 cup	quinoa	125 ml
8 cups	spinach (about 1 lb/454 g)	2 L
2	cans (7.5 oz/213 g each) salmon, drained	2
2 cups	sliced red pepper	500 ml
2 cups	grated carrot	500 ml

Dressing

4 tbsp	rice vinegar	60 ml
2 tbsp	honey	25 ml
1 tbsp	grated fresh ginger root	15 ml
1 tbsp	olive oil	15 ml

In a small saucepan bring water to a boil over high heat. Add quinoa, stir, then cover and simmer over low heat until quinoa is cooked and all of the moisture is absorbed, about 12 to 15 minutes. Remove lid, fluff quinoa with a fork; set aside to cool.

In a large mixing bowl toss cooled quinoa, spinach, salmon, red pepper and carrot.

In a small mixing bowl, whisk together rice vinegar, honey, ginger and olive oil.

Drizzle salad with dressing; toss to coat.

Serve immediately.

Serves 4.

Per 3 cups (750 ml) salad and 2 tbsp (25 ml) dressing: 364 cal, 30 g pro, 11 g total fat (2 g saturated fat), 37 g carb, 7 g fibre, 42 mg chol, 218 mg sodium

Excellent source of: vitamin C, vitamin D, vitamin E, vitamin K, calcium, magnesium, folate, iron, potassium, beta carotene
Very high source of fibre

Wheat Berry and Pomegranate Salad with Maple Dijon Dressing

Taste-testers loved this salad! The pomegranate seeds add a touch of sweetness, while the arugula lends a peppery taste. And the wheat berries, a whole grain, provide a nutty flavour and make this salad an excellent source of fibre.

Tip: Removing the seeds from a pomegranate can be a messy job. The best way to seed a pomegranate is to slice it into quarters. Using your hands, gently split open the fruit and use your fingers to gently pry the seeds away from the peel and white membrane. An easy way to separate the seeds from the membrane is to drop the seeds into a bowl of cold water—the seeds will sink to the bottom, and the membrane will float to the top.

Salad

1-1/2 cups	wheat berries, rinsed	375 ml
3 cups	water	750 ml
1-1/3 cups	diced Red Delicious apple, with skin on (about 1 large)	325 ml
1 cup	pomegranate seeds (about 2 medium)	250 ml
1/4 cup	sliced green onions	50 ml
1-1/2 cups	coarsely chopped arugula	375 ml

Dressing

3 tbsp	olive oil	50 ml
5 tbsp	apple cider vinegar	65 ml
2 tbsp	maple syrup	25 ml
1 tbsp	grainy Dijon mustard	15 ml
4 tbsp	100% pure unsweetened apple juice	60 ml
1/4 tsp	sea salt	1 ml
	freshly ground black pepper, to taste	

In a medium saucepan, bring water to a boil over high heat. Add wheat berries, stir, cover and simmer over low heat until wheat berries are tender, but still chewy, about 30 to 40 minutes. Remove from heat and drain any excess water. Rinse wheat berries under cold water.

In a large mixing bowl combine cooked wheat berries, apple, pomegranate seeds, green onions and arugula.

In a small mixing bowl whisk together olive oil, apple cider vinegar, maple syrup, mustard, apple juice, salt and pepper.

Pour dressing over wheat berry salad; toss to coat.

Cover and refrigerate for at least 2 hours before serving.

Serves 8.

Per 1 cup (250 ml) serving: 215 cal, 5 g pro, 6 g total fat (1 g saturated fat), 38 g carb, 6 g fibre, 0 mg chol, 103 mg sodium

Good source of: vitamin K
Low in sodium
Low in saturated fat
Low in cholesterol
Very high source of fibre

Seafood

Shrimp, Mango and Avocado Salad

If you avoid eating avocados due to their high fat content, think again. Avocados are an exceptional source of monounsaturated fat, which can help lower LDL cholesterol and boost heart health. What's more, avocados are also an excellent source of folate and potassium. Just stop at one helping to stay within your daily calorie limit!

2	avocados, peeled and diced	2
2	mangos, peeled and diced	2
1/3 cup	freshly squeezed lime juice	75 ml
1 tbsp	olive oil	15 ml
1/8 tsp	red pepper flakes	0.5 ml
1/4 tsp	sea salt	1 ml
1/2 lb	large cooked shrimp	226 g
2 tbsp	sliced green onion	25 ml
2 tbsp	finely chopped mint	25 ml
1/2 cup	finely chopped cilantro	125 ml

In a large mixing bowl combine avocado, mango, lime juice, olive oil, red pepper flakes, salt and shrimp. Gently toss to combine.

Sprinkle shrimp mixture with green onions, mint and cilantro.

Serve cold.

Serves 6.

Per 3/4 cup (175 ml) serving: 183 cal, 9 g pro, 10 g total fat (1 g saturated fat), 17 g carb, 5 g fibre, 74 mg chol, 189 mg sodium

Excellent source of: vitamin C, vitamin E, vitamin K, folate
Good source of: potassium
Low in saturated fat
High source of fibre

Soups

Beet, Apple and Ginger Soup

Beets may be well known for their deep reddish-purple hue, but it's their exceptional betaine and folate content that gives them top marks as a longevity food. One half-cup (125 ml) of cooked beets contains more than 30 percent of the recommended daily intake of folate. This quick and simple soup uses roasted beets to play up their natural sweetness.

Tip: This soup looks great when garnished with something to contrast its deep purple colour; try a dollop of low-fat yogurt or some shredded apple.

2	large beets, trimmed, peeled and quartered (about 1.8 lb/0.8 kg)	2
2 tbsp	canola oil	25 ml
1 cup	chopped onion	250 ml
5 cups	vegetable stock	1.25 L
2-1/2 cups	diced Red Delicious apple, peeled	625 ml
2 tbsp	minced ginger root	25 ml

Preheat oven to 375°F (190°C).

Rub beets with 1 tbsp (15 ml) canola oil; arrange on a baking sheet. Place in the oven; bake for 60 minutes, or until beets can be easily pierced with a fork but are still firm.

Remove from heat, cool and dice into 1-inch (2.5 cm) pieces.

In a large saucepan heat 1 tbsp (15 ml) canola oil over medium heat. Add onions and sauté for 8 to 10 minutes, or until golden brown. Add stock, diced beets, apples and ginger.

Cover and bring to a boil. Reduce heat and simmer for 20 minutes.

Using a hand blender, purée soup until smooth.

Serve warm.

Serves 6.

Per 1 cup (250 ml) serving: 135 cal, 3 g pro, 5 g total fat (0 g saturated fat), 21 g carb, 4 g fibre, 0 mg chol, 450 mg sodium

Excellent source of: folate
Good source of: magnesium, potassium
Low in saturated fat
Low in cholesterol
High source of fibre

Fresh Tomato Soup with Garlic and Basil

This light and healthy soup tastes best when made with fresh, locally grown tomatoes, in abundance during the summer months. This recipe clocks in at less than 100 calories and about 300 mg of sodium per serving—a fraction of the sodium in most store-bought brands.

1 tbsp	canola oil	15 ml
1 cup	chopped onions	250 ml
3	cloves garlic, finely chopped	3
6 cups	chopped fresh tomatoes	1.5 L
2 cups	water	500 ml
1/4 cup	fresh basil leaves, loosely packed	50 ml
1/2 tsp	salt	2 ml
	freshly ground black pepper, to taste	

Heat oil in a large saucepan over medium heat. Add onions; sauté for 8 to 10 minutes. Add garlic; sauté for another minute.

Add tomatoes, water, basil, salt and pepper. Cover and simmer over medium-low heat for 30 minutes.

Remove from heat, purée with a hand blender until smooth.

Serve hot.

Serves 4.

Per 1-1/2 cup (375 ml) serving: 84 cal, 2 g pro, 4 g total fat (0 g saturated fat), 12 g carb, 3 g fibre, 0 mg chol, 306 mg sodium

Excellent source of: vitamin K
Good source of: vitamin C, folate, potassium, beta carotene
Low in saturated fat
Low in cholesterol

Lemon Chickpea Soup

This high-fibre soup makes a perfect midday meal when combined with a whole-grain roll and side salad. If you don't have chickpeas, other mild-tasting beans work just as well, including white kidney beans.

2 tbsp	canola oil	25 ml
1 cup	diced onion	250 ml
1 cup	diced celery	250 ml
1 cup	finely diced carrots	250 ml
3	cloves garlic, finely chopped	3
6 cups	water	1.5 L
1/2 cup	white wine	125 ml
3 tbsp	rice vinegar	50 ml
2 tbsp	freshly squeezed lemon juice	25 ml
1	can (19 oz/540 ml) chickpeas, drained and rinsed	1
1	chicken or vegetable bouillon cube (11 g)	1
3	bay leaves	3

Heat oil in a large saucepan over medium heat.

Add onions; sauté for 8 to 10 minutes. Add celery and carrots; sauté for another 3 to 4 minutes. Add garlic; sauté for another minute.

Add water, wine, rice vinegar, lemon juice, chickpeas, bouillon and bay leaves. Cover and simmer over medium-low heat for 30 minutes.

Serve hot.

Serves 6.

Per 1-1/2 cup (375 ml) serving: 174 cal, 5 g pro, 6 g total fat (1 g saturated fat), 24 g carb, 5 g fibre, 0 mg chol, 600 mg sodium

Excellent source of: folate, beta carotene
Good source of: vitamin K
Low in saturated fat
Low in cholesterol
High source of fibre

Red Lentil Soup

Unlike some other dried legumes, which require a long soaking time, red lentils are surprisingly quick and easy to prepare. Best of all, they are high in iron and folate and an excellent source of fibre.

2 tbsp	canola oil	25 ml
2 cups	chopped onions, about 1 large	500 ml
2	cloves garlic, finely chopped	2
6 cups	water	1.5 L
1 cup	raw red lentils, rinsed	250 ml
1	chicken bouillon cube (11 g)	1
1/2 tsp	ground cumin	2 ml
1/2 tsp	turmeric	2 ml
1/4 cup	lemon juice, freshly squeezed	50 ml

Heat oil in a large saucepan over medium heat. Add onions; sauté for 8 to 10 minutes. Add garlic, sauté for another minute.

Add water, lentils, chicken bouillon, cumin and turmeric. Cover and simmer over medium-low heat for 30 minutes, or until lentils are cooked through.

Remove from heat, purée with a hand blender until smooth. Stir in lemon juice.

Serve hot.

Serves 4.

Per 1-1/2 cup (375 ml) serving: 271 cal, 13 g pro, 8 g total fat (1 g saturated fat), 38 g carb, 6 g fibre, 0 mg chol, 525 mg sodium

Excellent source of: folate, iron
Good source of: vitamin E, magnesium, potassium
Low in saturated fat
Low in cholesterol
Very high source of fibre

Roasted Garlic and Butternut Squash Soup

The bright orange colour of this soup is an indicator of its exceptional phyto-chemical content. Thanks to the butternut squash, it's packed with beta carotene as well as vitamins C and E. Even better, it contains less than 400 milligrams of sodium per serving, much less than in store-bought prepared soups.

2	heads garlic	2
1	medium butternut squash (about 1 kg)	1
1 tsp + 2 tbsp	canola oil	30 ml
2 cups	chopped onions	500 ml
6 cups	water	1.5 L
1	chicken bouillon cube (11 g)	1

Preheat oven to 375°F (190°C).

Gently remove papery skin from garlic bulbs and slice off a quarter-inch (5 mm) from the top of each. Place garlic on a baking sheet and drizzle with 1/4 tsp (1 ml) of the oil.

Slice squash in half lengthwise and scoop out seeds. Place squash cut-side up on the baking sheet with the garlic. Drizzle squash with 3/4 tsp (3 ml) of the oil.

Place baking sheet in oven; bake for 60 to 70 minutes, or until squash is cooked through and can easily be pierced with a fork.

Meanwhile, heat the last 2 tbsp (25 ml) of the oil in a large saucepan over medium heat. Add onions and gently sauté over medium-low heat until onions begin to brown and caramelize, about 20 to 30 minutes. Add water and chicken bouillon; bring to a boil.

Meanwhile, gently scoop out flesh of butternut squash and add to the saucepan.

Gently squeeze each clove of roasted garlic out of the skin; add to saucepan with squash.

Cover saucepan and simmer over low heat for 20 minutes.

Remove from heat, purée with a hand blender until smooth.

Serve hot.

Serves 6.

Per 1-1/3 cup (325 ml) serving: 139 cal, 3 g pro, 6 g total fat (0 g saturated fat), 23 g carb, 3 g fibre, 0 mg chol, 354 mg sodium

Excellent source of: vitamin E, beta carotene
Good source of: vitamin C, magnesium, folate, potassium
Low in saturated fat
Low in cholesterol

Sweet Potato Soup with Maple-Glazed Walnuts

This recipe provides a simple way to get your daily serving of bright orange vegetables. With both sweet potatoes and carrots, this soup is packed with the powerful antioxidant beta carotene. One serving contains a whopping 13 milligrams! It's also a good source of fibre, vitamin K and potassium.

Soup

2 tbsp	canola oil	25 ml
1 cup	diced onion	250 ml
1	sweet potato, peeled and diced (about 1.5 lb/0.67 kg)	1
2 cups	chopped carrots	500 ml
6 cups	water	1.5 L
1	chicken or vegetable bouillon cube (11 g)	1
1 tsp	nutmeg	5 ml
1 tsp	grated fresh ginger root	5 ml
	freshly ground black pepper, to taste	

Maple-glazed walnuts

1/4 cup	coarsely chopped walnuts	50 ml
1 tbsp	maple syrup	15 ml

Heat oil in a large saucepan over medium heat. Add onions; sauté for 8 to 10 minutes.

Add sweet potato, carrots, water, bouillon, nutmeg, ginger and pepper. Cover and simmer over medium-low heat for 30 to 40 minutes.

Meanwhile, in a small mixing bowl combine walnuts and maple syrup; toss to coat. Heat a skillet over medium heat; add walnut mixture and toast until fragrant and sticky, about 3 to 4 minutes. Set aside to cool.

When sweet potatoes and carrots are soft, remove from heat, purée with a hand blender until smooth.

Serve hot. Garnish soup with glazed walnuts.

Serves 6.

Per 1-1/3 cup (325 ml) soup and 1 tbsp (15 ml) walnuts: 207 cal, 3 g pro, 8 g total fat (1 g saturated fat), 33 g carb, 5 g fibre, 0 mg chol, 409 mg sodium

Excellent source of: potassium, beta carotene
Good source of: vitamin E, vitamin K, magnesium
Low in saturated fat
Low in cholesterol
High source of fibre

Side Dishes

Vegetables

Balsamic Grilled Bell Peppers

This recipe plays up the bright colours and sweet taste of bell peppers. I recommend using a mix of red, orange and yellow peppers—since they are the most colourful and contain the most vitamin C. Each serving contains less than 60 calories and 284 milligrams of vitamin C—more than half the amount I recommend for preventing age-related disease!

4	bell peppers	4
2 tsp	olive oil	10 ml
1 tbsp	balsamic vinegar	15 ml
1/8 tsp	sea salt	0.5 ml
	freshly ground black pepper, to taste	

Preheat grill over low heat.

Cut peppers in half lengthwise; remove tops, inner ribs and seeds.

In a small mixing bowl, combine olive oil, vinegar, salt and pepper. Add pepper, toss to coat. Set aside for 10 minutes.

Place peppers on grill; reserve any leftover marinade. Cook peppers for 8 to 10 minutes, turning two or three times.

Remove from heat, toss with reserved marinade. Serve warm.

Serves 4.

Per 2 pepper halves: 64 cal, 2 g pro, 3 g total fat (0 g saturated fat), 10 g carb, 2 g fibre, 0 mg chol, 80 mg sodium

Excellent source of: vitamin C
Good source: beta carotene
Low in sodium
Low in fat
Low in saturated fat
Low in cholesterol

Roasted Beets with Honey Balsamic Glaze

The same pigment that gives beets their vibrant colour is also responsible for many of their potent cancer-fighting properties. Preparing beets can be messy—use lemon juice to remove any stains that beet juice leaves on your hands, countertop and cutting board.

2	large beets, trimmed and peeled (about 1 3/4 lb/0.8 kg)	2
2 tbsp	olive oil	25 ml
1/8 tsp	sea salt	0.5 ml
2 tbsp	balsamic vinegar	25 ml
2 tbsp	honey	25 ml

Preheat oven to 375°F (190°C).

Slice peeled and washed beets in half lengthwise; cut into quarter-inch (5 mm) slices. Place beets in a large mixing bowl and toss with 1 tbsp (15 ml) olive oil and sea salt. Arrange beets in a single layer on a baking sheet. Place them in the oven and bake until the beets are firm but can easily be pierced with a fork, about 45 to 55 minutes.

Meanwhile, in a small saucepan whisk half (1 tbsp) of the olive oil together with the balsamic vinegar and honey. Bring the mixture to a rolling boil over medium-high heat, then remove from heat.

When beets are cooked, remove baking sheet from the oven and transfer the beets to a serving dish; drizzle the honey balsamic glaze over them. Serve warm.

Serves 6.

Per serving: 123 cal, 2 g pro, 5 g total fat (1 g saturated fat), 19 g carb, 3 g fibre, 0 mg chol, 154 mg sodium

Excellent source of: folate
Good source of: potassium
Low in saturated fat
Low in cholesterol

Roasted Broccoli

If you're looking for ways to get the kids—or even the adults—in your family to eat their greens, look no further! Roasting broccoli in the oven gives it a delicious nutty flavour and crispy texture. You may never go back to plain old steamed broccoli after trying this recipe—it's that good!

Tip: Cooking time can vary by a few minutes depending on your oven, so keep an eye on the broccoli to make sure it doesn't burn. If you're doubling the recipe, be sure to use a large baking sheet. Crowding the broccoli will prevent it from roasting properly.

6 cups	broccoli florets (about 1 large head of broccoli)	1.5 L
2 tbsp	olive oil	25 ml
1/4 tsp	coarse sea salt	1 ml
	freshly ground black pepper, to taste	

Preheat oven to 450°F (230°C).

Put broccoli florets in a large mixing bowl. Drizzle with olive oil. With clean hands, rub the olive oil into the broccoli to evenly coat it.

Season with salt and pepper.

Lay broccoli in a single layer on a large baking sheet.

Place in the oven and roast for 18 to 20 minutes, or just until the edges of the broccoli are brown and crispy and the stems are tender but not soft.

Remove from heat; serve warm.

Serves 4.

Per 1-1/2 cup (375 ml) serving: 105 cal, 4 g pro, 7 g total fat (1 g saturated fat), 9 g carb, 3 g fibre, 0 mg chol, 190 mg sodium

Excellent source of: vitamin C, vitamin K, folate
Good source of: vitamin E, potassium
Low in saturated fat
Low in cholesterol

Roasted Tomatoes with Herbes de Provence

This roasted tomato dish, inspired by my colleague Michelle Gelok's recent trip to France, is delicious when served with grilled salmon and steamed brown rice. Best of all, it's low in calories and high in vitamin C. If you don't have these herbs pre-mixed, you can make your own herbs de Provence blend using equal parts savory, fennel, basil and thyme.

4	large beef tomatoes	4
2 tsp	olive oil	10 ml
1/4 tsp	sea salt	1 ml
1 tsp	herbes de Provence	5 ml

Preheat oven to 350°F (180°C).

Using a small knife, remove stems from tomatoes. Cut tomatoes in half widthwise.

Gently place tomatoes, cut side up, on a baking sheet.

Drizzle tomatoes with olive oil; sprinkle with sea salt and herbes de Provence.

Bake for 40 to 45 minutes, or until the tomatoes are soft but still hold their shape.

Serve warm.

Serves 4.

Per 2 tomato halves: 42 cal, 1 g pro, 3 g total fat (0 g saturated fat), 5 g carb, 2 g fibre, 0 mg chol, 152 mg sodium

Low in fat
Low in saturated fat
Low in cholesterol

Sautéed Cherry Tomatoes with Garlic and Fresh Basil

This side dish takes less than 5 minutes to cook and is delicious eaten warm or cold. For the best flavour, be sure to use fresh, locally grown cherry tomatoes when they are in season.

2 tbsp	extra-virgin olive oil	25 ml
4 cups	cherry tomatoes	1 L
2	cloves garlic, roughly chopped	2
1/4 cup	fresh basil, roughly chopped	50 ml
2 tbsp	pine nuts	25 ml
	freshly ground black pepper, to taste	

Heat oil in a skillet over medium heat. Add tomatoes and sauté until they are warmed through—about 3 to 4 minutes. Add garlic and sauté for another minute.

Remove from heat. Stir in basil and pine nuts.

Serve warm.

Serves 4.

Per serving (1 cup/250 ml): 95 cal, 1 g pro, 10 g total fat (1 g saturated fat), 2 g carb, 1 g fibre, 0 mg chol, 2 mg sodium

Good source of: vitamin K
Low in sodium
Low in saturated fat
Low in cholesterol

Simple Sautéed Spinach

Spinach gets two thumbs up when it comes to nutrition. It's high in vitamin C, vitamin K, folate, iron, magnesium and potassium, and low in calories. And it's loaded with lutein to keep your eyes healthy as you age.

1 tbsp	olive oil	15 ml
2	cloves garlic, finely chopped	2
8 cups	spinach (about 1 lb/454 g)	2 L
2 tbsp	freshly squeezed lemon juice	25 ml
1/4 tsp	sea salt	1 ml
	freshly ground black pepper, to taste	

Heat oil in a large skillet over medium heat. Add garlic; sauté for 1 minute.

Add spinach, lemon juice, salt and pepper to skillet; cover and steam for 3 to 4 minutes, or until spinach is wilted. Remove from heat and serve immediately.

Serves 4.

Per 2/3 cup (150 ml) serving: 60 cal, 3 g pro, 4 g total fat (1 g saturated fat), 5 g carb, 3 g fibre, 0 mg chol, 236 mg sodium

Excellent source of: vitamin C, vitamin E, vitamin K, magnesium, folate, potassium, beta carotene
Good source of: iron
Low in saturated fat
Low in cholesterol

Spicy Sautéed Kale

With its unmistakable dark green curly leaves, kale is as attractive as it is nutritious. Gram for gram kale outshines most other leafy green vegetables, including spinach, Swiss chard and dandelion greens, when it comes to vitamins A, C, E and K. This recipe is a great way to introduce the leafy green vegetable into your diet if you're not familiar with it.

1 tbsp	olive oil	15 ml
2	cloves garlic, finely chopped	2
8 cups	kale, washed and trimmed, cut into bite-sized pieces	2 L
1/3 cup	water	75 ml
1 tbsp	red wine vinegar	15 ml
1/4 tsp	red pepper flakes	1 ml
1/4 tsp	sea salt	1 ml
	freshly ground black pepper, to taste	

Heat oil in a skillet over medium heat; add garlic and sauté for one minute.

Add kale, water, red wine vinegar, red pepper flakes, salt and pepper to skillet. Cover and steam for 10 to 12 minutes, or until kale is wilted and tender.

Remove from heat and serve immediately.

Serves 4.

Per 3/4 cup (175 ml) serving: 100 cal, 5 g pro, 4 g total fat (1 g saturated fat), 14 g carb, 3 g fibre, 0 mg chol, 205 mg sodium

Excellent source of: vitamin C, vitamin E, vitamin K, potassium, beta carotene
Good source of: magnesium, calcium, folate, iron
Low in saturated fat
Low in cholesterol

Zesty Sweet Potato Wedges

This is one of those easy-to-make recipes that guests of all ages will love. Turn the wedges once or twice during baking to prevent them from burning.

2	medium-sized sweet potatoes, each peeled and cut into 8 wedges	2
2 tsp	canola oil	10 ml
2 tsp	cumin seeds	10 ml
1/8 tsp	cayenne pepper, or to taste	0.5 ml
1/8 tsp	coarse sea salt	0.5 ml
	freshly ground black pepper, to taste	

Preheat oven to 375°F (190°C).

In a bowl, toss sweet potato wedges with canola oil, cumin seeds, cayenne, salt and pepper.

Spread onto a baking sheet and bake for 35 to 45 minutes, turning once or twice, until potatoes are slightly crispy and tender.

Remove from heat. Serve warm.

Serves 4.

Per serving (4 wedges): 89 cal, 1 g pro, 3 g total fat (3 g saturated fat), 14 g carb, 2 g fibre, 0 mg chol, 113 mg sodium

Excellent source of: beta carotene
Good source of: vitamin K

Whole Grains and Legumes

Nasi Goreng

A trip to the beaches of Bali inspired this variation on a traditional Indonesian fried rice dish. This version uses a small amount of heart-healthy canola oil and egg whites to keep the calories and cholesterol down. I've also swapped brown rice for white rice to boost fibre and antioxidants.

Tip: To yield 3 cups (750 ml) of cooked rice, bring 2 cups (500 ml) of water to a boil in a saucepan. Add 1 cup (250 ml) of brown rice. Cover and cook for 12 minutes or until all of the water is absorbed. Remove from heat and fluff with a fork.

Tip: Kecap manis is a type of Indonesian sweet soy sauce that resembles molasses. Look for it in the Asian section of grocery and specialty food stores.

2 tbsp	canola oil	25 ml
6	shallots, finely chopped	6
1 cup	chopped leek (about 1 leek)	250 ml
4 cups	shredded green cabbage	1 L
3 cups	cooked brown basmati rice	750 ml
1-1/2 tbsp	oyster sauce	20 ml
1-1/2 tbsp	kecap manis (sweet soy sauce)	20 ml
1/4 tsp	red pepper flakes	1 ml
2	egg whites, whisked	2

Heat oil in a skillet over medium heat. Add shallots; sauté for 12 to 15 minutes, or until brown and slightly crispy. Add the chopped leek; sauté for another 4 to 5 minutes.

Add cabbage and rice to skillet; continue to stir until heated through.

Add oyster sauce, kecap manis and red pepper flakes; mix ingredients together.

Continue to cook over medium-high heat, stirring frequently, until rice begins to get brown and crispy.

Add egg white; quickly mix ingredients together until egg white is absorbed and forms long strands.

Serve hot.

Serves 5.

Per 1 cup (250 ml) serving: 237 cal, 7 g pro, 7 g total fat (1 g saturated fat), 39 g carb, 3 g fibre, 0 mg chol, 351 mg sodium

Excellent source of: vitamin K, magnesium, folate
Good source of: vitamin C, potassium
Low in saturated fat
Low in cholesterol

Red Rice and Leek Casserole with White Wine and Lemon

Leeks don't often get the attention they deserve as a healthy food. Not only are they low in calories, they're also high in vitamin C and iron. A distant relative of the onion, leeks belong to the allium family of vegetables, which have been shown to play a role in cancer prevention and boost heart health.

1 tbsp	canola oil	15 ml
1 cup	sliced leeks	250 ml
3	cloves garlic, finely chopped	3
1-1/2 cups	water	375 ml
1/2 cup	white wine	125 ml
1/2 cup	red rice, rinsed	125 ml
1/2 cup	red lentils, rinsed	125 ml
1/2 cup	freshly squeezed lemon juice	125 ml
2	bay leaves	2
1/2 tsp	sea salt	2 ml
	fresh ground black pepper, to taste	

Preheat oven to 350°F (180°C).

Heat oil in a skillet over medium heat. Add leeks; sauté for 5 to 6 minutes. Add garlic; sauté for another minute. Remove from heat.

In a 13 x 9 inch (3.5 L) glass baking dish combine water, white wine, rice, lentils, lemon juice, bay leaves, salt, pepper and leek mixture. Stir to combine all ingredients.

Cover and bake for 60 to 70 minutes, or until most of the liquid is absorbed and rice is cooked through.

Serve warm.

Serves 4.

Per 1 cup (250 ml) serving: 229 cal, 10 g pro, 4 g total fat (0 g saturated fat), 36 g carb, 5 g fibre, 0 mg chol, 304 mg sodium

Excellent source of: magnesium, folate
Good source of: vitamin C, vitamin K, iron
Low in saturated fat
Low in cholesterol
High source of fibre

Entrees

Poultry

Baked Pita Pizza with Chicken, Spinach and Fresh Basil

Compared to store-bought pizza that can run upwards of 400 calories and 7 grams of saturated fat per serving, these personal-sized pizzas are much easier on the waistline and the arteries. Be creative and add your own combination of fresh vegetables, such as arugula instead of spinach or orange bell peppers instead of red peppers. Leftover Roasted Broccoli (p. 267) is another great topping!

4	whole-grain pitas (6-inch/15 cm)	4
1/4 cup	pizza sauce	50 ml
2	cloves garlic, finely chopped	2
2 cups	baby spinach, loosely packed	500 ml
1 cup	thinly sliced red pepper strips (about 1/2 large pepper)	250 ml
8 oz	cooked skinless, boneless chicken breast, shredded	226 g
1/2 cup	shredded fresh basil	125 ml
1/2 cup	sliced mushrooms	125 ml
1/4 tsp	red pepper flakes, or to taste	1 ml
1 cup	shredded low-fat cheese, such as mozzarella	250 ml

Preheat oven to 375°F (190°C).

Place pitas on a large baking sheet.

Evenly divide the sauce, garlic, spinach, red pepper strips, chicken, basil, mushrooms, red pepper flakes and cheese between the pitas.

Place pitas in the oven and bake until cheese melts and edges begin to brown, about 10 to 12 minutes. Remove from heat and serve hot.

Serves 4.

Per pita pizza: 349 cal, 36 g pro, 5 g total fat (2 g saturated fat), 42 g carb, 6 g fibre, 60 mg chol, 536 mg sodium

Excellent source of: vitamin C, vitamin K, calcium, magnesium, folate, potassium, beta carotene
Good source of: iron
Low in saturated fat
Very high source of fibre

Chicken and Arugula Sandwich with Lemon Chive Mayonnaise

So simple, yet so delicious! Taste-testers asked for seconds of this mouth-watering sandwich. Arugula, also known as rocket, makes for a delicious addition to salads and sandwiches. Like most salad greens, it's high in beta carotene, lutein and vitamin C, and very low in calories—half a cup of arugula contains less than 3 calories!

Lemon Chive Mayonnaise

1/4 cup	low-fat mayonnaise	50 ml
1/4 tsp	lemon zest	1 ml
1 tbsp	finely chopped chives	15 ml
1/4 tsp	sea salt	1 ml
	freshly ground black pepper, to taste	

Sandwich

8	thin slices dark rye bread	8
12 oz	cooked boneless, skinless chicken breast, sliced	340 g
1	tomato, sliced	1
2 cups	loosely packed arugula	500 ml

In a small bowl, combine mayonnaise, lemon zest, chives, salt and pepper.

Lightly toast rye bread. Lay bread on a clean work surface. Evenly distribute chicken, tomato, arugula and Lemon Chive Mayonnaise among 4 slices of bread. Top with remaining pieces of bread.

Serve warm.

Serves 4.

Per sandwich: 288 cal, 32 g pro, 6 g total fat (1 g saturated fat), 25 g carb, 3 g fibre, 76 mg chol, 579 mg sodium

Excellent source of: potassium
Good source of: vitamin K, magnesium
Low in saturated fat

Ginger Tomato Chicken Pasta

Tomatoes are high in vitamins A, C and K, but it's their lycopene content that has helped them gain "super food" status. Lycopene is a phytochemical that gives tomatoes their bright red colour and helps guard against prostate cancer and heart disease. Cooking tomatoes, such as in this recipe, helps break down the fibres of the fruit and boosts the amount of lycopene available for absorption.

2 tbsp	olive oil	25 ml
1 lb	skinless, boneless chicken breast, cubed	500 g
1/2 cup	sliced green onions (about 4)	125 ml
4	cloves garlic, finely chopped	4
4 cups	diced fresh tomatoes	1 L
1 cup	sliced mushrooms	250 ml
2 cups	sliced zucchini, in medallions	500 ml
2 tbsp	grated fresh ginger root	25 ml
1/4 tsp	dried red pepper flakes	1 ml
1/2 tsp	sea salt	2 ml
	freshly ground black pepper, to taste	
2 tbsp	fresh lemon juice	25 ml
4 cups	cooked whole-wheat pasta, such as linguine	1 L

Heat 1 tbsp (15 ml) of the oil in a skillet over medium heat. Add chicken and sauté for 12 to 15 minutes, or until cooked through.

Remove chicken from skillet, and set aside.

Heat the remaining 1 tbsp (15 ml) oil in the skillet over medium heat. Add green onions and garlic; sauté for 2 minutes until fragrant. Add tomatoes, mushrooms, zucchini, half of the ginger root, red pepper flakes, salt, pepper and diced chicken. Cover and simmer over medium-low heat for 20 minutes.

Remove from heat. Add cooked pasta to the skillet with vegetables. Add lemon juice and the rest of the fresh ginger root, and toss to coat.

Serve hot.

Serves 4.

Per 1 cup (250 ml) pasta and 2 cups (500 ml) sauce: 427 cal, 38 g pro, 10 g total fat (2 g saturated fat), 50 g carb, 8 g fibre, 67 mg chol, 382 mg sodium

Excellent source of: vitamin C, vitamin E, vitamin K, magnesium, folate, potassium
Good source of: iron, beta carotene
Low in saturated fat
Very high source of fibre

Grilled Chicken with Tomato Cilantro Citrus Salsa

Choosing skinless chicken breast is a simple way to cut calories and saturated fat. Gram for gram, skinless chicken breast has 36 percent less calories and 86 percent less saturated fat than chicken with the skin on. But skinless chicken breast doesn't have to be boring. This recipe combines skinless chicken breast with antioxidant-rich tomatoes and heart-healthy avocado for a perfect mid-summer meal.

Tip: This recipe is designed for the barbecue but can be easily brought indoors to your kitchen oven. Bake the chicken at 375°F (190°C) for 20 to 22 minutes or until cooked through.

4	boneless, skinless chicken breasts (4 oz/120 g each)	4
2 tbsp	freshly squeezed lime juice	25 ml
2 tsp	canola oil	10 ml
2 cups	diced fresh tomato	500 ml
1	avocado, diced	1
1/2 cup	coarsely chopped cilantro	125 ml
2 tbsp	freshly squeezed lime juice	25 ml
1/4 tsp	sea salt	1 ml
	freshly ground black pepper, to taste	

In a shallow dish, toss chicken breasts with lime juice and canola oil. Set aside for 10 to 20 minutes.

Meanwhile, preheat grill over medium-low heat.

Place chicken on grill and cook for 18 to 20 minutes, or until cooked through, turning every 4 to 5 minutes.

Meanwhile, in a small mixing bowl combine tomato, avocado, cilantro, lime juice, salt and pepper. Toss to combine.

Remove chicken from grill, and cover with tomato mixture. Serve immediately.

Serves 4.

Per chicken breast with 1/2 cup (125 ml) salsa: 307 cal, 26 g pro, 19 g total fat (4 g saturated fat), 8 g carb, 4 g fibre, 77 mg chol, 218 mg sodium

Excellent source of: vitamin K, potassium
Good source of: vitamin C, vitamin E, magnesium, folate
High source of fibre

Kasha Cabbage Rolls

This recipe is a new take on an old classic. By incorporating nutty-flavoured kasha (roasted buckwheat groats), these tasty cabbage rolls are high in fibre (13 g of fibre per serving) and still retain their disease-fighting cruciferous chemicals.

This recipe freezes quite well after it's baked, making it ideal for quick, stress-free dinners or a brown bag lunch.

12	medium-sized cabbage leaves	12
2 cups	onions, chopped	500 ml
3	cloves garlic, chopped	3
1 tsp	red pepper flakes	5 ml
1 tsp	salt	5 ml
1 tbsp	dried basil	15 ml
2 cups	kasha, cooked, cooled and rinsed	500 ml
2	eggs	2
1 lb	ground chicken, turkey or soy ground round	454 g
1/4 cup	ground flaxseed	50 ml
2	cans (28 oz/796 ml each) diced tomatoes	2
	freshly ground pepper, to taste	

Preheat oven to 375°F (190°C).

In a pot of boiling water, blanch cabbage leaves until slightly softened and wilted. Remove and shake off any water.

In a large bowl, combine onions, garlic, pepper flakes, salt, basil, kasha, eggs, ground poultry or soy and ground flax.

Spread one can of the tomatoes over the bottom of a large (4 L) Dutch oven.

To make each cabbage roll, scoop 1/2 cup (125 ml) of kasha mixture, place it in the centre of a cabbage leaf, then roll up the leaf over the filling, carefully tuck the ends under. Snugly arrange the cabbage rolls in a single layer over the bed of tomatoes in the Dutch oven pan.

Pour the second can of tomatoes over the rolls. Season with pepper.

Bake, covered, for 2 to 2 1/2 hours, or until the tomato mixture is bubbling and the meat is cooked through.

Serves 6.

Per serving (2 rolls): 377 cal, 26 g pro, 6 g total fat (1 g saturated fat), 63 g carb, 13 g fibre, 56 mg chol, 826 mg sodium

Excellent source of: fibre, vitamin A, vitamin C, folate, iron, magnesium, potassium
Good source of: calcium

Fish and Seafood

Braised Tilapia with Tomato Fennel Sauce

Fish, including tilapia, is an excellent source of protein that's low in cholesterol and saturated fat. Canada's Food Guide recommends that adults eat fish at least twice per week. If you're not familiar with fish, tilapia is a great place to start. Thanks to its mild taste and delicate white flesh it tends to be a crowd pleaser.

4 cups	diced fresh tomatoes	1 L
1/4 cup	white wine	50 ml
3	cloves garlic, finely chopped	3
2	medium fennel bulbs, trimmed and thinly sliced	2
1 tbsp	freshly squeezed lemon juice	15 ml
1 tsp	lemon zest	5 ml
1/2 tsp	sea salt	2 ml
	freshly ground black pepper, to taste	
4	tilapia fillets (4 oz/120 g each)	4

In a large skillet, combine tomatoes, white wine, garlic, sliced fennel, lemon juice, lemon zest, salt and pepper. Cover and bring to a boil over high heat. Reduce heat and simmer over low for 15 to 20 minutes until sauce is slightly watery.

Increase heat to medium. Gently nestle tilapia fillets on top of tomato mixture; cover. Continue to cook until fish is cooked through and flakes easily when tested with a fork, about 10 to 12 minutes.

Remove from heat and serve immediately.

Per fillet with 1 cup (250 ml) sauce: 192 cal, 26 g pro, 3 g total fat (1 g saturated fat), 17 g carb, 6 g fibre, 57 mg chol, 422 mg sodium

Excellent source of: vitamin C, magnesium, folate, potassium
Good source of: vitamin E, vitamin K, iron, beta carotene
Low in sodium
Low in fat
Low in saturated fat
Very high source of fibre

Halibut with Ginger, Sesame and Cilantro

There's a reason halibut is a favourite among fish lovers—it has firm white meat and a slightly sweet flavour. It also gets two thumbs up from a nutrition standpoint. Not only is it a lean source of protein, with 130 calories and less than 3 grams of fat per 120 gram serving, it's also an excellent source of vitamin D.

1 tbsp	canola oil	15 ml
1/4 cup	sliced green onions	50 ml
1 tbsp	grated fresh ginger root	15 ml
4	halibut fish fillets, 1-inch thick (4 oz/120 g each)	4
1/4 cup	freshly squeezed lime juice	50 ml
1/2 tsp	sesame oil	2 ml
1/2 cup	chopped cilantro	125 ml

Heat oil in a skillet over medium heat. Add onions and ginger; sauté for 2 minutes.

Add fish to skillet, skin side up. Drizzle with lime juice, then cover and continue to cook for 4 minutes.

Flip fish, cover again and continue to cook for another 2 minutes.

Flip fish again; this time gently remove skin with a spatula or fork; discard the skin.

Cover and continue to cook for another 3 to 4 minutes, or until fish is cooked through and flakes easily when tested with a fork.

Remove from heat. Drizzle the fillets with sesame oil and sprinkle with cilantro. Serve immediately.

Serves 4.

Per fillet (4 oz/120 g): 167 cal, 24 g pro, 7 g total fat (1 g saturated fat), 2 g carb, 0 g fibre, 36 mg chol, 64 mg sodium

Excellent source of: vitamin D, vitamin K, magnesium, potassium
Good source of: vitamin E
Low in sodium
Low in saturated fat

Salmon with White Wine, Lemon and Garlic

The Heart and Stroke Foundation of Canada recommends that adults consume fish, especially fatty fish such as salmon, at least twice a week. Salmon is not only packed with heart-healthy omega-3 fatty acids, it also leads the pack when it comes to vitamin D.

Tip: The natural oils from the salmon will release as the salmon cooks, coating the pan. If the pan begins to dry out, add a tablespoon or two (15 to 30 ml) of white wine or lemon juice to keep the fish from sticking.

2	cloves garlic, finely chopped	2
1/4 cup	white wine	50 ml
1/4 cup	freshly squeezed lemon juice	50 ml
4	salmon fillets, 1-inch thick (4 oz/120 g each)	4
2 tsp	canola oil	10 tsp
	lemon wedges, as garnish	

In a shallow dish, combine garlic, white wine and lemon juice. Place salmon, skin side up, in dish. Set aside to marinate for 20 minutes.

Heat oil in a skillet over high heat. Add salmon, skin side up. Cover, and reduce heat to medium. Cook for 3 minutes.

Flip salmon, and add lemon-wine marinade to skillet. Cover, and continue to cook for 5 minutes.

Flip salmon again, this time gently removing the skin with a spatula or fork; discard.

Continue to cook for 3 to 5 minutes, or until fish is cooked through and flakes easily when tested with a fork. Remove from heat.

Serve immediately, with a lemon wedge if desired.

Serves 4.

Per fillet: 244 cal, 23 g pro, 15 g total fat (3 g saturated fat), 2 g carb, 0 g fibre, 67 mg chol, 68 mg sodium

Excellent source of: vitamin D
Good source of: folate, potassium
Low in sodium

Sesame Salmon Wrap

The Canadian Cancer Society recommends that adults boost their intake of vitamin D during the long, dark winter months. Salmon is one of the few food sources naturally high in the "sunshine" vitamin. This wrap isn't just an excellent source of vitamin D, it's also very high in vitamin C, folate, vitamin K, calcium and potassium.

Tip: If you're packing these wraps for lunch, pack the salmon mixture, wrap and vegetables separately to keep them from getting soggy.

2	cans (7.5 oz/213 g each) salmon, drained	2
2 tbsp	sodium-reduced soy sauce	25 ml
2 tbsp	rice vinegar	25 ml
2 tbsp	freshly squeezed lime juice	25ml
1/2 tsp	wasabi paste	2 ml
1/2 tsp	sesame oil	2 ml
4	whole-grain tortilla wraps (10-inch/25 cm each)	4
2 cups	spinach, loosely packed	500 ml
2 cups	cucumber strips, thinly sliced (about 1/4 cucumber)	500 ml
2 cups	red pepper strips, thinly sliced (about 1 pepper)	500 ml
1/2 cup	sliced green onions	125 ml

In a small bowl, combine salmon, soy sauce, rice vinegar, lime juice, wasabi paste and sesame oil. Use the back of a fork to mash ingredients together.

On a clean work surface, lay out the four wraps. Gently arrange a layer of spinach on each wrap. Evenly distribute the salmon mixture, cucumber and red pepper strips among the four wraps.

To wrap tortillas, gently fold the bottom of the wrap over the filling, then fold one side over the filling and roll tightly.

Serve immediately.

Serves 4.

Per wrap: 380 cal, 31 g pro, 12 g total fat (5 g saturated fat), 36 g carb, 6 g fibre, 42 mg chol, 788 mg sodium

Excellent source of: vitamin C, vitamin D, vitamin E, vitamin K, calcium, magnesium, folate, potassium, beta carotene
Very high source of fibre

Thai Roasted Trout with Fresh Lime

Rainbow trout, with its silvery, speckled flesh and pink meat, is as beautiful as it is nutritious. Like other cold-water fatty fish, including salmon, it's an excellent source of omega-3 fatty acids that protect your heart and your telomeres.

4	rainbow trout fillets (4 oz/120 g each)	4
1/4 cup	freshly squeezed lime juice	50 ml
1 tbsp	rice vinegar	15 ml
1 tbsp	sodium-reduced soy sauce	15 ml
1 tbsp	brown sugar	15 ml
1 tsp	grated fresh ginger root	5 ml
1/4 tsp	sesame oil	1 ml

Preheat oven to 375°F (190°C).

In a small mixing bowl, combine lime juice, rice vinegar, soy sauce, brown sugar, ginger and sesame oil.

In a shallow baking dish, arrange trout fillets. Pour the lime juice marinade over the fillets.

Place the baking dish in the oven, uncovered. Bake for 30 to 35 minutes, or until fish is cooked through and flakes easily when tested with a fork.

Remove from heat and serve immediately.

Serves 4.

Per fillet: 178 cal, 24 g pro, 6 g total fat (2 g saturated fat), 5 g carb, 0 g fibre, 67 mg chol, 174 mg sodium

Excellent source of: vitamin D, potassium
Good source of: magnesium
Low in saturated fat

Wasabi and Ginger Baked Salmon

Wild or farmed? Pacific or Atlantic? While the health benefits of salmon are well known, there's much confusion around which type of salmon to choose. According to Sea Choice, Canada's sustainable seafood program and partner with the David Suzuki Foundation, wild Pacific salmon is the most environmentally friendly choice.

2 tsp	wasabi paste	10 ml
1 tbsp	water	15 ml
1 tbsp	rice vinegar	15 ml
1 tbsp	sodium-reduced soy sauce	15 ml
1 tbsp	brown sugar	15 ml
2 tbsp	freshly squeezed lime juice	25 ml
1 tbsp	grated fresh ginger root	15 ml
4	salmon fillets (4 oz/120 g each)	4

Preheat oven to 375°F (190°C).

In a small mixing bowl, combine wasabi, water, rice vinegar, soy sauce, brown sugar, lime juice and ginger root.

Place salmon, skin-side down, in a glass baking dish. Cover with wasabi ginger mixture. Cover and bake for 25 to 35 minutes, or until fish is cooked through and flakes easily when tested with a fork.

Remove from heat, serve immediately.

Serves 4.

Per fillet: 226 cal, 23 g pro, 12 g total fat (3 g saturated fat), 5 g carb, 0 g fibre, 67 mg chol, 202 mg sodium

Excellent source of: vitamin D
Good source of: potassium

Legumes and Soy

Baked Lentils with Cumin Yogurt Sauce

Lentils may be small in size but they're mighty when it comes to nutrition. Perhaps best known for their high-fibre content, lentils are also rich in protein, folate and iron. These baked lentils are delicious straight out of the oven, but they also taste great as leftovers the next day.

2 cups	water	500 ml
1 cup	green lentils, washed and rinsed	250 ml
1 cup	diced onion	250 ml
1/2 cup	quick oats	125 ml
1/2 cup	hot salsa	125 ml
1/4 cup	ground flaxseeds	50 ml
1	egg white	1
2	cloves garlic, finely chopped	2
1/2 tsp	salt	2 ml
1/4 tsp	red pepper flakes	1 ml
1-1/2 cups	low-fat (1% MF or less) plain yogurt or soy yogurt	375 ml
1/2 tsp	ground cumin	2 ml

Preheat oven to 375°F (190°C).

Heat water in a saucepan and bring to a boil. Add rinsed lentils, and bring back to a boil. Reduce heat, cover and simmer for 20 minutes, or until lentils are soft. Drain off any excess liquid. Set aside to cool.

In a large mixing bowl combine cooked lentils, onion, oats, salsa, flaxseeds, egg white, garlic, salt and pepper. Stir to combine well.

Transfer the lentil mixture into a glass baking dish. Using your hands, gently shape the mixture into a 9-inch-long (24 cm) loaf; bake it, uncovered, for 60 to 70 minutes, or until the edges begin to brown.

Meanwhile, in a small mixing bowl, combine yogurt and cumin.

Serve each slice of lentil loaf with a dollop of yogurt-cumin sauce.

Serves 6.

Per 1.5-inch (4 cm) slice and 1/4 cup (50 ml) yogurt sauce: 207 cal, 13 g pro, 3 g total fat (0 g saturated fat), 34 g carb, 7 g fibre, 1 mg chol, 387 mg sodium

Excellent source of: potassium
Good source of: iron
Low in fat
Low in saturated fat
Low in cholesterol
Very high source of fibre

Balsamic Glazed Mushroom and Soy Burgers

These meat-free burgers contain textured vegetable protein, a dehydrated meat alternative made from soybeans. Bob's Red Mill carries it in their line of dried goods and it's also available in the bulk section of most health food stores. The combination of sweet balsamic glazed mushrooms and nutty ground flaxseed makes for a delicious and healthy alternative to beef burgers. Taste-testers, including meat-lovers, couldn't get enough of these!

Tip: Serve these burgers in small whole-grain dinner rolls—or eat as open-faced sandwiches—topped with spinach, tomato, red onion slices and mashed avocado.

Tip: To bake burgers instead, preheat oven to 375°F (190°C). Place burgers on lightly oiled baking sheet and bake for 40 to 45 minutes, turning once, until they are cooked through.

2 cups	dry textured vegetable protein granules	500 ml
2 cups	sodium-reduced vegetable or chicken broth	500 ml
2 tbsp	canola oil	25 ml
2 cups	chopped onions	500 ml
3 cups	sliced brown mushrooms	750 ml
4	cloves garlic, finely chopped	4
2 tbsp	balsamic vinegar	25 ml
1	egg white	1
1/2 cup	ground flaxseed	125 ml
1/4 cup	quick oats	50 ml
1/4 cup	whole-wheat breadcrumbs	50 ml
1/2 tsp	red pepper flakes	2 ml
1/2 tsp	sea salt	2 ml
	freshly ground black pepper, to taste	
1 tsp	canola oil	5 ml

Place textured vegetable protein in a large mixing bowl.

In a saucepan, bring stock to a boil. Remove from heat and pour over textured vegetable protein. Stir together until all of the liquid is absorbed. Set aside.

Heat oil in a skillet over medium heat; add onions and mushrooms and sauté for 15 to 18 minutes, or until pan begins to dry out. Add garlic; sauté for another minute.

Remove skillet from heat; drizzle with balsamic vinegar.

Add warm mushroom balsamic mixture to textured vegetable protein and set aside to cool.

When textured vegetable protein and mushroom mixture is cool, add egg white, ground flaxseed, oats, breadcrumbs, red pepper flakes and salt and pepper. Stir ingredients together until mixed well and mixture begins to hold its shape.

Use a 1/3-cup measuring cup to scoop out mixture to form each burger. Firmly press ingredients together using your hands. Set formed burgers aside.

Heat oil in a skillet over medium heat. Add burgers and cook until brown and slightly crispy on the outside, about 5 to 6 minutes per side.

Makes 10 burgers.

Serves 10.

Per burger: 174 cal, 14 g pro, 6 g total fat (1 g saturated fat), 16 g carb, 6 g fibre, 0 mg chol, 163 mg sodium

Excellent source of: magnesium, potassium
Good source of: iron
Low in saturated fat
Low in cholesterol
Very high source of fibre

Chana Masala

Chana masala, a classic North Indian vegetarian dish, is a great way to boost your intake of fibre-rich chickpeas. I promise this recipe, cooked in a delicious broth of tomatoes, onions and traditional Indian spices, will be a hit, even with non-vegetarians. Serve it with a small piece of naan bread or some brown rice.

1 tbsp	canola oil	15 ml
1/4 tsp	cardamom seeds, removed from pods	1 ml
1 cup	finely diced onions	250 ml
2	cloves garlic, finely chopped	2
2 tsp	grated fresh ginger root	10 ml
2 cups	diced fresh tomatoes	500 ml
1	can (19 oz/540 ml) chickpeas, drained and rinsed	1
1/4 tsp	red pepper flakes	1 ml
1/2 tsp	ground cumin	2 ml
1/2 tsp	ground cardamom	2 ml
1/2 tsp	turmeric	2 ml
1	small cinnamon stick	1
1/2 cup	chopped cilantro	125 ml

Heat oil in skillet over medium heat. Add cardamom seeds; sauté for 1 to 2 minutes. Add onion; sauté for another 8 to 10 minutes. Add garlic and ginger; continue to sauté for another minute.

Add tomatoes, chickpeas, red pepper flakes, cumin, cardamom, turmeric and cinnamon stick; stir to combine. Cover and simmer for 20 minutes. If pan begins to dry out, add 1/4 cup (50 ml) water.

When chickpeas are heated through, remove the cinnamon stick. Serve hot.

Serves 4.

Per 3/4 cup (175 ml) serving: 188 cal, 6 g pro, 5 g total fat (0 g saturated fat), 31 g carb, 6 g fibre, 0 mg chol, 323 mg sodium

Excellent source of: folate
Good source of: vitamin K, magnesium, potassium
Low in saturated fat
Low in cholesterol
Very high source of fibre

Garlic and Rosemary Lentil Burgers with Warm Mushroom Gravy

Compared to other beans, lentils are relatively quick to prepare. They're a great meat alternative for vegetarians since they are high in protein, contain no saturated fat and are a source of fibre and iron. And of course, they're among my top 25 longevity foods!

Tip: Substitute dried rosemary with 1 tbsp (15 ml) of chopped fresh rosemary if you have it.

Lentil burgers

2 cups	vegetable stock	500 ml
1 cup	dried green lentils	250 ml
1 tbsp + 2 tsp	canola oil	15 ml + 10 ml
1 cup	coarsely chopped onions	250 ml
3	cloves garlic, crushed	3
1/2 cup	breadcrumbs	125 ml
1/2 cup	rolled oats	125 ml
1 tbsp	champagne vinegar	15 ml
1 tsp	dried rosemary	5 ml
1/2 tsp	red pepper flakes	2 ml
1/4 tsp	salt	1 ml
	freshly ground black pepper	

Gravy

2 tsp	canola oil	10 ml
1/2 cup	finely chopped onions	125 ml
1 cup	finely chopped mushrooms	250 ml
1 cup	water	250 ml
1/4 cup	white wine	50 ml
1 tsp	balsamic vinegar	5 ml
1/4 tsp	salt	1 ml
	freshly ground black pepper, to taste	
2 tbsp	flour	25 ml

To prepare lentil burgers, bring stock to a boil over high heat in a small saucepan. Add lentils and stir. Cover and reduce heat; simmer over medium-low heat for 25 minutes, or until lentils are soft, but still hold their shape. Remove from heat; drain any excess liquid. Set aside and cool.

Meanwhile, heat 1 tbsp (15 ml) of the canola oil in a skillet over medium heat; add onions and sauté until golden and soft, about 8 to 10 minutes. Add garlic, sauté for another 1 to 2 minutes or until fragrant. Remove from heat.

In a large mixing bowl combine lentils, sautéed onions and garlic, bread-crumbs, oats, vinegar, rosemary, red pepper flakes, salt and pepper. Using clean hands, mix ingredients together until they hold their shape.

Using a 1/3 cup (75 ml) measuring cup, divide lentil mixture into 8 portions. Using clean hands, firmly press each portion into a patty.

Heat the remaining 2 tsp (10 ml) of canola oil in a skillet over medium heat. Add lentil patties and cook until brown and slightly crispy, about 8 to 10 minutes.

Meanwhile, to prepare the gravy, heat another 2 tsp (10 ml) canola oil in a skillet over medium heat. Add onions and mushrooms and sauté for 12 minutes. Remove from heat.

In a small saucepan, combine sautéed mushroom and onions, water, wine, vinegar, salt and pepper over medium heat. Whisk in the flour. Bring ingredients to a boil until the mixture thickens. Remove from heat and drizzle over hot lentil patties.

Serve warm.

Makes 8 patties.

Serves 8.

Per patty with 2 tbsp (25 ml) gravy: 195 cal, 8 g pro, 5 g total fat (1 g saturated fat), 29 g carb, 5 g fibre, 0 mg chol, 237 mg sodium

Good source of: iron
Low in saturated fat
Low in cholesterol
High source of fibre

Sesame Ginger Stir-Fried Tofu and Bok Choy with Brown Rice

This high-fibre vegetarian dish is packed with flavour—and nutrients. It's an excellent source of vitamin C, folate, vitamin K, calcium, iron, magnesium, potassium and beta carotene! Brown rice takes 40 to 45 minutes to cook, so get it started before you begin prepping the vegetables. Once it's on the stove, take a few minutes to toast the sesame seeds for a slightly nuttier taste.

1 tbsp	canola oil	15 ml
4	cloves garlic, finely chopped	4
2 tbsp	grated fresh ginger root	25 ml
1 tsp	lemon zest	5 ml
8 cups	sliced bok choy, loosely packed	2 L
2 tbsp	oyster sauce	25 ml
2 tbsp	water	25 ml
4 tsp	sodium-reduced soy sauce	20 ml
2 tsp	freshly squeezed lemon juice	10 ml
1	block (454 g) medium-firm tofu, cut into 1-inch (2.5 cm) cubes	1
1 tsp	sesame seeds, toasted	5 ml
3 cups	cooked brown rice	750 ml

Set rice to cook according to the package directions.

Heat oil in a skillet over medium heat. Add garlic, ginger and lemon zest; sauté for 2 minutes.

Add bok choy, oyster sauce, water, soy sauce and lemon juice; stir-fry until bok choy begins to wilt, about 1 minute.

Add tofu, continue to stir-fry until tofu is heated through, about 3 to 4 minutes.

Remove from heat; sprinkle with sesame seeds.

Serve over brown rice.

Serves 4.

Per 3/4 cup (175 ml) brown rice and 1 1/4 cup (300 ml) bok choy mixture: 333 cal, 19 g pro, 11 g total fat (1 g saturated fat), 44 g carb, 6 g fibre, 0 mg chol, 526 mg sodium

Excellent source of: vitamin C, vitamin K, calcium, magnesium, folate, iron, potassium, beta carotene
Low in saturated fat
Low in cholesterol
Very high source of fibre

White Bean, Garlic and Arugula Wrap

White kidney beans, also known as Cannellini beans, are a staple of the Mediterranean diet and well known for their creamy texture and sweet taste. Besides these claims to fame, they are exceptionally nutritious. Here they're teamed with garlic, lemon and spicy arugula, a combination that makes for a mouth-watering wrap high in fibre and vitamin K.

1	can (19 oz/540 ml) white kidney beans, drained and rinsed	1
1 tbsp	olive oil	15 ml
2 tbsp	freshly squeezed lemon juice	25 ml
2 tbsp	chopped chives	25 ml
1	clove garlic, finely chopped	1
	freshly ground pepper, to taste	
4	whole-grain tortilla wraps (7-inch/18 cm each)	4
2 cups	loosely packed arugula, washed and rinsed	500 ml
1 cup	sliced tomato (about 1 medium tomato)	250 ml

In a small mixing bowl, combine kidney beans, olive oil, lemon juice, garlic and pepper. Using the back of a fork mash ingredients together until beans are smooth.

Arrange wraps on a clean work surface. Evenly spread bean mixture on the top third of each wrap. Evenly divide the arugula and tomato among the wraps.

To wrap tortillas, gently fold the bottom of the wrap over the filling, then fold one side up over the filling and roll tightly. Serve immediately.

Serves 4.

Per wrap: 237 cal, 12 g pro, 6 g total fat (1 g saturated fat), 37 g carb, 7 g fibre, 0 mg chol, 574 mg sodium

Excellent source of: vitamin K
Good source of: iron
Low in saturated fat
Low in cholesterol
Very high source of fibre

Salad Dressings, Condiments and Marinades

Ginger Green Tea Marinade

This marinade has a unique taste that goes well with chicken, white fish or scallops. Though this recipe can be made with whatever type of tea suits your taste—from ordinary Earl Grey to sweet and slightly rooibos tea—green tea will infuse this marinade with longevity-boosting power.

2	green tea bags	2
3/4 cup	boiling water	175 ml
2 tbsp	low-sodium soy sauce	25 ml
1 tbsp	piece ginger root, minced	25 ml
1 tbsp	lime juice, freshly squeezed	15 ml

In a glass measuring cup, pour boiling water over tea bag or, if you prefer, 1 tsp (5 ml) tea leaves. Let steep for 10 minutes. Remove tea bag or infuser (or strain loose tea from brew).

Add soy sauce, ginger root and lime juice to the tea. Pour over chicken, fish or scallops and marinate in the fridge for 1 to 2 hours.

Makes 1 cup.

Serves 4.

Per 1/4 cup (50 ml) serving: 6 cal, 0 g pro, 0 g total fat (0 g saturated fat), 1 g carb, 0 g fibre, 0 mg chol, 243 mg sodium

Honey Balsamic Dressing

A triple-duty recipe! Try this delicious salad dressing, rich in monounsaturated fat and alpha-linolenic acid (ALA), as a marinade for meat and vegetables, or as a topping for baked potatoes.

2 tbsp	extra-virgin olive oil	25 ml
1 tbsp	flaxseed oil	15 ml
3 tbsp	balsamic vinegar	50 ml
1 tbsp	honey	15 ml
1/2 tbsp	Dijon mustard	7 ml
1	clove garlic, minced	1

In a small bowl, whisk together olive oil, flaxseed oil, vinegar, honey, mustard and garlic.

Store in an airtight container in the fridge until ready to serve.

Serves 6.

Per 1 tbsp (15 ml) serving: 74 cal, 0 g pro, 7 g total fat (1 g saturated fat), 4 g carb, 0 g fibre, 0 mg chol, 17 mg sodium

Low in sodium
Low in saturated fat
Low in cholesterol

Spicy Grape and Ginger Chutney

This tasty chutney is a great addition to roasted poultry or pork tenderloin. It takes less than 15 minutes to prepare and is a great alternative to other condiments since it delivers plenty of flavour and antioxidants but little fat and sodium.

1 tbsp	canola oil	15 ml
1/2 cup	finely chopped onion	125 ml
1/3 cup	white wine	75 ml
1 tbsp	apple cider vinegar	15 ml
1 tsp	minced ginger root	5 ml
1/2 tsp	cinnamon	2 ml
1/8 tsp	red pepper flakes	0.5 ml
1/8 tsp	sea salt	0.5 ml
2 cups	halved seedless red grapes	500 ml

Heat oil in a saucepan over medium heat.

Add onion and sauté until soft, about 8 minutes.

Add wine, vinegar, ginger, cinnamon, red pepper flakes and salt to the saucepan and bring to a boil over high heat.

Add grapes to the saucepan, bring to a boil then reduce heat. Cover and simmer over low heat for 12 minutes.

Serve warm over grilled or baked chicken or pork.

Makes 1-1/2 cups (375 ml).

Per 2 tablespoon (25 ml) serving: 35 cal, 0.5 g pro, 1 g total fat (0 g saturated fat), 5.5 g carb, 0.5 g fibre, 0 mg chol, 30 mg sodium

Good source of: vitamin K
Low in sodium
Low in fat
Low in saturated fat
Low in cholesterol

Muffins

Chocolate Zucchini Muffins

Yes, chocolate is good for you! Cocoa beans used to make cocoa powder are an excellent source of antioxidants that might help keep blood pressure in check. These low-fat chocolatey muffins freeze well; just pop the extras in a resealable freezer bag and freeze to enjoy later.

2-1/2 cups	whole-wheat flour	625 ml
1/2 cup	oat bran	125 ml
3 tbsp	ground flaxseed	50 ml
1/3 cup	unsweetened cocoa powder	75 ml
2-1/2 tsp	baking powder	12 ml
1-1/2 tsp	baking soda	7 ml
1/4 tsp	salt	1 ml
1 tsp	cinnamon	5 ml
2 cups	shredded zucchini	500 ml
2/3 cup	low-fat (1% MF or less) milk or soy milk	150 ml
4	egg whites	4
2 tbsp	canola oil	25 ml
1/2 cup	white sugar	125 ml
1 tsp	vanilla extract	5 ml
1 tbsp	orange zest	15 ml

Preheat oven to 375°F (190°C).

In a large mixing bowl, combine flour, oat bran, ground flaxseed, cocoa, baking powder, baking soda, salt and cinnamon.

In another bowl, combine zucchini, milk, egg whites, canola oil, sugar, vanilla and orange zest.

Add wet ingredients to dry ingredients, mix just enough to combine.

Line a muffin tin with 16 small (10 cm) paper muffin cups. Pour 1/4 cup (50 ml) batter into each muffin cup.

Bake for 25 minutes or until cooked through (when a knife inserted in the centre comes out clean).

Makes 16 muffins.

Per serving (1 muffin): 133 cal, 5 g pro, 3 g total fat (0 g saturated fat), 25 g carb, 4 g fibre, 1 mg chol, 213 mg sodium

Good source of: magnesium
Low in saturated fat
Low in cholesterol
High source of fibre

Pumpkin Spice Muffins with Carrots and Blueberries

It's hard to believe these muffins have only 150 calories per serving. They're moist, colourful and taste great! And they're low in saturated fat and trans fat–free. Be sure to use pure pumpkin purée, not pumpkin pie filling, to keep the calories in check. Available in cans at the grocery store, the purée has about one-third of the calories of the pie filling, without added sugar, fat or spices.

Tip: Fresh or frozen blueberries work equally well in these muffins.

1 cup	whole-wheat flour	250 ml
1 cup	all-purpose flour	250 ml
2 tsp	baking powder	10 ml
1 tsp	baking soda	5 ml
1/2 tsp	salt	2 ml
1 tsp	nutmeg	5 ml
1 tsp	ground cloves	5 ml
1	egg	1
1	egg white	1
3/4 cup	brown sugar	175 ml
1 cup	pure pumpkin purée	250 ml
1 cup	shredded carrot (about 1 large)	250 ml
1/2 cup	low-fat (1% MF or less) milk or soy milk	125 ml
1/4 cup	canola oil	50 ml
1 tsp	vanilla	5 ml
1 cup	blueberries	250 ml
1 tbsp	brown sugar	15 ml

Preheat oven to 375°F (190°C).

In a large mixing bowl, combine flour, baking powder, baking soda, salt, nutmeg and cloves. Set aside.

In a separate large mixing bowl, whisk together egg and egg white until frothy, about 30 seconds. Add brown sugar and whisk until ingredients are combined. Add pumpkin, carrots, milk, canola oil and vanilla; whisk together.

Add dry ingredients to wet ingredients and mix just enough to combine. Add blueberries, gently folding them into the batter.

Line a muffin tin with 16 small (10 cm) paper muffin cups. Pour 1/4 cup (50 ml) batter into each muffin cup, sprinkle top with brown sugar.

Bake for 22 minutes, or until cooked through (when a knife inserted in the centre comes out clean).

Makes 16 muffins.

Per muffin: 149 cal, 3 g pro, 4 g total fat (1 g saturated fat), 26 g carb, 2 g fibre, 11 mg chol, 211 mg sodium

Excellent source of: beta carotene
Low in saturated fat
Low in cholesterol

Raspberry Ginger Muffins

The combination of raspberries and fresh ginger makes these muffins irresistible! Unlike many store-bought muffins, these contain 100% whole-grain flour, low-fat milk, egg whites and just a touch of canola oil. As a result they have less than 150 calories each. Consider making extra—they won't last long!

1 cup	whole-wheat flour	250 ml
1 cup	all purpose flour	250 ml
3/4 cup	sugar	175 ml
1-1/2 tsp	baking powder	7 ml
1/2 tsp	baking soda	2 ml
1/2 tsp	salt	2 ml
1	egg	1
1	egg white	1
1 cup	low-fat (1% MF or less) milk or soy milk	250 ml
1/4 cup	canola oil	50 ml
1 tbsp	grated fresh ginger root	15 ml
1 tsp	vanilla	5 ml
1-1/3 cups	raspberries	325 ml
2 tbsp	quick oats	25 ml
1 tbsp	granulated sugar	15 ml

Preheat oven to 375°F (190°C).

In a large mixing bowl, combine flour, sugar, baking powder, baking soda and salt. Set aside.

In a separate large mixing bowl, whisk together egg and egg white until frothy, about 30 seconds. Add milk, canola oil, ginger and vanilla, and whisk together.

Add dry ingredients to wet ingredients, mixing just enough to combine. Add raspberries, gently folding them into the batter.

In a small bowl, combine oats and sugar. Set aside.

Line a muffin tin with 16 small (10 cm) paper muffin cups. Pour 1/4 cup (50 ml) batter into each muffin cup, sprinkle top with oat and brown sugar mixture.

Bake for 20 to 22 minutes, or until cooked through (when a knife inserted in the centre comes out clean).

Makes 16 muffins.

Per muffin: 144 cal, 3 g pro, 4 g total fat (1 g saturated fat), 24 g carb, 2 g fibre, 11 mg chol, 155 mg sodium

Low in saturated fat
Low in cholesterol

Desserts

Chocolate Fruit Fondue

Chocolate fondue recipes usually call for heavy cream, a source of cholesterol-raising saturated fat. This recipe skips the cream, making it slightly thicker but much lower in fat than most recipes. While the recipe calls for regular semi-sweet or unsweetened chocolate, you can also use plain or flavoured specialty dark chocolate bars, such as orange, mint, espresso or green tea. Buy dark chocolate with 70% cocoa solids; the higher the cocoa solids the greater the concentration of antioxidants!

Tip: A double boiler is two saucepans that stack on top of each other. The bottom saucepan is filled with simmering water, while the top saucepan is filled with food, in this case chocolate, and is melted from the heat below. If you don't have a double boiler, make your own; fill a small saucepan with 1 to 2 inches of water and bring to a boil. Place a stainless steel bowl over the mouth of the pan. Add the chopped chocolate to the bowl and continue to stir until the chocolate is melted and smooth.

1 cup	chopped dark chocolate (about 140 g)	250 ml
4 cups	mixed fruit, diced (such as strawberries, mango, apples, banana, kiwi or pineapple)	1 L

Using a double boiler, melt chocolate until warm and smooth, stirring continuously.

When chocolate is melted, remove from heat and serve immediately with fresh fruit.

Serves 4.

Per serving of 1 cup (250 ml) mixed fruit and 2 tbsp (25 ml) chocolate: 302 cal, 5 g pro, 18 g total fat (10 g saturated fat), 44 g carb, 4 g fibre, 0 mg chol, 4 mg sodium

Excellent source of: vitamin C, potassium
Good source of: iron
Low in sodium
Low in cholesterol
High source of fibre

Appendix 1

A guide to vitamins and minerals

Use the following guide to choose nutrient-rich foods. For each vitamin and mineral, you'll learn your recommended daily allowance (RDA)—how much you need to consume every day—and foods that provide relatively large amounts of each nutrient. Note the different requirements for males (M) and females (F) in the table.

Key vitamins	RDAs	Best food sources
Vitamin A	F: 700 mcg Pregnancy: 770 mcg Breastfeeding: 1300 mcg M: 900 mcg	Liver, oily fish, milk, cheese, eggs Beta carotene: carrots, sweet potato, winter squash, broccoli, kale, spinach; apricots, peaches, mango
Vitamin B1 *(thiamin)*	F: 1.1 mg Pregnancy: 1.4 mg Breastfeeding: 1.4 mg M: 12 mg	Pork, liver, fish, whole grains, wheat germ, enriched breakfast cereals and breads, legumes, nuts
Vitamin B2 *(riboflavin)*	F: 1.1 m Pregnancy: 1.4 mg Breastfeeding: 1.6 mg M: 1.3 mg	Milk, yogurt, cheese, fortified soy and rice milk, meat, eggs, legumes, nuts, whole grains
Vitamin B3 *(niacin)*	F: 14 mg Pregnancy: 18 mg Breastfeeding: 17 mg M: 16 mg	Red meat, poultry, fish, liver, eggs, dairy products, peanuts, almonds, enriched breakfast cereals, wheat bran

Key vitamins	RDAs	Best food sources
Vitamin B6	F: Age 19–50: 1.3 mg F: Age 50+: 1.5 mg Pregnancy: 1.9 mg Breastfeeding: 2.0 mg M: Age 19–50: 1.3 mg M: Age 50+: 1.7 mg	Red meat, poultry, fish, liver, eggs, legumes, nuts, seeds, whole grains, leafy green vegetables, bananas, potatoes, avocados
Vitamin B12	2.4 mcg Pregnancy: 2.6 mcg Breastfeeding: 2.8 mcg	Milk, poultry, fish, eggs, dairy products, fortified soy and rice milk
Folate	400 mcg Pregnancy: 600 mcg Breastfeeding: 500 mcg	Lentils, legumes, seeds, cooked spinach, asparagus, artichokes, orange juice
Vitamin C	F: 75 mg (110 mg for smokers) Pregnancy: 85 mg Breastfeeding: 120 mg M: 90 mg (125 mg for smokers)	Citrus fruit & juices, kiwi, cantaloupe, strawberries, broccoli, cauliflower, cabbage, tomato juice, bell peppers
Vitamin D	1000–2000 IU (international units)* Pregnancy: 2000 IU*	Fluid milk, egg yolks, oily fish, fortified soy and rice milk
Vitamin E	15 mg (22 IU) Pregnancy: 15 mg Breastfeeding: 19 mg	Vegetable oils, nuts, seeds, soybeans, whole grains, wheat germ, avocado, leafy green vegetables
Vitamin K	F: 90 mcg Pregnancy: 90 mcg Breastfeeding: 90 mcg M: 120 mcg	Green peas, broccoli, leafy green vegetables, cabbage, liver

*Represents the current recommended intake to reduce cancer risk. This amount is above the official RDA, which is now considered too low.

mg: milligram; mcg: microgram

Key minerals	RDAs	Best food sources
Calcium	Age 9–18: 1300 mg Age 19–50: 1000 mg Age 50+: 1200 mg Pregnancy: 1000 mg Breastfeeding: 1000 mg	Dairy products, fortified soy and rice milk, broccoli, leafy green vegetables, almonds, legumes, tofu, canned salmon (with bones), sardines, fortified fruit juice
Iron	F: Age 9–13: 8 mg F: Age 14–18: 15 mg F: Age 19–50: 18 mg F: Age 50+: 8 mg Pregnancy: 27 mg Breastfeeding: 9 mg M: Age 9–13: 8 mg M: Age 14–18: 11 mg M: Age 19+: 8 mg	Red meat, poultry, tuna, salmon, eggs, enriched breakfast cereals, whole grains, baked beans, lentils, blackstrap molasses, raisins
Magnesium	F: Age 9–13: 240 mg F: Age 14–18: 360 mg F: Age 19–30: 310 mg F: Age 30+: 320 mg Pregnancy: 350–360 mg Breastfeeding: 310–320 mg M: Age 9–13: 240 mg M: Age 14–18: 410 mg M: Age 19–30: 400 mg M: Age 30+: 420 mg	Whole grains, almonds, Brazil nuts, sunflower seeds, legumes, tofu, leafy green vegetables, prunes, figs, dates
Potassium	4700 mg Pregnancy: 4700 mg Breastfeeding: 5100 mg	Bananas, oranges, orange juice, cantaloupe, peaches, avocado, broccoli, Brussels sprouts, spinach, tomato juice, lima beans, peas
Chromium	F: Age 9–13: 21 mcg F: Age 14–18: 24 mcg F: Age 19–50: 25 mcg F: Age 50+: 20 mcg Pregnancy: 30 mcg Breastfeeding: 45 mcg M: Age 9–13: 25 mcg M: Age 14–50: 35 mg M: Age 50+: 30 mcg	Meat, fish, poultry, whole grains, dark chocolate, mushrooms, green peppers, green beans, spinach, apples, bananas, orange juice

mg: milligram; mcg: microgram

Key minerals	RDAs	Best food sources
Selenium	55 mcg Pregnancy: 60 mcg Breastfeeding: 70 mcg	Brazil nuts, shrimp, salmon, halibut, crab, fish, pork, organ meats, wheat bran, whole-wheat bread, brown rice, onion, garlic, mushrooms
Zinc	F: 8 mg Pregnancy: 11 mg Breastfeeding: 12 mg M: 11 mg	Beef, pork, lamb, yogurt, milk, wheat bran, wheat germ, whole grains, enriched breakfast cereals, legumes, pumpkin seeds, cashews

mg: milligram; mcg: microgram

Appendix 2

The Longevity Diet Daily Food and Nutrient Tracker

Tracker: Check off nutrient-rich food choices:

Protein ☐　　　Beta carotene ☐　　　Vitamin C ☐　　　Vitamin E ☐

Vitamin K ☐　　　Calcium ☐　　　Magnesium ☐

Time of day you ate	Foods eaten (see sample entry for a breakfast)	Portion Size	Number of Longevity Diet food group choices
BREAKFAST *Time:* 7:30	All Bran Cereal Whole-grain toast Yogurt, 1% Raspberries Almonds	1/2 cup 1 slice 3/4 cup 1 cup 6	1 Starchy Food Choice 1 Starchy Food Choice 1 Milk/Milk Alternative Choice 1 Fruit Choice 1 Fat/Oil Choice
BREAKFAST *Time:*			

Time of day you ate	Foods eaten (see sample entry for a breakfast)	Portion Size	Number of Longevity Diet food group choices

SNACK

Time:

_____

_____

_____

_____

_____

_____

_____

_____

LUNCH

Time:

_____

_____

_____

_____

_____

_____

SNACK

Time:

_____

_____

_____

_____

_____

_____

_____

_____

Time of day you ate	Foods eaten (see sample entry for a breakfast)	Portion Size	Number of Longevity Diet food group choices

DINNER

Time:

_____

_____

_____

_____

_____

_____

_____

_____

_____

Assess Your Food and Nutrient Tracker

Each day, take a moment to reflect what you wrote down by answering the following questions:

Did you reach your daily target for food group choices?

(Depending on the calorie level of your Longevity Diet meal plan, you may not need to check all the boxes.)

Protein Food Choices ☐ ☐ ☐ ☐ ☐ ☐ ☐ ☐ ☐
Milk/Milk Alternatives Choices ☐ ☐ ☐
Starchy Food Choices ☐ ☐ ☐ ☐ ☐ ☐ ☐
Fruit Choices ☐ ☐ ☐
Vegetable Choices ☐ ☐ ☐ ☐ ☐ ☐
Fat & Oil Choices ☐ ☐ ☐ ☐ ☐ ☐
Water (cups) ☐ ☐ ☐ ☐ ☐ ☐ ☐ ☐ ☐ ☐ ☐ ☐ ☐
(Targets: 9 cups for women, 13 cups for men)

Did you drink any alcoholic beverages?

Yes ☐ No ☐ How many? _____
(Remember your weekly upper limit: 7 drinks for women, 9 drinks for men)

How many calories did these beverages add to your diet?

_____

Did you eat anything off your plan?

Yes ☐ No ☐ What? _____
(Remember, you're allowed one treat or splurge per week.)

Did you rate your hunger level before, halfway through and after eating your meals?

Yes ☐ No ☐
What did you learn?

_____

Did you plan your meals and snacks in advance?

Yes ☐ No ☐

Did a lack of planning influence your food choices or how much you ate?

Yes ☐ No ☐

Did any emotions prompt you to overeat?

Yes ☐ No ☐
If so, what were they?

_____

_____

_____

How can you prevent these emotions from influencing your food intake tomorrow?

_____

_____

_____

_____

What will you do differently tomorrow, if anything?

_____

_____

_____

_____

Appendix 3

The Longevity Diet Health Measurement Tracker

To learn how to take your measurements correctly, and how to calculate your body mass index, refer to page 194 in Chapter 10.

	Week 0	Month 3	Month 6	Month 12
Body Measurements				
Weight (lbs or kg)				
Body Mass Index (BMI)				
Waist (inches)				
Hips (inches)				
Waist-Hip Ratio (WHR)				
Chest/Bust (inches)				
% Body Fat				
Aging Biomarkers				
Blood pressure (mm Hg)				
Fasting glucose (mmol/L)				
Fasting insulin (mmol/L)				
Total cholesterol (mmol/L)				
LDL cholesterol (mmol/l)				
HDL cholesterol (mmol/)				
Triglycerides (mmol/L)				
C-reactive protein (mg/L)				

References

Chapter 1

1. Statistics Canada. Life expectancy at birth and at age 65, by sex, Canada. Available at: www.statcan.gc.ca/daily-quotidien/100223/t100223a1-eng.htm.
2. Fraser GE and DJ Shavlik. Ten years of life: Is it a matter of choice? *Arch Intern Med* 2001; 161(13):1645–1652.
3. Khaw KT, Wareham N, Bingham S, Welch A et al. Combined impact of health behaviours and mortality in men and women: The EPIC-Norfolk prospective population study. *PLoS Med* 2008 Jan 8; 5(1):e12.
4. McGue M, Vaupel JW, Holm N and B Harvald. Longevity is moderately heritable in a sample of Danish twins born 1870–1880. *J Gerontol* 1993 Nov; 48(6):B237–244.
5. Perls TT, Wilmoth J, Levenson R, Drinkwater M et al. Life-long sustained mortality advantage of siblings of centenarians. *Proc Natl Acad Sci USA* 2002 Jun 11;99(12):8442–8447.
6. Terry DF, Nolan VG, Andersen SL, Perls TT and R Cawthon. Association of longer telomeres with better health in centenarians. *J Gerontol A Biol Sci Med Sci* 2008 Aug; 63(8):809–812.
7. Atzmon G, Cho M, Cawthon RM, Budagov T et al. Evolution in health and medicine Sackler colloquium: Genetic variation in human telomerase is associated with telomere length in Ashkenazi centenarians. *Proc Natl Acad Sci USA* 2010 Jan 26; 107 Suppl 1:1710–1717.
8. Cassidy A, De Vivo I, Liu Y, Han J et al. Associations between diet, lifestyle factors, and telomere length in women. *Am J Clin Nutr* 2010; Mar 10. [Epub ahead of print doi:10.3945/ajcn.2009.28947].

Chapter 2

1. Poulain M, Pes GM, Grasland C, Carru C et al. Identification of a geographic area characterized by extreme longevity in the Sardinia island: The AKEA study. *Experimental Gerontology* 2004; Vol. 39(9):1423–1429.
2. Science Daily. Goats' milk is more beneficial to health than cows' milk, study suggests. July 31, 2007. Available at: www.sciencedaily.com/releases/2007/07/070730100229.htm.

3. Tsugane S, Tsuda M, Gey F and S Watanabe. Cross-sectional study with multiple measurements of biological markers for assessing stomach cancer risks at the population level. *Environ Health Perspect* 1992; 98:207–210.

4. Suzuki M, Wilcox BJ and CD Wilcox. Implications from and for food cultures for cardiovascular disease: Longevity. *Asia Pacific J Clin Nutr* 2001; Vol. 10(2):165–171.

5. Okinawa Centenarian Study. Okinawa's centenarians. April 17, 2009. Available at: okicent.org/cent.html.

6. Statistics Canada. 2006 Census: Portrait of the Canadian population in 2006: Highlights. September 22, 2009. Available at: www12.statcan.gc.ca/census-recensement/2006/as-sa/97-550/p1-eng.cfm.

7. Sho H. History and characteristics of Okinawan longevity food. *Asia Pacific J Clin Nutr* 2001; Vol. 10(2):159–164.

8. Willcox DC, Willcox BJ, Todoriki H, Curn DJ and Suzuki M. Caloric restriction and human longevity: What can we learn from the Okinawans? *Biogerontology* 2006; Vol. 7(3):173–177.

9. Weindruch R and RS Sohal. Seminars in medicine of the Beth Israel Deaconess Medical Center. Caloric intake and aging. *N Engl J Med* 1997; Vol. 337(14):986–994.

10. Willcox DC, Willcox BJ, Sokolovsky J and S Sakihara. The cultural context of "successful aging" among older women weavers in a northern Okinawan village: The role of productive activity. *J Cross Cult Gerontology* 2007; Vol. 22(2):137–165.

11. Goto A, Yasumura S, Nishise Y and S Sakihara. Association of health behaviour and social role with total mortality among Japanese elders in Okinawa, Japan. *Aging Clin Exp Res* 2003; Vol. 15(6):443–450.

12. Willcox BJ, Willcox DC, He Q, Curb JD and M Suzuki. Siblings of Okinawan centenarians share lifelong mortality advantages. *J Gerontol A Biol Sci Med Sci* 2006; Vol. 61(4):345–354.

13. Takata H, Suzuki M, Ishii T, Sekiguchi S and H Iri. Influence of major histocompatibility complex region genes on human longevity among Okinawan-Japanese centenarians and nonagenarians. *Lancet* 1987; Vol. 2(8563):824–826.

14. Beeson LW, Mills, PK, Phillips RL et al. Chronic disease among Seventh-day Adventists, a low risk group. *Cancer* 1989; Vol. 64:570–581.

15. GE Fraser. Associations between diet and cancer, ischemic heart disease, and all-cause mortality in non-Hispanic white California Seventh-day Adventists. *Am J Clin Nutr* 1999; Vol. 70(suppl):532S–538S.

16. Fraser GE and DJ Shavlik. Ten years of life: Is it a matter of choice? *Arch Intern Med* 2001; 161(13):1645–1652.

17. Kahn HA, Phillips RL, Snowdon DA and W Choi. Association between reported diet and all-cause mortality: Twenty-one-year follow-up on 27,530 adult Seventh-Day Adventists. *Am J Epidemiol* 1984; Vol. 119(5):775–787.

18. Appleby PN, Key TJ, Thorogood M, Burr ML and J Mann. Mortality in British vegetarians. *Public Health Nutr* 2002; Vol. 5(1):29–36.

19. Chang-Claude J, Frentzel-Beyme R and U Eilber. Mortality pattern of German vegetarians after 11 years of follow-up. *Epidemiology* 1992; Vol. 3(5):395–401.

20. Fraser GE. Associations between diet and cancer, ischemic heart disease and all-cause mortality in non-Hispanic white Californian Seventh-day Adventists. *Am J Clin Nutr* 1999; Vol. 70(Suppl):532S–538S.

21. Jacobsen BK, Knutsen SF and GE Fraser. Does high soy milk intake reduce prostate cancer incidence? The Adventist Health Study (United States). *Cancer Causes Control* 1998; Vol. 9(6):553–557.

22. Singh PN, Lindsted KD and GE Fraser. Body weight and mortality among adults who never smoked. *Am J Epidemiol* 1999; Vol. 150(11):1152–164.

23. Kahn HA, Phillips RL, Snowdon DA and W Choi. Association between reported diet and all-cause mortality: Twenty-one-year follow-up on 27,530 adult Seventh-Day Adventists. *Am J Epidemiol* 1984; Vol. 119(5):775–787.

24. Lindsted KD, Tonstad S and JW Kuzma. Self-report of physical activity and patterns of mortality in Seventh-day Adventist men. *J Clin Epidemiol* 1991; Vol. 44(4–5):355–364.

Chapter 3

1. Nusselder WJ, Franco OH, Peeters A and JP Mackenbach. Living healthier for longer: Comparative effects of three heart-healthy behaviours on life expectancy with and without cardiovascular disease. *BMC Public Health* 2009; Vol. 9:487.

2. Lee IM and RS Paffenbarger Jr. Associations of light, moderate, and vigorous intensity physical activity with longevity. The Harvard Alumni Health Study. *Am J Epidemiol* 2000; Vol. 151(3):293–299.

3. Sun Q, Townsend MK, Okereke OI, Franco OH et al. Physical activity at midlife in relation to successful survival in women at age 70 years or older. *Arch Intern Med* 2010; Vol. 170(2):194–201.

4. Cherkas LF, Hunkin JL, Richards JB, Gardner JP et al. The association between physical activity and leukocyte telomere length. *Arch Intern Med* 2008; Vol. 168(2):154–158.

5. Melov S, Tarnopolsky MA, Beckman K and A Hubbard. Resistance exercise reverses aging in human skeletal muscle. *PLoS One* 2007; 5:1–9.

6. Gallicchio L and B Kalesan. Sleep duration and mortality: A systematic review and meta-analysis. *J Sleep Res* 2009; Vol. 18(2):148–158.

7. *Ibid.*

8. Giltay EJ, Geleijnse JM, Zitman FG, Hoekstra T and EG Schouten. Dispositional optimism and all-cause and cardiovascular mortality in a prospective cohort of elderly Dutch men and women. *Arch Gen Psychiatry* 2004; Vol. 61(11):1126–1135.

9. Nabi H, Koskenvuo M, Singh-Manoux A, Korkeila J et al. Low pessimism protects against stroke: The Health and Social Support (HeSSup) prospective cohort study. *Stroke* 2010; Vol. 41(1):187–190.

10. Rasmussen HN, Scheier MF and JB Greenhouse. Optimism and physical health: A meta-analytic review. *Ann Behav Med* 2009; Vol. 37(3):239–256.

11. Roy B, Diez-Roux AV, Seeman T, Ranjit N et al. Association of optimism and pessimism with inflammation and hemostatis in the Multi-Ethnic Study of Atherosclerosis (MESA). *Psychosom Med* 2010; Vol. 72(2):134–140.

12. Baumann A, Filipiak B, Stieber J and Lowel H. Family status and social integration as predictors of mortality: A 5-year follow-up study of 55 to 74-year old men and women in the Augsburg area. *Z Gerontol Geriatr* 1998; Vol. 31(3):184–192.

13. Zunzunegui MV, Béland F, Sanchez MT and A Otero. Longevity and relationships with children: The importance of the parental role. *BMC Public Health* 2009 Sep 18; 9:351.

14. Giles LC, Gloneck GFV, Luszcz MA and GR Andrews. Effect of social networks on 10 year survival in very old Australians: The Australian longitudinal study of aging. *J Epidemiol Community Health* 2005; Vol. 59(7):574–579.

15. Adapted from "Stay Socially Connected." AARP. Available at: www.aarp.org/health/brain/takingcontrol/stay_socially_connected.html.

Chapter 4

1. Prior RL and G Cao. Antioxidant capacity and polyphenolic components of teas: Implications for altering in vivo antioxidant status. *Proc Soc Exp Biol Med* 1999; Vol. 220(4):255–261.

2. Paolisso G, Ammendola S, Del Buono A, Gambardella A et al. Serum levels of insulin-like growth factor-I (IGF-1) and IGF-binding proteins-3 in healthy centenarians: Relationship with plasma leptin and lipid concentrations, insulin action and cognitive function. *J Clin Endorcinol Metab* 1997; Vol. 82(7):2204–2209.

3. Paolisso G, Barbieri M, Rizzo MR, Carella C et al. Low insulin resistance and preserved beta-cell function contribute to human longevity but are not associated with TH-INS genes. *Exp Gerontol* 2001; 37(1):149–156.

4. Paolisso G, Gambardella A, Ammendola S, D'Amore A et al. Glucose tolerance and insulin action in healty centenarians. *Am J Physiol* 1996; Vol. 270(5 Pt 1):E890–894.

5. Taguchi A, Wartschow LM and MF White. Brain IRS2 signaling coordinates life span and nutrient homeostasis. *Science* 2007; Vol. 317(5836):369–372.

Chapter 5

1. Sabate J, Oda K and E Ros. Nut consumption and blood lipid levels. *Arch Intern Med* 2010; Vol. 170(9):821–827.

2. Detopoulou P, Panagiotakos DB, Antonopoulou S et al. Dietary choline and betaine intake in relation to concentrations of inflammatory markers in healthy adults: The ATTICA study. *Am J Clin Nutr* 2008; Vol. 87(2):424–430.

3. Halvorsen BL, Carlsen MH, Phillips KM et al. Content of redox-active compounds (ie, antioxidants) in foods consumed in the United States. *Am J Clin Nutr* 2006; Vol.84(1):95–135.

4. Gates MA, Tworoger SS, Hecht JL, De Vivo I, Rosner B and SE Hankinson SE. A prospective study of dietary flavonoid intake and incidence of epithelial ovarian cancer. *Int J Cancer* 2007; Vol. 121(10):2225–2232.

5. Desch S, Kobler D, Schmidt J, Sonnabend M et al. Low vs. higher-dose dark chocolate and blood pressure in cardiovascular high-risk patients. *Am J Hypertens* 2010; Mar 4. [Epub ahead of print].

6. Taubert D, Roesen R, Lehmann C, Jung N and E Schömig. Effects of low habitual cocoa intake on blood pressure and bioactive nitric oxide: A randomized controlled trial. *JAMA* 2007; Vol. 298(1):49–60.

7. Grassi D, Necozione S, Lippi C, Croce G, Valeri L, Pasqualetti P, Desideri G, Blumberg JB and C Ferri. Cocoa reduces blood pressure and insulin resistance and improves endothelium-dependent vasodilation in hypertensives. *Hypertension* 2005; Vol. 46(2):398–405.

8. Hu FB, Stamppfer MJ, Manson JE, Rimm EB et al. Dietary intake of α-linolenic acid and risk of fatal ischemic heart disease among women. *Am J Clin Nutr* 1999; Vol. 69(5):890–897.

9. Albert CM, Kyungwon O, Whang W, Manson JE et al. Dietary α-linolenic acid intake and risk of sudden cardiac death and coronary heart disease. *Circulation* 2005; Vol. 112(21):3232–3238.

10. Djoussé L, Arnett DK, Carr JJ, Eckfeldt JH, Hopkins PN, Province MA, Ellison RC; Investigators of the NHLBI FHS. Dietary linolenic acid is inversely associated with calcified atherosclerotic plaque in the coronary arteries: The National Heart, Lung, and Blood Institute Family Heart Study. *Circulation* 2005; Vol. 111(22):2921–2926.

11. Thompson LU, Rickard SE, Orcheson LJ, Seidl MM. Flaxseed and its lignan and oil components reduce mammary tumor growth at a late stage of carcinogenesis. *Carcinogenesis* 1996; Vol. 17(6):1373–1376.

12. Chen J, Power KA, Mann J, Cheng A and LU Thompson. Flaxseed alone or in combination with tamoxifen inhibits MCF-7 breast tumor growth in ovariectomized athymic mice with high circulating levels of estrogen. *Exp Biol Med* (Maywood) 2007; Vol. 232(8):1071–1080.

13. Buck K, Zaineddin AK, Vrieling A, Linseisen J and J Chang-Claude. Meta-analyses of lignans and enterolignans in relation to breast cancer risk. *Am J Clin Nutr* 2010; 92(1):141–153.

14. Denmark-Wahnefried W, Polascik TJ, Georges SL, Switzer BR et al. Flaxseed supplementation (not dietary fat restriction) reduces prostate cancer proliferation rates in men presurgery. *Cancer Epidemiol Biomarkers Prev* 2008; Vol. 17(12):3577–3587.

15. Fleischauer AT, Poole C and L Arab. Garlic consumption and cancer prevention: Meta-analyses of colorectal and stomach cancers. *Am J Clin Nutr* 2000; Vol. 72(4):1047–1052.

16. Galeone C, Pelucchi C, Levi F et al. Onion and garlic use and human cancer. *Am J Clin Nutr* 2006; Vol. 84(5):1027–1032.

17. Sun CL, Yuan JM, Koh WP and MC Yu. Green tea, black tea and breast cancer risk: A meta-analysis of epidemiological studies. *Carcinogenesis* 2006; Vol. 27(7):1310–5. Epub 2005 Nov 25.

18. Paganga G, Miller N and CA Rice-Evans. The polyphenolic content of fruit and vegetables and their antioxidant activities. What does a serving constitute? *Free Radic Res* 1999, Vol. 30(2):153–162.

19. Brown L, Rimm EB, Seddon JM et al. A prospective study of carotenoid intake and risk of cataract extraction in U.S. men. *Am J Clin Nutr* 1999; Vol. 70(4): 517–524.

20. Morris MC, Evans DA, Tangney CC et al. Associations of vegetable and fruit consumption with age-related cognitive change. *Neurology* 2006; Vol. 67(8):1370–1376.

21. Knoops KT, de Groot LC, Fidanza F, Alberti-Fidanza A et al. Comparison of three different dietary scores in relation to 10-year mortality in elderly European subjects: The HALE project. *Eur J Clin Nutr* 2006; Vol. 60(6):746–755.

22. Knoops KT, de Groot LC, Kromhout D, Perrin AE, Moreiras-Varela O et al. Mediterranean diet, lifestyle factors and 10-year mortality in elderly European men and women: The HALE project. *JAMA* 2004; Vol. 292(12):1433–1439.

23. Fruit juice may cut Alzheimer's risk. Mayo Clin Health Letter. 2009 Feb; Vol. 27(2):4.

24. Mullen W, Marks SC and A Crozier. Evaluation of phenolic compounds in commercial fruit juices and fruit drinks. *J Agric Food Chem* 2007; Vol. 55(8):3148–3157.

25. Farzaneh-Far R, Lin J, Epel ES, Harris WS et al. Association of marine omega-3 fatty acid levels with telomeric aging in patients with coronary heart disease. *JAMA* 2010; Vol. 303(3):250–257.

26. Morris MC, Evans DA, Bienias JL et al. Consumption of fish and n-3 fatty acids and risk of incident Alzheimer disease. *Arch Neurol* 2003; Vol. 60(7):940–946.

27. Kalmijn S, Launer LJ, Ott A et al. Dietary fat intake and the risk of incident dementia in the Rotterdam Study. *Ann Neurol* 1997; Vol. 42(5):776–782.

28. Richards JB, Valdes AM, Gardner JP, Paximadas D et al. Higher serum vitamin D concentrations are associated with longer leukocyte telomere length in women. *Am J Clin Nutr* 2007; Vol. 86(5):1420–1425.

29. Jacobsen BK, Knutsen SF and GE Fraser. Does high soy milk intake reduce prostate cancer incidence? The Adventist Health Study (United States). *Cancer Causes Control* 1998; Vol. 9(6):553–557.

30. Trock BJ, Hilakivi-Clarke L and R Clarke. Meta-analysis of soy intake and breast cancer risk. *J Natl Cancer Inst* 2006; Vol. 98(7):459–471.

31. Willis LM, Shukitt-Hale B, Cheng V and JA Joseph. Dose-dependent effects of walnuts on motor and cognitive function in aged rats. *Br J Nutr* 2009; Vol. 101(8):1140–1144.

Chapter 6

1. Richards JB, Valdes AM, Gardner JP, Paximadas D, Kimura M et al. Higher serum vitamin D concentrations are associated with longer leukocyte telomere length in women. *Am J Clin Nutr* 2007; Vol. 86(5):1420–1425.

2. Hall LM, Kimlin MG, Aronov PA, Hammock BD et al. Vitamin D intake needed to maintain target serum 25-hydroxyvitamin D concentrations in participants with

low sun exposure and dark skin pigmentation is substantially higher than current recommendations. *J Nutr* 2010; Vol. 140(3):542–550.

3. Devore EE, Grodstein F, van Rooij FJ, Hofman A et al. Dietary antioxidants and long-term risk of dementia. *Arch Neurol* 2010; Vol. 67(7):819–825.

4. Xu Q, Parks CG, DeRoo LA, Cawthon RM, Sandler DP and H Chen. Multivitamin use and telomere length in women. *Am J Clin Nutr* 2009; Vol. 89(6):1857–1863.

5. Kaluza J, Orsini N, Levitan EB, Brzozowska A et al. Dietary calcium and magnesium intake and mortality: A prospective study of men. *Am J Epidemiol* 2010; Vol. 171(7):801–807.

6. Farzaneh-Far R, Lin J, Epel ES, Harris WS et al. Association of marine omega-3 fatty acid levels with telomeric aging in patients with coronary heart disease. *JAMA* 2010; Vol. 303(3):250–257.

7. Xu Q, Parks CG, DeRoo LA, Cawthon RM, Sandler DP and H Chen. Multivitamin use and telomere length in women. *Am J Clin Nutr* 2009; Vol. 89(6):1857–1863.

Chapter 7

1. Singh PN, Sabate J and GE Fraser. Does low meat consumption increase life expectancy in humans? *Am J Clin Nutr* 2003; Vol. 78(suppl):526S–532S.

2. Larsson SC and A Wolk. Meat consumption and risk of colorectal cancer: A meat-analysis of prospective studies. *Int J Cancer* 2006; Vol. 119(11):2657–2664.

3. Norat T, Lukanov A, Ferrari P and E Riboli. Meat consumption and colorectal cancer risk: Dose-response meat-analysis of epidemiological studies. *Int J Cancer* 2002; Vol. 98(2):241–256.

4. Rohrmann S, Hermann S and J Linseisen. Heterocyclic aromatic amine intake increases colorectal adenoma risk: Findings from a prospective European cohort study. *Am J Clin Nutr* 2009; Vol. 89(5):1418–1424.

5. Aune D, Ursin G and MB Veierod. Meat consumption and the risk of type 2 diabetes: A systematic review and meta-analysis of cohort studies. *Diabetologia* 2009; Vol. 52(11):2277–2287.

6. Vang A, Singh PN, Lee JW, Haddad EH and CH Brinegar. Meats, processed meats, obesity, weight gain and occurrence of diabetes among adults: Findings from Adventist Health Studies. *Ann Nutr Metab* 2008; Vol. 52(2):96–104.

7. Cross AJ, Ferrucci LM, Risch A, Graubard BI, Ward MH, Park Y, Hollenbeck AR, Schatzkin A and R Sinha. A large prospective study of meat consumption and colorectal cancer risk: An investigation of potential mechanisms underlying this association. *Cancer Res* 2010; Vol. 70(6):2406–2414.

8. Welsh JA, Sharma A, Abramson JL, Vaccarino V et al. Caloric sweetener consumption and dyslipidemia among US adults. *JAMA* 2010; Vol. 303(15):1490–1497.

9. Jakobsen MU, Dethlefsen C, Joensen AM, Stegger J et al. Intake of carbohydrates compared with intake of saturated fatty acids and risk of myocardial infarction: Importance of the glycemic index. *Am J Clin Nutr* 2010; Vol. 91(6):1764–1768.

10. Statistics Canada. Table 3: Average daily sodium intake (milligrams), by age group and sex, Canada excluding territories, 2004 and United States, 2001–2002. Available at: www.statcan.gc.ca/pub/82-003-x/2006004/article/sodium/t/4060652-eng.htm.

11. Allen NE, Beral V, Casabonne D, Kan SW, Reeves GK, Brown A, Green J; Million Women Study Collaborators. Moderate alcohol intake and cancer incidence in women. *J Natl Cancer Inst* 2009; Vol. 101(5):296–305.

Chapter 8

1. Colman RJ, Anderson RM, Johnson SC, Kastman EK et al. Caloric restriction delays disease onset and mortality in rhesus monkeys. *Science* 2009; Vol. 325(5937):201–214.

2. Walford RL, Mock D, Verdery R and T MacCallum. Calorie restriction in biosphere 2: Alterations in physiologic, hematologic, hormonal, and biochemical parameters in humans restricted for a 2-year period. *J Gerontol A Biol Sci Med Sci* 2002; Vol. 57(6):B211–224.

3. Fontana L, Meyer TE, Klein S and JO Holloszy. Long-term calorie restriction is highly effective in reducing the risk for atherosclerosis in humans. *Proc Natl Acad Sci USA* 2004; Vol. 101(17):6659–6663.

4. Cangemi R, Friedmann AJ, Holloszy JO and L Fontana. Long-term effects of calorie restriction on serum sex-hormone concentrations in men. *Aging Cell* 2010; Vol. 9(2):236–242.

5. Redman LM, Heilbronn LK, Martin CK, Alfonso A, Smith SR, Ravussin E; Pennington CALERIE Team. Effect of calorie restriction with or without exercise on body composition and fat distribution. *J Clin Endocrinol Metab* 2007; Vol. 92(3):865–872.

6. Larson-Meyer DE, Newcomer BR, Heilbronn LK, Volaufova J, Smith SR, Alfonso AJ, Lefevre M, Rood JC, Williamson DA, Ravussin E; Pennington CALERIE Team. Effect of 6-month calorie restriction and exercise on serum and liver lipids and markers of liver function. *Obesity* (Silver Spring) 2008; Vol.16(6):1355–1362.

7. Fontana L, Villareal DT, Weiss EP, Racette SB, Steger-May K, Klein S, Holloszy JO; and the Washington University School of Medicine CALERIE Group. Calorie restriction or exercise: Effects on coronary heart disease risk factors. A randomized, controlled trial. *Am J Physiol Endocrinol Metab* 2007; Vol. 293(1):E197–202.

8. Weiss EP, Racette SB, Villareal DT, Fontana L, Steger-May K, Schechtman KB, Klein S, Holloszy JO; Washington University School of Medicine CALERIE Group. Improvements in glucose tolerance and insulin action induced by increasing energy expenditure or decreasing energy intake: A randomized controlled trial. *Am J Clin Nutr* 2006; Vol. 84(5):1033–1042.

9. Racette SB, Weiss EP, Villareal DT, Arif H, Steger-May K, Schechtman KB, Fontana L, Klein S, Holloszy JO; Washington University School of Medicine CALERIE Group. One year of caloric restriction in humans: Feasibility and effects on body composition and abdominal adipose tissue. *J Gerontol A Biol Sci Med Sci* 2006; Vol. 61(9):943–950.

10. Heilbronn LK, de Jonge L, Frisard MI, DeLany JP, Larson-Meyer DE, Rood J, Nguyen T, Martin CK, Volaufova J, Most MM, Greenway FL, Smith SR, Deutsch WA, Williamson DA, Ravussin E; Pennington CALERIE Team. Effect of 6-month calorie restriction on biomarkers of longevity, metabolic adaptation, and oxidative

stress in overweight individuals: A randomized controlled trial. *JAMA* 2006; Vol. 295(13):1539–1548.

11. Peeters A, Barendregt JJ, Willekens F, Mackenbach JP, Al Mamun A, Bonneux L; NEDCOM, the Netherlands Epidemiology and Demography Compression of Morbidity Research Group. Obesity in adulthood and its consequences for life expectancy: A life-table analysis. *Ann Intern Med* 2003; Vol. 138(1):24–32.

12. Fontaine KR, Redden DT, Wang C, Westfall AO and DB Allison. Years of life lost due to obesity. *JAMA* 2003; Vol. 289(2):187–193.

13. Hofer T, Fontana L, Anton SD, Weiss EP, Villareal D, Malayappan B and C Leeuwenburgh. Long-term effects of caloric restriction or exercise on DNA and RNA oxidation levels in white blood cells and urine in humans. *Rejuvenation Res* 2008; Vol. 11(4):793–799.

Chapter 9

1. Food and Nutrition Board, Institute of Medicine, National Academies. Dietary reference intakes (DRIs): Estimated energy requirements (EER) for men and women. Available at: iom.edu/en/Global/News%20Announcements/~/media/Files/Activity%20Files/Nutrition/DRIs/DRISummaryListing2.ashx.

General Index

Recipe Index

HEALTHY LIVING BOOKS BY
LESLIE BECK RD

LESLIE BECK RD
The Complete A-Z
NUTRITION
Encyclopedia
A Guide to Natural Health

MANAGE OVER 75
HEALTH CONDITIONS NATURALLY WITH
•HEALTHY DIET STRATEGIES
•VITAMINS AND MINERALS
•NATURAL HEALTH PRODUCTS

FOODS THAT FIGHT DISEASE

A Nutrition Guide
to Staying Healthy
for Life

Leslie Beck RD

WHAT TO EAT TO HELP PREVENT
Cancer, Stroke, Type 2 Diabetes, High Blood Pressure,
High Blood Cholesterol, Osteoporosis, Heart Disease

10 STEPS TO HEALTHY EATING

Boost Energy,
Manage Weight and
Prevent Disease
with the Right Foods

Leslie Beck RD

"Everything you need to know to get healthy
and stay healthy by eating right."

Featuring recipes created by the
best kitchen

THE NO-FAIL DIET

The Easy 4-Step
Plan for Permanent
Weight Loss

Leslie Beck RD

A NUTRITIONALLY BALANCED
12-WEEK PLAN TO HELP YOU:
• reach your healthy weight
• boost your energy level
• stay healthy as you age

"Canada's nutrition guru."

HEART HEALTHY FOODS FOR LIFE

Preventing Heart
Disease through
Diet and Nutrition

Leslie Beck RD

THE COMPLETE NUTRITION GUIDE FOR WOMEN

Staying Healthy
with Diet, Nutrients
and Supplements

Leslie Beck RD

"Everything you need to know to get healthy and stay
healthy is eating right." —Christiane Northrup, MD

THE COMPLETE NUTRITION GUIDE TO MENOPAUSE

Natural Strategies
to Manage Symptoms,
Control Weight
and Stay Healthy

Leslie Beck RD

AVAILABLE WHEREVER BOOKS ARE SOLD